Smithsonian Series in Ethnographic Inquiry
WILLIAM L. MERRILL AND IVAN KARP, SERIES EDITORS

Ethnography as fieldwork, analysis, and literary form is the distinguishing feature of modern anthropology. Guided by the assumption that anthropological theory and ethnography are inextricably linked, this series is devoted to exploring the ethnographic enterprise.

Advisory Board

ANTHONY D. BUCKLEY AND MAR

CATHERINE KENNEY

Negotiating Identity

Rhetoric,
Metaphor,
and
Social
Drama
in
Northern
Ireland

Smithsonian
Institution
Press

Washington
and
London

Portions of this book first appeared, in different form, as: Anthony D. Buckley, "Walls within Walls: Religion and Rough Behavior in an Ulster Community," *Sociology* 18, 1 (1984); Anthony D. Buckley, "Bad Boys and Little Old Ladies: Youth and Old Age in Two Ulster Villages," *Ethnologia Europaea* 17 (1987); Anthony D. Buckley, "Playful Rebellion: Social Control and the Framing of Experience in an Ulster Community," *Man* (n.s.) 18 (1983); Anthony D. Buckley, "'The Chosen Few': Biblical Texts in the Regalia of an Ulster Secret Society," *Folk Life: The Journal of the Society of Folk Life Studies* 29 (1985–86); Anthony D. Buckley, "Collecting Ulster's Culture: Are There *Really* Two Traditions?" in R. A. Gailey, ed., *The Use of Tradition: Essays Presented to G. B. Thompson* (Cultra: Ulster Folk and Transport Museum, 1988); and Anthony D. Buckley and Mary Catherine Kenney, "Cultural Heritage in an Oasis of Calm: Divided Identities in a Museum in Ulster," in Ullrich Kockel, ed., *Culture, Tourism, and Development* (Liverpool: University of Liverpool Press, 1994). All are reprinted with permission of the original publishers.

Copy Editor: Susan A. Warga
Production Editor: Duke Johns
Designer: Linda McKnight

Library of Congress Cataloging-in-Publication Data
Buckley, Anthony D.
   Negotiating identity : rhetoric, metaphor, and social drama in Northern Ireland / Anthony D. Buckley and Mary Catherine Kenney.
      p.   cm.
   Includes bibliographical references (p.   ) and index.
   ISBN 1-56098-520-8.
   1. Northern Ireland—History—1969–   .   2. Northern Ireland—Social conditions—1969–   .   3. Ethnicity—Religious aspects—Christianity.   4. Rhetoric—Social aspects—Northern Ireland.   5. Ethnology—Northern Ireland.   6. Irish—Ethnic identity.
   I. Kenney, Mary Catherine.   II. Title.
   DA990.U46B8   1995
   305.8'009416—dc20   94-47184

British Library Cataloguing-in-Publication Data is available

Manufactured in the United States of America
02 01 00 99 98 97 96 95   5 4 3 2 1

Contents

Contents

To
Linda
and
Cornelia

Preface

The authors of this volume met in 1985, when M. C. Kenney was studying the role of processions in urban Belfast and A. D. Buckley was studying the Orange Order, an association that organizes such processions. That year differed from many others in that a higher-than-usual proportion of its processions dissolved into riot. So it happened that Buckley and Kenney found themselves together watching crowds of people throwing stones and bottles, usually at policemen. This volume reflects their discussions as they traveled to and from these mind-forming experiences, as well as their conversations about their more general fieldwork in urban and rural areas of Ulster.

There is a stylistic problem in collaborating to write a book of anthropology. While it is possible to discuss and come to an agreement about theoretical matters, the field research of an anthropologist is very much an individual endeavor. Anthropology differs from many of the other social sciences in that a central figure in the resulting description is the individual anthropologist. Sometimes, therefore, in a collaborative work, one finds oneself writing as two people; but sometimes one must write as a single individual. Some chapters will, therefore, be *joint* chapters, the authors being referred to either together as *we* or separately as Buckley and Kenney. In other chapters, however, the fieldwork is that of a named individual, who will refer to him- or herself as *I*. In each of these chapters, however, while the fieldwork was undertaken by one individual, the theory that informs the chapter was developed jointly.

There is another sense in which all social anthropology is a collaboration. This study has been totally dependent upon the kindness and generosity of our informants, who came forth liberally with tea, sandwiches, and cakes, as well as information. These individuals, whether from the Upper Tullagh, Listymore, or different parts of Belfast and South Antrim or elsewhere, were universally open-handed.

Our thanks are also due especially to Mrs. Linda Buckley and Dr. Reg Byron, who supported our work throughout. Buckley wishes particularly to acknowledge his debt to his employer, the Ulster Folk and Transport Museum, for which his own ethnographic fieldwork was undertaken, and to his colleagues, who provided an endless stream of useful ideas and inspiration. Much of the raw data of his research, particularly audio field recordings, photographs, and documents, are now lodged in the museum's archives. Special thanks and admiration are due to Mrs. Lorraine Lawrence, who unflinchingly prepared much of the text with great cheerfulness and thoroughness. Kenney is especially grateful to Billy, Tom, and Linda of the Donegall Pass Youth Club, and Brian, Tom, and Stephanie from the Concord Community Centre, for introducing her to the ways of life characteristic of Belfast neighborhoods.

We do not, of course, expect that all our informants will agree with all our judgments. But even where our comments are somewhat critical, they arise primarily out of the fondness we have for Northern Ireland and its people.

In our work in Northern Ireland, neither of us has felt any need to espouse either of the great historical political causes of nationalism and unionism. Our conclusions are inevitably drawn in the context of particular observations. By taking part in one set of worlds, one avoids participating in others. Buckley has studied in Ulster since 1975, and most of his recent research has been among Protestants, generally away from the more troubled areas; Kenney's main period of field research was for only two years (1984–86), and it focused on a particularly troubled Catholic area. This research emphasis may be taken as a sign of bias, but such a conclusion would be unwarranted. The truth is that one cannot study everything everywhere. We believe that our conclusions apply generally to people on both sides in Northern Ireland. We like and admire people on both sides of the historical divide, and our only political aspiration for the province is that its people will find a greater measure of peace.

The aim of this book is to show how specific individuals construct their own identities in concrete and immediate circumstances. The focus for the study is not, therefore, the unfolding of the troubles or the development of Northern Ireland's history. Rather, the area's macrohistory, which includes both the distant and the more recent past, provides a background to the actions we describe. Unfortunately for this kind of analysis, the macrohistorical events that provide the background for action do nevertheless progress and unfold.

While this undoubtedly gives the lie to an ahistorical, synchronic anthropology that tries to see society as existing in a timeless present, it does not invalidate an attempt to understand how individuals act in particular circumstances.

After the conclusion of our field research, and as the writing of this book drew toward its completion, the political atmosphere in Northern Ireland was emphatically changed, first by the Downing Street Declaration of December 1993 and then even more drastically in the next year by the declaration of a ceasefire by most of the different paramilitary organizations. Despite this, we have clung to the use of the ethnographic present in describing the situations we found. This allows us to focus on the individuals we met rather than on the developing historical process.

In any case, our judgment is that the fundamental situation that gave rise to and perpetuated Ulster's troubles remains much as it ever was. The history of Ulster has been punctuated by periods of trouble and periods of peace; there is every reason to suppose that we are entering just another phase of a familiar cycle. In particular, there still remain deeply ingrained patterns of social interaction that divide one ethnic group from the other. Unless constant attention is paid, by population and government, over a period of decades to redress the impact of this division, any settlement achieved by politicians is likely to be fragile.

Particularly in matters relating to ethnicity, the population of Northern Ireland has been dealt a difficult hand. Despite these well-known difficulties, there is in the north of Ireland a degree of tolerance and goodwill often lacking in other societies fraught with ethnic tension. Our hope is that this book will contribute in the long term to the peace and goodwill that so many people in Ulster wish to see realized.

Anthony D. Buckley
Mary Catherine Kenney

1
Negotiating Identity in Ulster

This book is about the way people in Northern Ireland define themselves and each other. Studies of identity in other parts of the world sometimes avoid issues of nationality, religion, or ethnicity, but after a quarter of a century of bitter ethnic conflict in Northern Ireland, these issues have come to dominate the topic, to the near exclusion of all else. This study too will focus on matters relating to that conflict, but we shall shift the emphasis away from that of earlier studies and link ethnicity to the nonethnic elements in a person's identity.

Identities are not timeless abstractions that exist outside the very specific worlds in which individuals live their lives. This ethnographic study will look at the way individuals negotiate definitions of themselves and other people during day-to-day interactions.

In this chapter we will first show how the nationalism, unionism, and Marxism of past writers on Ireland have given way to an emphasis on internal conflict and ethnicity. We next look at cultural difference, exploring the role of distinctively ethnic culture in relation to social and political division. There will be discussion of how an ethnic group claims ownership of certain kinds of intellectual property — for example, when people say, "This is part of *our* culture." And we shall show how enthusiasts or experts act as curators, conserving this property for the wider group.

Our case, however, is that ethnic identity and conflict arise from patterns of social interaction. We adopt an idea from urban anthropology, that the interaction that gives rise to identity takes place within relatively discrete situations, relationships, or "worlds." We argue that a person's identity is a "social construction" and from moment to moment is subject to negotiation.

This chapter will look at the debates about Irish identity in anthropological and other texts. It will show why we have adopted our special outlook and will introduce the places and people we ourselves have studied. The next chapter will put the topic of identity in Ulster in comparative and theoretical perspective.

The People or Peoples of Ireland

In his magisterial review *Interpreting Northern Ireland,* John Whyte (1991) discerns four distinctive models of the conflict in Ireland: *traditional nationalist, traditional unionist, traditional Marxist,* and *two-community* or *internal-conflict.* Of these, he says, the last has recently come to dominate. Whyte believes that the two-community approach influences even those writers who adhere to one of the traditional models, and that this has given rise to the current interest in ethnicity and identity in the north of Ireland.

Whyte sums up the traditional nationalist view of Northern Ireland in two propositions: "(1) the people of Ireland form one nation; and (2) the fault for keeping Ireland divided lies with Britain" (Whyte 1991, 117). For example, Gallagher writes:

> Britain based her partition policy on divergences she herself created and fostered among the Irish people. Other democratic nations have had similar problems to those of Ireland. These have been solved, with justice to all concerned and within a framework of the national units in question, because no powerful neighbour set out to prevent a settlement by exploiting internal differences. (Gallagher 1957, 88)

Close to this nationalist view is the traditional Marxist one, which stems from James Connolly. Connolly's views, in this respect, are similar to those of Lenin (1916). He writes that the British Empire was "the most aggressive type and resolute defender of capitalism" (quoted in Ryan 1948, 9). To defeat capitalism in Ireland, he says, one must first break the link with Britain.

Like the non-Marxist nationalists, Connolly blames the failure of northern Protestants to join the national cause upon successive governments in London. Unlike them, he believes these governments acted on behalf of the employing classes, who discriminated against Catholic workers and small farmers in favor of Protestants, and therefore "created a feeling of common interests between the slaves and the slave drivers" (quoted in Ryan 1948, 102).

Nationalist and Marxist writers differ sharply from unionists. The former have emphasized the inherent unity of the Irish people and/or of its working class. Unionist writers have typically insisted that the Catholic and Protestant peoples of Ireland are fundamentally divided or opposed. This view (e.g., McNeill 1922; Shearman 1942, 1948) claims for the Protestant people the same right of self-determination that nationalists claim for Ireland as a whole. Unionists see the present state of Northern Ireland as legitimated by the will of the majority of people living in the province. It regards southern Irish claims to the north as a kind of imperialism. The fearfulness unionists express in their attitude toward the Irish Republic is well described by what journalists call the "siege mentality."

With the coming of the troubles in the 1960s, these traditional models fell increasingly into disrepute. Whatever might have been true in the past, neither the British nor the Irish government, nor yet the employing classes, can any longer be seen as prime movers in fomenting violence. Pressures for or against Irish unity come most strongly not from Dublin or London but from the indigenous population of Northern Ireland itself. As a result, there has evolved a new interpretation that sees the source of conflict to be within Northern Ireland itself, and stresses the existence of two communities and an internal conflict (Whyte 1991).

The best definition of this approach (Poole 1983) highlights two key (and parallel) expressions: "the double minority" and "the double majority." Poole points out that Catholics and Protestants are each a minority and a majority, but in relation to different territorial units. In Northern Ireland Catholics are a minority, but they form a majority in Ireland as a whole. Protestants, conversely, are in a majority in the north, but would form a minority in any future united Ireland. The territorial arrangement preferred by each side, therefore, is the one in which its own side would dominate.

The purer forms of this new analytical perspective refuse to take sides in the conflict. In practice, however, few writers show such detachment. Many note the importance of the idea of internal conflict but continue to adopt a recognizably nationalist, unionist, or Marxist position.

Unionists have had little adjustment to make, since unionism has always emphasized the divided nature of Irish society. Nationalists have shifted their position more sharply. Fennell (1983, 1985, 1986, 1989), for example, is emphatically a nationalist writer, but he freely acknowledges a separate unionist or British identity in Ireland. So too with the Marxists. Bell (1990) adopts something of a traditional line, claiming that discrimination and the inspiration of Britain's imperial past together forged Protestant working-class identity. He

3

knows, nevertheless, that the conflict he describes (between gangs of youths) is defined by ethnicity rather than by class. Other Marxist writers have traveled uncharted paths; for example, there has been a well-argued strand of Marxist unionism that for a time was very influential (BICO 1971, 1972). According to this somewhat eccentric hypothesis, the Protestants of the north represent a progressive, industrial proletarianism, in contrast to the Catholic agrarianism of the south.

Despite tending to revert to older issues, the internal-conflict approach has brought with it important practical implications. Above all, it has turned away from history. It seeks the source of and the solutions to present conflicts in the present (which can be changed) and not in the past (about which one can do nothing). It has also diverted at least some of the debate away from the question of which side in the conflict is right and which wrong. The interest is more in satisfying the hopes and soothing the fears of the two conflicting groups.

Identity as a Social Construct: Culture and Interaction

The internal-conflict approach has also created in Irish studies a scholarly interest in identity, especially ethnic identity. Wallis et al. (1986) argue that Protestants and Catholics in Northern Ireland are *ethnic* groups because, unlike *racial* groups, whose members are defined by their physical features, Ulster's groups are defined by cultural differences. Thus, there has been a shift of emphasis to the study of ethnicity and the role of culture in the definition of ethnic identity.

There have been two broad approaches to the role of culture and cultural difference in the formation of ethnic identity in Ulster. Both have found their way into more popular debate. One view emphasizes the extent and depth of the differences that separate the two cultures or traditions: Catholic and nationalist, Protestant and unionist. This version of the model is exceedingly popular (see Lundy and MacPoilin 1992). It has, indeed, become part of the vocabulary of the troubles. The expression "two traditions," with its unthinking emphasis on cultural differentiation, is now widely used to refer to the two ethnic groups (see, for example, Major and Reynolds 1993). An especially articulate expression of this idea is that of Lyons (1979). He asserts, however, that Northern Ireland has not *two* cultures, but *three*: Anglican, Presbyterian, and Catholic. According to this view, at the heart of the social conflict is cultural division.

A challenge to this kind of approach comes from Akenson's book *Small Differences* (1991). Akenson uses, as a test case, data on nineteenth-century Irish migrants in the New World and Australasia. He finds that in matters of culture, Protestant and Catholic migrants differed scarcely at all. Different patterns of behavior found among separate migrant groups, he says, arose out of the dissimilar situations in which they found themselves. Contrary to what was said both at the time by observers and subsequently by historians, differences between migrants did not reflect any cultural contrasts stemming from Ireland (Akenson 1991, chap. 1). Irish culture, whether Protestant or Catholic, was very flexible. Migrants could adapt it to fit whatever new circumstances they happened to confront.

An obvious question arising from Akenson's findings is that if the cultural differences that divide Catholic from Protestant in Ireland were (and by implication are) so few, then what is the nature of the so-called sectarian divide? Akenson's answer is derived from Barth (1969). The divide arises, he says, out of patterns of social interaction that maintain social boundaries (see also Whyte 1986). Among these patterns of interaction, as we ourselves shall strongly argue, is participation in activities of expressive culture peculiar to one's own ethnic group. More centrally, however, the divide comes from patterns of discrimination and segregation that shape the whole social fabric. These include constraints on intermarriage, residence, education, and employment. *Cultural* identity, says Akenson, quoting Freud, is the "narcissism of small differences" (see Freud 1921, 1930).

We shall steer a middle course between these two opposed sets of opinions. Wallis et al. (1986) are correct to say that cultural differences have their place. However, we agree with Akenson and Barth that social interaction and boundary maintenance are central. Identity, we believe, whether ethnic or otherwise, is a social construct (Berger and Luckman 1966) and is negotiated during social interaction. We also claim (following Mead 1934; see also Burkitt 1991) that much social interaction is *symbolic* interaction, which includes social drama (Burke 1957; Turner 1982) and exchanges of rhetoric (Billig 1985). In such interaction, cultural differences, while small and not making up the whole picture, still have a significant place.

It is also true, however, that many important patterns of interaction leading to ethnic identity and conflict in Northern Ireland have little to do with cultural difference. Most important of all is the discouragement, even prohibition, of intermarriage. Lee (1981) says that as few as 1.2 percent of marriages contracted in Northern Ireland in 1971 were mixed. Although there is some evidence that this proportion is increasing, endogamy remains a central feature of the social life of Northern Ireland.

In part, restrictions on intermarriage have come about because of formal disapproval from certain churches—notably the Roman Catholic Church, but also some of the smaller Protestant churches (Robinson 1992, 11). More important has been the popular desire to maintain social distance between the two sides (McFarlane 1978, 1986), a desire reinforced by pressure from family, friends, and neighbors. Robinson's study of cross-community marriages (1992), the fullest to date, contains many sad little stories of star-crossed lovers confronting tensions and difficulties that range from what people call "coolness" to complete estrangement from friends, neighbors, and kin. Most people seem also to believe (though firm evidence is, perhaps inevitably, ambiguous) that mixed couples risk physical intimidation, including murder. Certainly, as a precaution, all the mixed couples known to us personally keep their numbers and addresses out of the telephone directory.

The importance of this endogamy rule on Northern Irish society can scarcely be overestimated. For the individual, the effect is that all his kin, his spouse's kin, his children, grandchildren, parents, and grandparents; the brothers and sisters of all these people; and the spouses and in-laws of all *these* people are likely to belong to the same major segment of society as the person himself. It is the rule of endogamy that makes ethnic identity in Ulster an ascribed identity. And while there is some space to negotiate ethnic identity in Ulster, it is the rule of endogamy that makes this space so confined.

The lack of intermarriage *incorporates* the ethnic groups. It makes plausible the idea that they are descended from two similarly distinct groups of people that existed in the past (see chapter 3). It ensures that each group has a corporate nature and a history that is distinct from the histories of the individuals who make it up. In effect, endogamy splits society into two.

The few mixed marriages make only a slight dent in the picture. The children of such a marriage will, in the course of time, lean to one side or the other and gain an ethnic identity, usually reinforced in the next generation. It is not too difficult to find someone who has a Catholic grandparent but who nevertheless has an unambiguously Protestant identity (or vice versa).

Important consequences flow from the prohibition of marriage between ethnic groups. One is a general tendency toward social segregation. This is particularly potent in spheres that affect the socialization of children. Whyte (1986) argues that segregation in schools is even more important than the marriage rule in maintaining the social division. There is segregation, of course, in churches, which provide an important focus for recreation, particularly in rural areas and particularly among women and children (McFarlane 1986, 99). Among adults, divisions in recreational life continue in the many segregated social clubs. There is also a tendency, stronger in some places than others, toward residential segregation (see chapter 5). This is enhanced by a perceived need to achieve security in the face of civil disturbance.

Social segregation also interacts with economic and political competition. Individuals often seek employment, business contacts, and other forms of help through such nonbureaucratic means as family connections, old-boy networks, and friendships (see Leyton 1975). Many such networks, based upon families, schools, churches, and social clubs, are ethnically homogeneous. Through the attempt to ensure that members of one's own side occupy influential positions in government and commerce, rivalry between the ethnic groups for prestige, power, and influence becomes inevitable.

If thus far we agree with Akenson and Barth in emphasizing social boundaries, we do not wish to overlook cultural differences. At least two kinds of difference are relevant here. One has been widely dealt with in Northern Irish ethnography. It concerns ethnic stereotyping, and particularly how it is possible to tell whether somebody is a Protestant or a Catholic. The second is not so familiar. It is the notion of intellectual property.

The stereotyping of Protestants and Catholics has been much discussed in the literature on Northern Ireland (see, for example, Buckley 1982; Burton 1978; Donnan and McFarlane 1986; Harris 1972, chap. 8; O'Donnell 1977). It is a complex issue and will be discussed further, especially in chapter 12. Here we shall confine ourselves to a much-quoted section of a valuable ethnography by Burton (1978).

Burton describes some of the cultural cues by which his informants can tell whether a stranger is a Catholic or a Protestant. For example, certain Christian names and surnames are identified as Catholic (he mentions the Christian names Colm, Gerard, Kieran, Liam, Sean, and Seamus, and the surnames Cooney, Lynch, McGuinness, and Murphy); others (Billy, Ian, Sammy; Armstrong, Craig, Maxwell, Taylor, Thompson) are Protestant. Discovering which school a person attended or in which district a person lives can provide important clues. So can the use of certain expletives: "Holy Mother," "sweet Jesus," and "Jesus, Mary, and Joseph" are common among certain kinds of Catholics. And Burton claims that there are more subtle social and even physical differences that enable somebody to "tell which foot a person digs with" (Burton 1978, 37–67).[1]

There are other examples, such as well-known differences in the way the alphabet is recited. Catholics usually pronounce *a* as "ah" and *h* as "haitch," in contrast to Protestants, who say "ay" and "aitch." In the 1970s (and no doubt sometimes today) this phenomenon provided a useful rule of thumb for gangs of youths, who used it to decide whether a passer-by should be beaten up. "Tell us your alphabet," they would say.

In addition, an Ulster Protestant is likely to prefer the term *Ulster* and avoid expressions such as "the six counties" or "the north of Ireland." In a similar way, some nationalists insist on the older name for the city of Derry, while many Protestants insist on calling it Londonderry (often to make a point). These problems with terminology make it difficult to refer innocently to "the province" without seeming to reveal some preconception or bias.

This last little controversy, incidentally, brought fame to a local radio personality through a running joke on his Londonderry-based radio show. He called the city "Derry stroke Londonderry" (Derry/Londonderry) or "Stroke City." Since his own name was Gerry Anderson, he referred to himself as "Gerry stroke Londongerry." People in Northern Ireland are highly aware of the absurdities in their own situation. They do not always want casual acquaintances to know their ethnic affiliation. Inhabitants of Derry (or Londonderry) face an extra problem in that they reveal themselves whenever they speak of their hometown. Anderson's catchphrase raised an ironic eyebrow at one solution to this daily dilemma.

Burton's findings about "telling" are important, but one should be wary of overstating their significance. Cultural cues belong to the whole of social life, not just to ethnicity, and are used to differentiate between all sorts of types of person. In a shop, for example, cultural cues will identify which of the people there is the shopkeeper and which are the customers. When one wishes to hail a taxi, cultural cues will identify which driver it is appropriate to wave at and which not. There is an important point here. While cultural cues are often necessary to a person's identity — the shopkeeper puts on an apron, and the taxi driver puts a sign on his car so others will know who he is — these cues are not the only elements in that identity; they are not even the most important. An apron does not make someone a shopkeeper.

So too one must not exaggerate the importance of cultural cues when speaking of Catholic or Protestant identities. A woman does not have a Northern Irish Catholic identity merely because her name is Mary and she lives in a Catholic area of Belfast. She may turn out to be an American anthropologist, for example. Such a person may (if she wants) learn enough of the local culture to *pretend* to be a Northern Irish Catholic. It is not, however, her distinctive culture — her dialect, her church attendance, her interest in music — that constitutes her ethnic identity. It is the fact that she has or does not have family, school, or other connections to particular people. Without the correct connections, her pretense would soon be found out.

The fact that cultural differences are what distinguishes members of these two groups may justify to social scientists the use of the term *ethnicity*. The existence of cultural differences, however, does not explain the existence of the two groups, nor why they have divergent political aims. Much more important are the habitual patterns of social interaction, reinforced by social control, that maintain social boundaries. It is these that have caused a division in society. And it is the social division that has created a need for distinctive cultural markers so that people can tell which person is on which side.

More important than the phenomenon of "telling" is the idea that an ethnic group owns what Harrison (1992) calls "intellectual property." People in Ulster, as in most other ethnically divided societies, say of a particular tradition, belief, or cultural item, "This is part of our culture." The kind of intellectual (or cultural) property we are concerned with here is expressive culture: specialist knowledge of ceremonial or ritual, knowledge of history, and specialist skills such as dance, sport, or music.

Much of the culture identified with Irish nationalism has become well known worldwide, but there is also much distinctively unionist culture. On the nationalist side there is, for example, an excellent and thriving tradition of Irish music and dance, and the sports of Gaelic football and hurling (or hurley); sometimes individuals claim (or imply) that the rich traditions of oral narrative and folk custom in Ireland belong to the nationalist side (Ballard 1988). Unionists have tended to differentiate their own culture by eschewing those activities that have become identified as "Irish." Nevertheless, they too have distinctive traditions of music — especially marching bands, but also the impressive though underrated Lambeg drum. These are associated with popular festivals, of which the Twelfth of July is the most important. There has recently grown up an association that strives to assert the equal importance of the Ulster Scots dialect of English with the Irish language. And it is important to note that there are distinctive religious traditions on both sides. All of these activities are quite complex, and a few will be discussed in later chapters.

In practice, these activities and systems of ideas are looked after by particular individuals, whom we shall refer to as curators. Usually these are amateur enthusiasts, but occasionally they are professionals. Frequently these people come together in specialist organizations, which must be cared for similarly. For example, the religious traditions of each side are cared for by the clergy of the different churches, and also by the more active members of congregations.

Historical traditions and also certain ritual and ceremonial practices are conserved by the more active members of such bodies as the Orange Order or the Ancient Order of Hibernians. There are traditions of dance, looked after by a number of different dance organizations. Irish sport has the Gaelic Athletic Association. Irish music has Cómhaltas Ceoltóiri Éireann. The "British culture" of Ulster — mainly historical traditions — is sustained by the Ulster Society. There are also individuals who publish books or give lectures, or whose stories are collected by folklore collectors, but who are less formally organized. In their curatorial role, associations and individuals such as these collectively (though sometimes as rivals) conserve the culture of their own ethnic group. The curators allow people who have a more peripheral interest in and a more superficial understanding of the subject to participate occasionally.

In addition to expressive culture, there are also intellectual traditions that are more narrowly political. Political traditions are under the care of the political parties, the paramilitary groups, and such associations as the Orange and Hibernian orders. Each of these bodies has its own distinctive traditions, rhetoric, and styles of practice, with which it tries to attract the allegiance of segments of the ethnic group it serves. Among the political parties that compete for the allegiance of Protestants in Ulster are the Ulster Unionist Party and the Democratic Unionist Party. The Social Democratic and Labour Party and Sinn Féin compete for the votes of Catholics. There is also the Alliance Party, whose members are drawn from both sides. The paramilitary groups include the loyalist (i.e., unionist) Ulster Defence Association and Ulster Volunteer Force, and the republican (i.e., nationalist) Provisional Irish Republican Army.

The fact that comparatively small numbers of individuals — enthusiasts and professionals — are curators of the cultural property of each ethnic group has major significance, explaining not only why Akenson (1991) is correct when he says that the cultural differences that separate Catholic and Protestant are few, but also why these small differences are so important.

The overwhelming majority of people allow their distinctive expressive culture (that is, that belonging to their own ethnic group) to have only a small impact on their lives. Most of the time they are concerned with other things. On special occasions, however, they can avail themselves of the culture, which is cared for on their behalf by specialists. Thus somebody can attend a church most Sundays, but have little interest in doctrine, which she leaves to others to understand. Someone can be a member of the Orange Order but do little more than pay a membership fee, attend the occasional meeting, and turn up at the annual processions. The complexity of the rituals, the historical traditions, and the organizing can be left to others for whom the need to preserve some aspect of their culture is an all-consuming passion. For most people, a distinctive ethnic culture is firmly in the background of their lives: they cheer the local hurling team on an occasional Sunday, but take no further interest in the game the rest of the time. And, of course, there are many who hardly ever go to church, belong to no political or cultural organizations, and watch no sport.

It is worth noting that this attitude toward intellectual property is not peculiar to ethnic culture alone. Northern Ireland is very much part of cosmopolitan society, with a rich culture that includes everything from astrology to angling, paragliding to pigeon racing, needlework to nuclear physics, woodworking, xylophone playing, yachting, and zoology. In each case there are experts and enthusiasts who act as tradition-bearers or curators of the tradition. In each case, too, other individuals with differing degrees of interest will observe or take part in some way. In this respect, distinctively Northern Irish or Irish culture (indeed, any ethnic culture) is merely part of a more general pattern.

Figure 1. The McPeake family, curators of a musical tradition. (Courtesy of the Ulster Folk and Transport Museum)

Figure 2. Irish traditional musicians. (Courtesy of the Ulster Folk and Transport Museum)

The main difference between distinctively ethnic culture and forms of culture associated with recreational, occupational, and other groups is that many people are effectively prevented from participating in the former. In principle, anyone may become a butcher or learn needlework. The same is much less true of the cultures that belong to the two major ethnic groups in Northern Ireland. Since nobody is willing to give up those parts of culture that have a direct practical use, it means that the *distinctive* culture of each side does not include those elements of culture that form the backbone of most day-to-day existence. Distinctive culture tends to be restricted to expressive culture, usually leisure activities.

The importance of the curators of specifically ethnic culture is, however, out of all proportion to their numbers. It may be that many people do not play or even attend games of hurling; do not understand the rites of the Orange Order; do not know very much about the Battle of the Boyne; find the doctrines of their church difficult to understand; do not speak more than a few words of the Irish language; only occasionally listen to a Lambeg drum; or cannot tell the difference between a hornpipe and a jig. Nevertheless, the fact that organi-

Figure 3. Irish dancers. (Courtesy of the Ulster Folk and Transport Museum)

zations and networks devoted to the cultivation of such activities are sustained by enthusiasts and experts ensures that the members of the ethnic group have a focus — or, indeed, an array of competing foci — for their allegiance.

As well as being foci for allegiance, such bodies may also be curators of the ethnic group's rhetoric. They may even (sometimes only at crucial moments) acquire a position of influence or power, acting as spokesmen for the group and upholding the group's interests. A spectacular example of such a body is the Orange Order, whose primary activities are ritual and ceremonial. This body, especially from the 1920s to the 1970s, provided an influential network whereby the opinions of ordinary Protestant men could, at key moments, exert pressure on senior Unionist Party politicians. When they gathered for their regular lodge meetings, the Protestant men of any given locality would discuss the news of the day. They might then transmit their views to the local Member of Parliament, whether at Westminster or, formerly, at the provincial Parliament at

Stormont in Belfast. Until the early 1970s, no Unionist Party politician could regularly oppose this well-organized body of local opinion and hope to keep his seat.

There has been some discussion about whether the two sides in Ulster are really two nationalities or whether they are better defined by their religious affiliations (Taylor 1984; Wright 1973). Attitude surveys also have tried to find out whether individuals believe themselves to be Irish, British, Ulster, or some combination of these national identities (e.g., Moxon-Browne 1983; Rose 1971). While it would be absurd to deny the importance of either national or religious allegiance in the definition of ethnic identity, there is a need for clarification of the relationship among them.

A person is a Catholic and a nationalist, for instance, because he was born into a particular set of people. Only seldom does he join a group of people because he has come to accept a set of beliefs or other cultural practices. Take the case of church allegiance, the biggest and most obvious source of cultural diversity in Ulster. Churches do, of course, differ culturally. They have different rituals, different beliefs, different histories; their priests or ministers wear different robes or vestments; they are organized in different forms of church polity. Individuals, however, only occasionally become members of a particular church because they share its specific religious beliefs or other parts of its distinctive culture. On the contrary, they share in that church's distinctive culture because they are members of that church already.

Allegiance to a church, like ethnic identity, is usually something a person is born with. Part of the connection between ethnic identity and religion comes from the fact that most people are introduced to church membership by their parents. It is possible to be Protestant or Catholic, even Presbyterian or Church of Ireland, without ever attending church services. Furthermore, in Northern Ireland changing one's church does not allow one to change one's ethnic status. A Protestant who "turns" to Catholicism is a former Protestant; he is not wholly a Catholic. There are many atheists and people who are members of non-Christian groups such as Baha'i or Divine Light who are readily identifiable also as Protestants or Catholics. There is much truth in the old Ulster joke, "Are you a Catholic atheist or a Protestant atheist?" So while membership in a congregation, and hence religious belief and practice, may indeed give a major clue to a person's ethnic allegiance, his Protestantism or Catholicism is more properly seen as arising out of his social and most specifically his family relationships.

Our claim, then, is that grounding ethnicity in cultural differences is misleading. Despite this, the activity of minorities who seek to sustain what they call "our culture" or "our traditions" can be crucially important.

We do not, of course, wish to create the impression that we think social interaction and culture are in some sense opposed. Patterns of church or school attendance, for example, are patterns of social interaction, but they are also grounded in cultural rules. Rituals, riots, historical commemorations, and other social dramas are all culturally structured. All such interaction consists largely of the exchange of culturally produced symbols. Also, without the cultural cues described by Burton (1978), it would be impossible to tell who is a Catholic and who a Protestant, making it impossible to sustain the patterns of discrimination that constitute the ethnic division.

What we question is an approach that gives the cultural *differences* between the two groups an undue prominence. Much more important is the way culture (both that which differentiates and that which does not) is actually *used* in specific and concrete situations of social interaction.

An Ethnographic Approach to Identity

The two authors of this book are, respectively, urban and rural anthropologists. Kenney concentrated upon Ardoyne, an "urban village" in north Belfast, where she was mainly interested in public demonstrations. Buckley worked in the two villages of Long Stone and Killycarnon, which make up the well-defined area of Listymore in County Londonderry.[2] In part because of their collaboration, each author found it necessary to supplement this material with information drawn from other places. They came also to question some of the assumptions underpinning the opposition between urban and rural anthropology.

Listymore is on the north coast of Northern Ireland. It comprises the two small villages of Killycarnon and Long Stone, together with the surrounding countryside. Killycarnon is a small seaside resort. There are several pubs, small hotels, and boarding houses, some shops, and three caravan sites (trailer parks where visitors rent or keep mobile homes so they may visit for a vacation). There are also tennis courts and a golf course, but, rather deliberately, few other tourist amenities. Many of its houses have the scrubbed, somewhat nautical look found in the seaside towns of the British Isles. Even at the summer's height, Killycarnon is seldom inundated with tourists. Killycarnon has two churches: the one in the center is Church of Ireland, and the other, on the edge of the village, is Presbyterian. There is a Masonic Hall and an Orange Hall. Despite a sizable working-class housing estate, Killycarnon is a quiet, respectable, middle-class village.

In contrast, the ethos of the village of Long Stone is working-class. Long Stone lies about two miles inland from Killycarnon. Until the 1950s it was a mill village, with several nearby "scutch mills" processing locally grown flax. When the Northern Irish linen industry collapsed (it has only recently and on a much smaller scale been revived), several old mills were turned into dwellings for the middle class. Others become derelict. Long Stone also has a Church of Ireland, a Presbyterian church, an interdenominational, fundamentalist mission hall, and an Orange Hall. The village has a few remaining older houses, formerly occupied by mill workers, but is dominated by modern public housing controlled by the Northern Ireland Housing Executive.

The countryside around the two villages is, of course, agricultural. The flat and fertile coastal plain is arable and is also used for cattle raising. This gives way to a hillier area suitable only for sheep farming.

Overlooking the area are the ruins of the castle occupied by the former landlord, Sir Charlesworth Beck. At the turn of the twentieth century, farmers in Ireland had the chance to buy the land they were leasing from the landlords. As a result, the last Sir Charlesworth left the area in the 1920s. Despite this, there is still a medley of memories of the landlords, some happy, others more bitter.

The ethnic composition of the entire Listymore area is mainly Protestant, though in recent years the number of Catholics has increased. There is only one Catholic church building in the area. It lies in an inaccessible part of the country, surrounded by a clump of houses occupied mainly by Catholics. Within living memory, people say, there used to be only two Catholic families in Long Stone. Now there are many more. Local Protestants allege that these Catholics were allowed in by the Northern Ireland Housing Executive. This important, nonelected public body is responsible for public housing all over Northern Ireland. Unlike earlier forms of local government, the Housing Executive does not allow local people to have a decisive say in who may live locally.

If, as its inhabitants sometimes say, Listymore was in the past somewhat self-contained, this is not true today. Apart from agriculture and tourism, the main sources of employment lie outside the immediate area. A nearby city can be easily reached by car, bus, or train. As in most seaside towns in the area, university students occupy the tourist flats of Killycarnon during the off season. There are also university staff members scattered between the two villages. A nearby prison provides employment, particularly for people living in Long

Stone. Individuals even travel longer distances to work in Belfast and London-derry (sixty and thirty miles, respectively).

Listymore undoubtedly has its internal tensions. Not least among these is a continuing conflict between the wealthier and better-educated population of Killycarnon and young men from the poorer, "rougher" village of Long Stone. To an extent this antagonism is also evident in the garish graffiti on walls, pro-claiming stridently loyalist affiliations. Despite these tensions, Listymore has been generally free from the worst excesses of Northern Ireland's violence. As its inhabitants say to strangers, Listymore is "a quiet place."

In stark contrast is Ardoyne. Ardoyne, in north Belfast, has a reputation as an urban stronghold of the republican movement, which includes the political party Sinn Féin and the paramilitary Provisional IRA. The residents of this working-class Catholic area have witnessed many incidents of political and communal violence in the years since the present troubles began.

Soldiers first came to Ardoyne in 1969 to protect the Catholic residents from the murderous assaults of mobs coming from neighboring Protestant districts. They remained to confront the IRA within the borders of this urban Catholic enclave. The inhabitants of Ardoyne have long been noted for their militant Irish nationalist political loyalties. In the streets and front gardens of Ardoyne, there has been a quarter of a century of almost daily urban guerilla activity, with correspondingly violent operations by the British army.

Various urban ethnographers (Burton [1978], Feldman [1991], Sluka [1989], and others) have concentrated on the role of the IRA in Catholic districts of Belfast. Their work has been in the Falls Road area, but also in Ardoyne. Darby (1986, 1988) and Weiner (1980) also included work on less-violent aspects of life. Of these urban studies, one of the most engaging has been *Formations of Violence*, by Alan Feldman (1991). Feldman's book is not ordinary ethnography, based on participant observation. It is a work of oral historiography, informed by a social theory derived from such writers as Foucault, Girard, and Nietzsche. Feldman's tape-recorded informants are almost all actual or former members of different paramilitary groups. The topics these people discuss include the practicalities of killing and maiming. Despite the lack of participant observation and an overcomplicated theory, the book's flashes of brilliance and remarkable quotations make it a classic of Irish anthropology.

Kenney's fieldwork in Ardoyne was much concerned with the (often anti-sectarian) community action groups and projects in both republican and loyalist districts of Belfast. Her Ardoyne informants were not, therefore, personally involved in violence, though some had relatives in prison for their connection to paramilitary groups. This is a common situation in Ardoyne, where, as in other Catholic areas of Northern Ireland, the rate of unemployment is said to be over fifty percent. A focus on informants who are not involved with republicanism sheds a special light on ordinary experience and the role of paramilitary groups in Belfast neighborhoods. Ardoyne residents are uniformly Irish nationalists. Nevertheless, many express ambivalent attitudes toward political violence and the domination of the area by the paramilitarists.

The contrast between peaceful Listymore and war-torn Ardoyne corresponds to the generally sharp division found between the findings of rural and urban anthropologists in Ulster. Rural anthropology has, with few exceptions, emphasized the peaceful nature of rural communities. The emphasis on peace is so central to rural studies that it appears on many title pages. Harris's classic study (1972) tells of both *Prejudice and Tolerance* in rural Tyrone. Buckley called his 1982 study of the Upper Tullagh *A Gentle People: A Study of a Peaceful Community*. And Bufwack (1982) writes of a *Village without Violence*. Leyton (1975, 1976) asks not why the village he calls Aughnaboy in County Down is so violent, but why it is so peaceful. He speaks of ideals of "common humanity," and his central theme is that the people of Aughnaboy are, despite their differences, *The One Blood*.

All these rural studies, in sharp contrast to the urban studies, have shown that ethnic identity is never the only relevant identity a person has. They show as well that allegiances are shifting things. Kane (1968), writing of County Donegal, discusses loyalties based on locality rather than ethnicity. She says these shift according to the immediate situation in which a person finds himself. McFarlane (1978) considers allegiances forged through gossip. These too, and the opinions expressed, are not fixed — they depend on the situation.

An aim of this collaborative study is to bridge the gulf between urban and rural studies in the anthropology of Ulster. The benign mood of the rural studies sits too uneasily with the barbarity described in the urban studies. We find the relation between violent and peaceful activity to be a subtle and complex one. We shall show that the models by which people in Northern Ireland define harmonious, neighborly, friendly, and loving situations often imply the existence of a harsher, unloving world outside.

Writing of a peaceful rural society in Tyrone, Harris (1972) attributes the intensity of good intracommunity relationships to the relative antagonism between the ethnic groups. In the more violent settings with which Kenney is familiar, the same intense friendliness to insiders and hostility to enemies is, perhaps, more emphatically present.

Beyond this, individuals from any environment will proclaim the need to use harsh methods to protect the benign aspects of the world that are so precious to them. Thus, for example, a respectable, middle-class, middle-aged woman told Kenney that Christ Himself came "not to bring peace but the sword." She used this to justify political violence, in this case by Protestants. More familiarly, someone may carelessly remark, "We must fight for peace."

There is a need, therefore, to show how the culture of Northern Ireland can accommodate such friendliness while simultaneously sustaining violence. The usual solution of ethnographers has been to study either violence in the city or peace in the country. We believe that though the contrast between town and country in Northern Ireland can sometimes be stark, there is still a continuity between them. Our collaboration will permit us to look at the construction of identity through both violent and peaceful interactions in an assortment of settings, including both rural and urban.

Ethnography in Modern Society

The dichotomy between rural and urban approaches to anthropology creates another, perhaps more fundamental problem in Irish (and other) ethnography. This is the question of what it means to do ethnography — to do a community study — in a modern or postmodern society such as Northern Ireland. We are not convinced that the typical solutions employed by ethnographers in the past are the only or the best solutions to these problems.

There is a tradition in Irish anthropology of studying small, discrete, isolated communities. Such groups can be examined without the intrusion of too much complexity. Among Ireland's ethnographers, Harris (1972) and Leyton (1975) have studied quite small townships; Kane (1968, 1979) and Brody (1971) chose remote communities in the depopulated west of Ireland; Messenger (1969, 1989) and Fox (1963, 1966, 1968, 1978) worked in the islands of Aran and Tory; and Buckley's first study in Ireland (1982), like the more celebrated work of Scheper Hughes (1979a, 1979b), was set at the end of a long peninsula.

The anthropological passion for the remote and discrete must surely set off alarms. There is, as Harris (1984) suggests, a popular ideology of community in Ireland, and this finds its way into scholarship. Whelan notes a surge of intellectual interest in Irish "local" places. He advocates a harnessing of the "power of place" to counterbalance the "fading rhetoric" of nationalism (Whelan 1992). This development is suspect. In modern societies, people do not live like characters in an Agatha Christie novel, sealed away in remote villages or on islands or at the ends of peninsulas.

Kenney's initial approach to Ardoyne did not suffer from the same limitation. Ardoyne, being an urban village, provided a well-defined area. It is, however, well recognized that the notion of an urban village is a solecism. The concept was introduced to counter the notion that people in cities live lives of soulless anonymity (Gans 1962). And this idea arose, in turn, as an attempt to contrast the supposed qualities of towns and villages. In many ways, the people who live in an urban Belfast village such as Ardoyne are more cut off from outside society than people who live in country areas. But nobody takes seriously the idea that the whole of social life in a modern city takes place within the ghetto walls.

When Listymore was first chosen as a site for research, though, it was certainly selected because it seemed compact and discrete. Only gradually did it emerge that this was an illusion. One major fact was the main railway line that links Listymore with both Belfast and Derry, the two largest cities in the province. But even apart from that, there was easy access to the nearby towns by road. Listymore, it turned out, was not at all isolated. It was actively part of modern society.

Nor is this peculiar to Listymore. The high rate of emigration from Ireland is legendary, but there is also a high rate of immigration. More than nine percent of the people living in Northern Ireland in 1971, for example, were born outside the province (Compton 1978, 32). And there is also a steady rate of internal migration within Northern Ireland, particularly from west to east and from the country to the towns (Compton 1978, 33). All these migrations have set up networks based on kinship, friendship, and other relationships; these networks are not only provincewide but also international.

Add to this the existence of motor cars, railways, airlines, televisions, fax machines, and telephones, and the significance of the locality is much diminished. It was pretty obvious that there were countless rural communities such as Listymore that were far from being isolated from cosmopolitan urban life. In consequence, the whole enterprise of "doing a community study" was called into question. It became more and more clear that Listymore could only be studied using approaches drawn from urban studies.

The unsatisfactoriness of making too local a study in Listymore is most obvious when one studies members of large organizations. The churches or the Orange Order, for example, are local bodies only in a restricted sense. At a wholly local level, the Orange lodges in Listymore hold only a very limited interest for their members. The more active members fret over raising enough funds to repair their hall and to pay the local property tax. Most ordinary members turn out only three or four times a year for the annual parades, only some of which are organized locally. The elaborate symbolism of the Order and its rituals and emblems are sustained by a network of ritual specialists, called "lecturers," whose interactions transcend local boundaries. Indeed, the main point of being an Orangeman is to participate in a provincewide (in some respects worldwide) network. To confine a study of the Orange Order only to Listymore, therefore, was to impose a needless restriction.

So too with religion. For example, the leader of the weekday meetings at the fundamentalist mission hall in Listymore lives locally, but he owns a shop in a town some eighteen miles away (see chapter 4). There, on Sundays, he and his wife attend a Pentecostalist congregation. More generally, fundamentalism, like Anglicanism, Presbyterianism, or Catholicism, draws its ideas, often very directly, from a complex international network. Again, to ignore this and confine oneself to a wholly local study seemed unnecessary.

We now believe that the correct approach to rural studies is to employ methods more usually employed in the anthropology of cities. Since Wirth's early studies (1938, 1956), there has been a recognition that city dwellers do not live their lives in bounded communities. City people shift continually from one geographically and socially separate situation to another.

There has, of course, been a discovery that even in urban areas there "continue to exist" comparatively discrete "urban villages" (Gans 1962). This mode of discourse about urban areas, however, was predicated on the view (usually linked with the name of Redfield [1947]) that rural settlements are radically different from cities. We, on the contrary, doubt the worth of this dichotomy.

A good modern example of an urban study is that of Finnegan (1989), who studied the musical life of the English city of Milton Keynes. Finnegan says that in Milton Keynes there are many different and separate musical worlds. There is the jazz world, the brass-band world, the world of folk music, several worlds of classical music, and so forth. Each of these worlds is little understood by participants in the others. And each has its distinctive conventions. They diverge over the proper modes of learning, transmission, composition, and performance.

Although Finnegan's study is an example of urban, not rural, anthropology, one can use her method in a rural setting. In Listymore, there is Irish folk music, country and western, Lambeg drumming, different forms of classical music, "Scottish" pipe bands, and other forms of music, too. Each kind of music has its own discrete world, and none of these worlds is confined within Listymore. As with religion or the Orange Order, these forms of music could not be sustained if they existed only in Listymore. Each depends on the specific world that exists provincewide or beyond. The two villages of Listymore are wholly interconnected with the rest of the social universe; if they were not surrounded by countryside, they would be called urban villages.

Most urban ethnography in Northern Ireland has studied some bounded social group or institution whose members have something in common. Thus Bell (1990) attached himself to a loyalist flute band in a housing estate in Londonderry. He, however, felt the need to augment his study with a questionnaire-based study of a broader sample of schoolchildren. Murray (1985) worked in two schools serving adjacent districts in west Belfast, observing pupils and staff. Feldman's study (1991) is of a tightly closed world that includes little more than the paramilitary groups, their victims, and the security forces. His study is not at all confined to particular geographical locations, for, by their nature, even the strongest of the paramilitary groups are not *numerically* dominant in any small geographical area. Their worlds, therefore, cross the boundaries of small communities.

To explore identity in all its richness, one must abandon the rural anthropologist's obsession with a sense of place. Instead, one must study within particular worlds. These are only sometimes rooted in localities. Some of the worlds we study here are firmly set in Listymore or Ardoyne. Others are not. In chapter 3, for example, we look at "ethnic history" (Smith 1984). This history has been generated by individual specialists, and is sustained mainly by enthusiasts within particular organizations. It is not found especially in Listymore or Ardoyne (or anywhere else), though it has an impact in these places. It is, in fact, most readily approached through written texts. Chapter 4 explores how patterns found in ethnic and other forms of history are also to be discovered in discourse within Listymore about contemporary social life.

Chapter 5 *is* concerned with place, but its subject is the definition of territory in Ardoyne. Chapter 6 is also rooted in place, this time in Listymore. It deals with the way wholly local considerations are bound up with ideas of authority and rebellion in domestic and recreational situations.

Chapters 7 and 8 consider the relationship between identity and religious experience and belief, and explore aspects of the world of fundamentalism. Fundamentalism is important in the life of Listymore, as it is elsewhere. However, it proved much easier to study this world in suburban Belfast, where fundamentalists are more numerous.

Chapters 9 and 10 describe various kinds of disruptive behavior and the way that these too relate to identity. Though some of these descriptions are firmly set in Listymore and Ardoyne, others belong to particular places only contingently. And the discussion of the symbolism of the Royal Black Institution in chapter 11 is not located in any special place.

There is here an important theoretical point. If individuals construct their identities during social interaction, they do so as they move from discrete world to discrete world. Also important is the fact that, even within any specific world, identities are defined and redefined against a background of successive situations and relationships. And when people make representations of their identities, they describe themselves, directly or by implication, against any one of countless different backgrounds. The constant redefinition of identity takes place, in part, to suit the purposes of the person who makes the definitions. For some purposes, a sense of place is crucial to an understanding of what goes on there; for other purposes, it is totally irrelevant.

In a modern society, an individual moves from world to world. One person will put a lot of work into the construction and maintenance of a particular world (Finnegan 1989), while another person will just be passing through. No one, however, constructs his or her identity (or that of another person) in abstraction. This theoretical perspective echoes field experience. In fieldwork, one does not often discover single "communities." Working in the field, the researcher one day meets a woman in her home; the next day, watches a procession; the day after, goes to church; and then, the next day, meets some people in a pub. These encounters have for the researcher a sense of immediacy and facticity. "Communities," in contrast, have an abstract quality. They become less and not more real the more they are studied.

Our contention is that individuals define themselves and others in the kinds of situations that researchers (but also quite ordinary people) continually meet in daily life. These are the concrete situations of immediate and small-scale interaction. We have tried, therefore, not to put too much faith in prearranged interviews. It is important to consider also those interactions that we did not ourselves set up, and in which we were not ourselves leading participants. People do define their identities in the interactive process of the formal interview, but it is a mistake to see interviews as typical forms of interaction. We recognize, of course, that much can be gained through interviews (see, for example, Buckley 1985; Feldman 1991). Still, we agree with Tonkin (1992) that it is often better to watch the production of even quite formal "texts" in a genre and a setting with which the informant is familiar.

Our research takes account of the fact that individuals move quickly from one world to another, and that not every world is confined to a single locality. If we had clung to the fiction that Listymore and Ardoyne were somehow the all-embracing loci of the social lives of the people who live there, the result would of course have been tidier, as it also would have been had we used only an oral-history approach.

In an individualistic, postmodern society in which individuals constantly leap from one social setting to another, the ethnographer must no longer look at integrated, structured communities, for none exist. Instead, he or she must look at specific texts and specific interactions. It is here that identities are de-scribed, dramatized, and given shape. It is here that a person can define himself or herself in a structured and meaningful framework through patterns of social interaction.

2

Some
Theoretical
Remarks

Two opposite ideas are central to the study of identity. First is the complexity of the knowledge we can have of an individual. Second is the idea that a person is not many people but only one.

Suppose you meet someone and learn that she is an Ulster Protestant. You may later discover that this same person is also a judo champion, a violinist, and a mother of two. At first, the listing of the elements that define a person is a mere categorization. It involves only semantic labels. But when one applies any kind of lemon-squeezing analysis, the subject overflows with complexity.

Suppose this woman really is a "judo champion" or a "violinist." Each of those labels implies that she occupies a place in an entire world of action and interaction. At its simplest, to identify somebody is to pigeonhole or label them, but it quickly becomes much more that this. Each label places that person in an elaborate moral and social context, containing both natural objects and other people.

One of the worlds within which the woman may live is the one pinpointed in the popular phrase "she lives in a world of her own." Most people live at least a proportion of their lives in a world (or in any one of several worlds) of their own. Such a world, like other worlds, is one where there is a kind of social interaction. In this case, the social interaction is of a reflexive nature. In such a world a person converses with herself.

As the woman shifts from world to world, or from situation to situation within any one of these worlds, her identity will also shift. She will not only be classified differently; she will also act differently, and will play a different part in relation to each different world or situation. Individuals, therefore, do not just have a single identity. They have multitudinous partial identities.

The second idea, opposed to the first, is that no matter how many different roles a person may play, no matter how many statuses he may occupy, there is only one unified, essential person, who always remains the same.

Cohen (1994) argues this last point strongly. He claims that a reflexive self-consciousness works to provide an individual with a unified self. This self is a synthesis of the different personae that arise during particular social interactions. He claims further that for any individual, a sense of self exists prior to any given social interaction. A more unified composite self-image allows the individual to be one of the authors of the interaction, and hence one of the authors of his own evolving identity.

Our opinion differs slightly from Cohen's. We maintain that at specific times, individuals will indeed construct representations of themselves that embrace a range of different personae. Such representations are unlikely to be as complete, unified, or integrated as Cohen seems to suggest. We shall show in chapter 12 not only that synthetic, apparently unified versions of the self are found in an introspective, reflexive self-consciousness, but also that such representations of self are presented to other people. We shall note, however, that these more-integrated versions of the self rarely provide anything that could pass for a truly complete view of the self. Nevertheless, we agree with him that, both in social interactions and in isolated introspection, individuals do strive to define and present themselves not as a series of unconnected, fragmented personae, but as more unified and integrated wholes.

This chapter is not concerned directly with Northern Ireland. It is divided into three main sections, which set the theoretical scene of the book. The first section will suggest that identity is the knowledge one person has of another, or the knowledge a person has of himself or herself. This knowledge is defined within an assortment of frames. The frames, in turn, can be divided into two broad categories: *operational* and *rhetorical*. Operational frames guide action, enabling people to achieve particular goals. Rhetorical frames try to persuade other people of the truth of a view of the world, and of the definition of the people and objects within that view.

Identity is a form of knowledge, and so the second section of this chapter will briefly address a perennial problem in the sociology of knowledge: the problem of relativism. It will show how a contrast between rhetorical and operational models can rescue a relativistic anthropology from the perils of self-refutation.

The third section will argue that the frames that define identities are partially structured by means of metaphor. This section will also suggest how an individual can have many separate and incompatible partial identities, while still seeming to remain (to himself and to others) the selfsame individual.

Operational and Rhetorical Frameworks

The starting point, in the spirit of Akenson (1991) and Barth (1969), is that individuals define themselves and other people when they act and interact with others. During action and interaction, individuals define the boundaries of situations, relationships, institutions, and "worlds." The identities of individuals are, in turn, negotiated within these bounded frames.

These ideas rest upon several assumptions. We assume that identity is a form of knowledge. Further, we say knowledge is a "social construct" (Berger and Luckman 1966). Also, knowledge about any topic — a person, object, event, etc. — is defined within a context or "frame" (Goffman 1975). Finally, we say that frames are defined with either operational or rhetorical purposes.

The term *framework* or *frame* comes from the work of Bateson (1955). It was also developed by Goffman in his book *Frame Analysis* (1975). A frame provides background information against which specific objects, events, or people — past, present, or future, real or fictional — are given definition. Such a frame can identify persons for either rhetorical or operational purposes. Because of the number and complexity of human purposes, the number of possible frames that may define any individual, situation, or relationship can be very large indeed.

In drawing attention to the distinction between rhetorical and operational frames, we underline a major contrast made by Goffman. This is the opposition between *real* or *actual* identity and *virtual* identity: between the identity a person really has, and the one that he or she tries to persuade others that he or she has (Goffman 1968, 12). This issue is intricate because expressions of virtual identity (that is, rhetoric) become, in rituals, ceremonials, and other genres of social drama, occasions for the forging of real identities.

The framing of a situation or relationship is usually purposive: a frame will be defined with the operational goal of achieving some desired objective. The frame therefore indicates a set of actions appropriate to the situation and to the reaching of the goal. For example, if a woman decides in the street to buy a newspaper, she must define the steps necessary to achieve this objective. She must identify that *this* shop (and not another one) sells newspapers. She must decide, before crossing the road, that particular drivers are, or are not, driving slowly enough to allow her to reach the shop safely, and so forth.

Such a framed definition of reality is sometimes (but more often not) spelled out in a written, spoken, or other description. Frequently, a person simply understands the situation in a nonverbal manner and acts accordingly. The framework provides knowledge of the actor in relation to other objects and people. We shall call such a framework or model of reality an *operational model* (Caws 1978) or an *operational framework*.

In performing even a simple task, such as buying a newspaper, there is an important social element to the definitions of identity that occur. In asking to buy a paper, the woman defines her own identity potentially as a customer. The other person is similarly defined as a newspaper vendor. But it is only when these virtual identities are mutually confirmed by means of a (perhaps tacit) negotiation that the relationship and the two identities are given a measure of objectivity or reality (Berger and Luckman 1966, 65ff.). In some cases, the reality of a person's identity may be of long duration. In other cases, as with the identity of a customer, it can be quite fleeting.

Sometimes a virtual identity is not confirmed by others, who will claim that a person's identity lacks reality. Sometimes one group of people will confirm an identity while others will deny it. For example, a man may regard himself as a freedom fighter and persuade his friends to agree with this definition. Other people — for example, the police — may see his activities as merely criminal and strive to lock him up.

Insofar as there is agreement on the nature of a person and what he does, then this identity gains "objectivity" (see Berger and Luckman 1966, 74ff.). Thus everyone may agree, for example, that the freedom fighter/criminal does indeed break the law. This definition of the person is a social construction, but it has objectivity. To the extent, however, that no agreement exists, the identity remains virtual or rhetorical.

Not all identities, however, arise simply out of operational frameworks. Sometimes someone will create a framed *representation* of reality and present it to another person with the aim of changing his definition of a particular piece of reality. Such a framework or model of reality we call a *rhetorical frame* or a *rhetorical model*. By its nature, and in contrast with an operational frame, a rhetorical frame *must* take the form of a representation.

Rhetorical models of the world are, of course, employed for pragmatic ends: they are a "level of organization" (Goldman 1970) within an operational model. As an example, a man might take part in gossip (exchanging rhetorically framed descriptions of other people) with the aim of being friendly to the person he is speaking to (McFarlane 1978). Indeed, many friendships consist of little more than exchanges of rhetorically framed messages. Other forms of rhetoric may be used in similar ways. A man might decide to attend religious rituals (which also provide framed descriptions of aspects of reality) because he judges that by going to church he will enlarge his circle of friends. In each case, his knowledge of the world (that engaging in a kind of conversation or going to church may perhaps improve his social life) has been framed for an operational purpose.

Such an operational framework is quite different from the framed definitions of reality contained in the *content* of the gossip or the religious rituals. The operational model (which suggests that a certain kind of interaction will give rise to friendship) is organized at one level. The largely rhetorically framed content of the descriptive or ritual interaction is organized at a different level (Goldman 1970; see also Hofstadter 1980). It is important to note that the relationships formed around the gossip, religious ritual, or other rhetoric will probably be real enough. But for the relationship to work, it is not necessary that the content of the rhetoric itself be true.

Many relationships and institutions, and hence identities, are created incidentally or in passing. They come into being during social interactions as actors strive to achieve their own diverse goals, defining their identities operationally in relation to these aims.

Other interactions, however, consist largely of dramatizations. Dramatizations have the aim of demonstrating that specific structured relationships, institutions, situations, and hence identities exist. Here, at its simplest, one person will act out an identity within a frame. Another person will then either affirm or deny the identity thus dramatized.

The point here originates from Evans-Pritchard (1965), who argued that ritual can itself *constitute* social relations. Ritual is not always, as Durkheim (1977) had said, only an *expression* of preexisting social relations. Girard (1989) has also argued that social solidarity arises out of ritual. He, however, holds that violently sacrificial rites are needed to constitute social solidarity, human sacrifice being especially efficacious! This is not a view we share.

We claim that definitions not only of social solidarity, but also of other kinds of social relationship, arise from all kinds of ritual and quasi-dramatic interactions. Such social drama (Burke 1957; Turner 1982) can range from the most grandiose ritual or ceremonial to quite commonplace exchanges such as conversation, a greeting, or a smile. All such drama makes a rhetorical statement about the nature of the world and the individual's place in it.

When one person presents himself to another, there are strong elements of both experiment and persuasion in the presentation. A greeting, for example, is an invitation to another person to confirm the existence of a friendly relationship. The greeting dramatizes a virtual relationship, and a set of virtual identities within the framework of that relationship. It is only when the greeting is confirmed (in this case by being returned) that the identities within the frame of the relationship become a reality. The initial greeting is, therefore, a persuasive or rhetorical gesture. It marks only a virtual set of identities. It is also an experimental act, inviting the other person to confirm that a particular opinion of the relationship is true. When confirmed, and when later supported by other, similar interactions, the relationship and the identities cease to be virtual ones. They acquire reality. In later chapters we shall look at quasi-dramatic interactions that are unfriendly. But even here there is a need for an affirmation of the nature of the identities thus defined. By such affirmation, virtual identities become real.

A feature of the social frames that define the identities of people is their moral quality (Goffman 1975, 22). When a person or a set of actions is placed in a particular frame, that person or those actions are defined as "good" or "bad," worthy of reward or worthy of punishment. The goodness or badness of a person or action can be redefined by shifting it from one frame to another (see chapter 4). According to how a person is defined in a frame, so will he or she be rewarded or punished.

Another feature of the presentation and definition of self is that it involves power. In presenting oneself to another person, one effectively invites the other to affirm the reality or validity of a particular framework. This framework will also often implicitly or explicitly define the other person, to the other's advantage or disadvantage. Important questions to be considered in any given interaction therefore include: Who benefits most from any given definition? Who has the power to do the defining?

Power can, of course, come from the naked use of physical force, and to live in Northern Ireland is to be aware of this fact. Physical force, however, is only the crudest form of power. Power more generally can be considered to be control over some resource. Such resources include what Marx called the means of production, but they extend to quite intimate matters. As Waller showed (1937; see also Leslie 1979), power commonly resides with the person (or group) who has the least interest in sustaining a given definition of a relationship or situation. The person who has the greater interest in maintaining a definition of a situation or relationship can, therefore, be exploited. The power that "comes out of the barrel of a gun," whether a terrorist's or a policeman's, is just a special case of this. It derives from the pain that could result if one did not acquiesce in the gun-holder's definition of a given situation. The gun in the other's hand increases one's interest in complying.

An action in a social drama, therefore, tries rhetorically to persuade another person to acquiesce in the truth of that definition. The success of one's rhetoric may sometimes depend only upon one's skills as a rhetorician, but sometimes it will depend on one's comparative power. (Taylor 1985 gives an excellent historical example of social drama in the west of Ireland where both power and skill were intertwined.)

It does not follow that because some statement or dramatization has a rhetorical aim, it is necessarily deceitful or untrue. When a lawyer claims that her client is not guilty, she may be stating what is actually the truth. In the same way, the car described by a salesman's rhetoric may in fact turn out to be as good as the salesman says it is. It is the same in the different genres of representation that we shall consider here.

We will show how agreed-upon facts can be framed and reframed to produce different versions of Irish life, past and present. These differently framed accounts have different rhetorical implications. Thus there are several versions of Irish history, but few disagreements about the *facts* of Irish history. Similarly, there are alternative versions of the ordinary events of everyday life.

In rhetorical presentations (in social life we are all rhetoricians) people will only sometimes tell a lie. Except where one's ends are systematically dishonest, to stoop to lying usually indicates desperation or mere incompetence. Similarly, rhetoric is not always a mere gloss on preexisting social facts. A few identities, of course — among them the ethnic identities of Ulster — have an edificelike solidity: they cannot be wished away just by changing one's mind. Most rhetoric, however, has a vitality of its own. The rhetoric of a lawyer can transform the identity of a free man into that of a convict. The rhetoric of a politician can create, sustain, or destroy a social institution. So too with the sorts of interactions described in this book. For example, gossip can cause listeners to relate differently to the people being described: they may no longer be seen as friends. And, as McFarlane has shown (1978), gossip itself may be a piece of social drama. Through it, a speaker and a listener can create or recreate a momentary or long-lasting set of identities.

In conversation, and in the other ceremonies, rituals, riots, and more commonplace interactions described in this book, the interaction often focuses in a kind of rhetoric. Through the interaction, however, the facticity of identity is often created.

The subject of rhetoric is almost as old as Western thought itself. Protagoras is famous for saying, "There are two sides to every question" (see Billig 1985, 97; Nill 1985, 29–30). This opinion, via Hegel, found its way into Marxist thought. Marx claimed that much philosophical, religious, and economic knowledge reflects the self-interest of specific social and economic groups. He called this knowledge *ideology* (Engels and Marx 1845–46), a form of rhetoric whose aim is to convince others of the justice of a particular cause. Sometimes, too, rhetoric can be a kind of self-deception. When, for example, someone has little objective worth, he may use rhetoric reflexively to convince himself that he has at least some (perhaps imaginary) value (Marx 1844, 115–16).

Nowadays, discussions of rhetoric are important to any study of the sociology of knowledge (Billig 1985; Toulouse 1985). Since Protagoras, the discussion has moved forward: it is better now to say not that there are *two* sides to every question. Rather, anything — animals, objects, people, social groups, gods — can be represented in *dozens* of different ways. The representation that is created is likely to be to the advantage or comfort of the person who creates it.

Our argument is that rhetoric has major significance in the social construction of identity. First, rhetorical knowledge about people and about their place in different frameworks exists in its own right. Second, the presentation of rhetorical views of the world plays a big part in the operational models through which people construct their real identities.

The Problem of Relativism

The idea that knowledge is a social construct; that the social and physical worlds can be defined in different ways; that the purpose of defining the world is often rhetorical; and that the alleged truth or falsehood of any proposition is merely relative to the place of the speaker or listener in the physical or social universe: all these issues raise a knotty theoretical problem that should be addressed, at least briefly. This is the problem of relativism.

Woolgar and Pawluch identify the problem of relativism (or of constructivism) in a series of essays. They say that constructivism is "ironical" in the way it treats knowledge, and that it casts doubt on the truth of the knowledge being studied. Worse, it casts doubt on *all* knowledge, including the knowledge of relativists or social constructivists themselves: "Relativism implies all forms of knowledge are untrue. Relativism is a form of knowledge. Therefore, relativism is untrue" (Woolgar 1983; Woolgar and Pawluch 1985a, 1985b).

The arguments of social constructivists, therefore, have the form of an antinomy. They are comparable to the paradox of Epimenides the Cretan, who said, "All Cretans are liars" (a statement that if true is therefore untrue, and that if untrue is therefore true);[1] or to that of Alexander Chase, who said, "All generalizations are false — including that one." On the face of it, say Woolgar and Pawluch, constructivism is a solipsism, a self-refuting hypothesis, a form of ontological gerrymandering.

Badly formed theories are subject to paradoxes, or what Hofstadter calls "strange loops" (Hofstadter 1980, 684ff.). Any theory of humanity must have the capacity to be reflexive: it must be applicable to or compatible with the self-definition of both the theorist and the theory. When one applies this test to the more extreme forms of relativism, these theories can be shown to be self-refuting (see Dixon 1977).

We wish, therefore, briefly to consider Woolgar and Pawluch's problem. We suggest that one can begin to escape from it by differentiating between operational and rhetorical representations of the world.

Writers suspicious of relativism have sometimes shown a slightly wicked tendency to relativize the study of knowledge itself. They have pushed the argument into a downward spiral of self-refutation. Such a trick is readily achieved by claiming that sociologists or historians of knowledge hold views that are themselves social constructions, or a form of rhetoric, or both.

One element in relativism is the view that the knowledge, beliefs, and culture found in different parts of the world are all equally valuable or true. Ebel (1986) has elegantly criticized this idea. He considers relativistic writers from Montaigne and Voltaire to Boas and Mead. None of them, he says, wants to give a dispassionate account of foreign societies. They want instead to criticize their own. Stein (1986) similarly says relativism is a rhetoric used by liberals who want to get back at racists.

Jacobs (1987), in a different vein, criticizes relativistic theories of science. Giving the sociology of knowledge a dose of its own self-refuting, relativistic medicine, he says the theories of Popper (1959), Kuhn (1962) and Feyerabend (1975) are rooted in the theorists' own political presuppositions, which he calls Whiggish, Jacobin/Marxist, and Trotskyist, respectively.

If all these criticisms are true, then not only this volume but also the whole enterprise of studying knowledge is fatally flawed. By a strange twist to the paradox, even the critics of relativism and social constructivism would be refuted. For it is by a relativistic critique that relativism is itself attacked.

Woolgar and Pawluch's problem has implications far beyond the sociology of knowledge. When we sit on a jury listening to lawyers; when we hear a politician's speech; when we listen to a used-car salesman: in all these situations, and in others less prototypical, we take proper account of the fact that the views we hear are rhetorical. We know they reflect the speaker's social situation. We know these people are trying to persuade. An epistemological critique of relativism, which requires us *not* to exercise such critical judgment, is too harsh. We would have to abandon not only a useful sociological method but also an invaluable social skill. We need to find a way out of the logical spiral of self-refutation while leaving intact our ability to evaluate rhetorical and other statements when we encounter them.

Two paths out of the difficulty suggest themselves. The first is an idea inherent in the work of Berlin and Kay (1969) but developed elsewhere (e.g., Berlin 1978; Brown 1977; Collier et al. 1976; Rosch 1972, 1977a, 1977b, 1978; Rosch et al. 1976). This body of research suggests that at certain basic levels of abstraction, both the perception and the naming of objects are much the same for people the world over, with linguistic and other cultural differences making little difference. This work implies that all descriptions of the world can be translated into a basic "language" in which people point at objects and name them. Such a language is common to all human beings. It is what allows people to make at least approximate translations from one language to another. It also provides a protected level (Hofstadter 1980, 688) of perception, free from socially constructed fictions. This protected level of perception ensures that people see, touch, and feel a world that is much the same for everyone.

The second idea, dependent upon the first, is that even in more abstract knowledge, there is a tendency to objectivity. This idea relies upon the distinction between forms of knowledge that are rhetorical (Billig 1985) and those whose aims are directly pragmatic or operational (Caws 1978). The distinction can be clarified by an example. A rhetorical frame is one used by a car salesman to *persuade* a prospective customer. Whatever the real condition of the car, the salesman will highlight its good points and minimize its faults. An operational frame, in contrast, is the one the customer uses when *making a decision*. Here the customer will not exaggerate or minimize the car's qualities. On the contrary, he wants to know if the car is *really* any good.

Operational frames tend toward objectivity. Suppose a man crosses the road, or bets on a horse, or buys a car. There will be quite clear criteria that demonstrate whether the operational frame he used was good enough for the purpose: Did he get safely to the other side? Did the horse come in first? Does the car in fact run well?

One should, of course, emphasize that even operational frameworks only *tend* toward objectivity. They can be called into question, either by the facts or by the views of other people. There are often several competing operational frameworks defining reality. An actor may therefore not be certain which of several actions is appropriate. A given operational framework can be better or worse than others; it can simply be mistaken or untrue; or its success may be wholly fortuitous. Also, a person may have mixed motives that cloud his objectivity in any given case.

Nevertheless, in selecting a proper course of action, a person is to some degree motivated by a desire to get his facts right. It is this objective tendency in operational models that gives the lie to the more extreme forms of relativism. It is easy, perhaps especially for scholars, to forget that beyond thought lies a real world, which brings real pleasure and real pain. Often the practical judgments people make lead successfully to pleasure. This does seem to show that conceptual frameworks can, at least sometimes, grasp genuine truths about the relation of real people to objects in the world.

The notion of an operational frame relates directly to individual identity. When a person acts he also defines himself. When, for example, a man drives his car down a particular street to reach his house, he places himself in a practical relation to his car, to the street, to other cars, to pedestrians, to his house, and so forth. At that moment, he knows himself to be a specific person who exists in relation to particular framed circumstances. If his actions are successful, if they achieve their desired goal — that is, if he reaches his home safely — there is in this very success proof that, within its incomplete limits, the operational framework (though not necessarily its rhetorical justification) was true. The partial identities of himself and the other people and objects within that framework correspond to an objective reality.

So too when, by his actions, a person dramatizes that he is a particular kind of individual. A man might, for example, wave to greet a friend across the street, dramatizing to the friend and to onlookers that he is indeed the other person's friend. In such a case, the dramatization may be an invitation to the other to confirm the existence of that relationship. If the dramatization is confirmed by the other, then he can assume that the relationship, and hence their identities within that relationship, exist. If denied, it will show that the actor's view of his emergent relationship with the other is mistaken: the relationship does not in fact exist or has perhaps lapsed. Thus, even in the fluid world of human relationships, a social reality can be subject to pragmatic testing.

Stein (1986, 159), quoting Erikson (1974, 103), makes a distinction between *relativism* and *relativity*. Relativism, he says, is the view that every individual has his own distinctive version of the universe, depending on his place in it. Relativity is the theory of Einstein. But relativity starts from relativism. It goes on, though, to build a theory that will predict what the universe will look like for any observer, no matter how he moves or where he stands. The study of identity, conceived as part of the sociology of knowledge, must at least contribute to such a relativity. It must account for the views of different actors, no matter where they stand or what their object. A study that assumes a measure of relativism in human knowledge can, therefore, avoid a spiral of self-refutation.

Even a successful theory of knowledge will remain, so to speak, the theorist's own view, reflecting his or her position in the world. No doubt some people will accept or refute a particular account merely because it provides the wrong sort of rhetoric, favorable to one cause or unfavorable to another. It is, however, also possible for people to judge a theory with the same objectivity they use when they cross the road or buy a car. A theory can be judged according to whether it provides a useful and accurately framed version of the evidence presented.

Metaphor and the Interrelatedness of Frameworks

We have argued that the frameworks that define identities change with each new social interaction. Because of this, an individual is likely to shift among myriads of different partial identities from moment to moment. In this section we shall begin to explain why, despite constantly shifting identities, a person is still thought to be the selfsame individual.

In brief, the argument is as follows: The frameworks used to define identity, whether for pragmatic purposes or for rhetorical ones, are often structured by the same few metaphors. Also, partial identities, and the frames that define them, often act as metaphors for one another. In consequence, the frameworks that define particular partial identities are often very similar to each other. Because of the similarity among frameworks, an individual often occupies a similar place in each of the different frameworks that define his identity.

On particular occasions, therefore, and for specific purposes, a person may find it possible to demonstrate that these partial identities are, at least in principle, unified and compatible. At these moments, several different facets of identity will be presented simultaneously, with one partial identity being presented through the presentation of another. As well as constructing, at different times, particular partial identities, a person may also, at other times, present himself or herself as a unified, multifaceted human being.

The first point of the argument is that the frameworks that define identity are remarkably similar. Piellon (1984), for example, considers several different forms of Irish discourse. He looks at novels and short stories by Irish writers, pastoral letters from Irish bishops, and the speeches of Irish trade unionists. In all of these writings, individuals and types of people are defined. Piellon shows how these texts, from three apparently quite different Irish settings, participate in the same "ideological" patterns.

The main reason for the similarity is that these different discourses are improvised from and partially structured by recurring prototypes or metaphors (Lakoff and Johnson 1980; Schon 1979). Not all these metaphors have wholly identical structures, but they do readily translate into one another, creating mixed metaphors of enormous usefulness.

Quite apart from the study of life in Ireland, students of human thought have long argued that the basis for the higher forms of knowledge lies in metaphors. They are also spoken of as "prototypes" or "good examples" or "archetypes" or "paradigms" (e.g., Ardener 1970; Barnes 1969; Beck 1978; Buckley 1985; Fernandez 1974, 1975; Giovannini 1981; Kuhn 1962; Lakoff and Johnson 1980; Menola-Kallio 1984; Ortony 1979; Willis 1972).

The classic (one might say paradigmatic) statement of this approach was that of Thomas Kuhn (1962). Kuhn suggests that scientific knowledge is derived from paradigms. Though later criticized in matters of detail, Kuhn's work remains outstanding as a pioneering work of genius.

Examples of paradigms are to be found in all the natural and human sciences. In the physical sciences, the movements of electrons in relation to other subatomic particles are classically structured in a conceptual framework metaphorically derived from the solar system. Certain psychological theories now situate human thoughts and actions in a framework that defines them as similar to the output of a computer. An old and occasionally recurring metaphor in the social sciences sees society as "evolving" through successive stages, like a biological organism. Another social scientific tradition describes human activity through mixed biological and mechanistic metaphors, as though it "functioned" like a body or even a steam engine (see Boyd 1979; Kuhn 1962, 1979). This approach to the study of knowledge, relating specific knowledge to paradigms, has also been found useful in African studies (see Buckley 1985; Willis 1972). And the pervasiveness of metaphor in the daily life of the West has been most clearly stated by Lakoff and Johnson, whose 1980 book has the evocative title *Metaphors We Live By*.

Among the metaphors to be considered here are those that give definition not only to social situations but also to the human body and individual self. There is a substantial literature on the relevance of the body both as an object of thought and as a tool for thinking (see chapter 3). Much of this has concentrated on the use of the body as a metaphor for society or for social groups. Such an approach has been criticized, sometimes with justice, for its tendency to regard the body as *only* a metaphor, unimportant in its own right (Buckley 1985, 182ff.).

Feldman's study of Northern Irish paramilitarists places a central emphasis on the human body and upon an image closely related to the body, the *sanctuary*. Feldman regards sanctuary as inherently a spatial concept. This he derives from Foucault, for whom power is itself spatialized, the body being a spatial unit constructing sites of domination. When Feldman perceives the body to be a metaphor or a symbol, it is a domestic or other *territory* that is thus defined.

We do not dispute Feldman's approach, except in matters of emphasis. We shall ourselves consider space with its sanctuaries as having been defined by body-based images. Not least among the metaphors that define social relationships are images of rape, of spirit and flesh, and of disease. These, we shall show, are similar to other images, such as those of the temple and, famously, of the siege, that Northern Irish people use to define social relationships. These images differentiate and organize not merely physical space but also social space between an "inside" and an "outside" (see chapter 3).

Where we disagree with Feldman is in considering this spatial approach to be the *only* approach to the body, or to society. There are other body-based metaphors that also play an important part in defining human relationships and identities. One is the dichotomy between the rational head and the sensual loins. Another is the well-known Pauline idea that social groups have "members" (e.g., Rom. 12:4). All these are important to the definition of human identities and relationships, but none of them is *spatial* in its implications.

Feldman's emphasis on physical territory, on physical sanctuary, and on the physical body itself, with all its excretions and vulnerabilities, is ideal for a study of violence. Our study, however, is not of violence but of identity. We do not want to restrict ourselves to the conversations of violent men. We need a less confining theory, one that will still embrace Feldman's insights.

Apart from body-based imagery, it is also true that any one type of identity or any one defining framework can become a metaphor for another. Thus men are sometimes described as "children"; employers are described as "paternalistic" or "tyrannical"; a classroom may be "in revolt," and so forth. It seems, for example, that the mass media in Sweden depict sports heroes as though they personify the alleged "Swedish national character" (Ehn 1989). These "national" characteristics, however, are better seen as the traits of a certain social class (Frykman 1989). Meaning is therefore piled on meaning, and each identity takes its shape from its relation to other identities.

In a similar way, we too shall emphasize the idea that images drawn from social class are used to construct and define ethnicity. Thus, people defined as "English" are often upper-class Ulster people (see chapters 6 and 7), and typically "Catholic" characteristics are often better described as those of working-class people (see chapter 12).

Because of the similar ways in which partial identities are defined, it becomes possible for an individual to present himself, on particular occasions, as having a single, integrated (if multifaceted) personality. An individual is liable to perceive a likeness or contingency between his place in one frame and his place in another. It also becomes possible for individuals to construct operational strategies that can be applied to quite different situations. In the same way, operational and rhetorical representations have features that fit together. As will be clear in chapter 12, individuals will therefore blend their partial identities together into seemingly integrated wholes.

Concluding Remarks

A person's identity is defined in frames constructed for operational or rhetorical purposes during specific social interactions. Conceptualizations, descriptions, and dramatizations, not only of fleeting incidents but also of historical events and long-standing relationships and institutions, provide structured contexts within which individuals and their actions are understood and given definition.

Tonkin (1992, 51ff.), writing of oral history, has drawn attention to the concept of *genre* (see also Kratz 1989). We wish to extend this concept to include not only different types of representation but also other kinds of interaction. There are, indeed, very many genres through which individuals create framed versions of reality, which in turn define individual identities. Often a specific genre of representation or other social practice can become a type of intellectual or other cultural "property" (Harrison 1992). In such a case, a genre may be cared for on behalf of a wider community by a group of enthusiasts or professionals. This volume will explore some of the many genres used by people in Northern Ireland to define their own and other people's identities. Among the genres of interaction we shall consider are history and other narratives, religious ritual, playfulness, riot, and the pictorial symbolism of a secretive society, as well as nonrepresentational ways of defining urban territory through violence. We shall also try to place the book itself in a framework provided by the fact that one of the authors is a curator in a Northern Irish museum.

Identities, we have suggested, are defined within the frameworks provided by the actors' own understanding of particular relationships, institutions, situations, or worlds. Actors switch among worlds, situations, relationships, and purposes with great rapidity. The number of possible frameworks that may define any person's identity can therefore be infinite.

Cohen (1994), however, shows that a person will typically be aware of a self that is broader than those partial identities that belong in narrow and immediate social settings. Individuals also bring to social interaction preexisting skills, experiences, recollections, goals, purposes, interests, and agendas. Each interacting individual may have one or several conscious representations of himself — composite identities — that exist prior to a particular interaction and which will always have an impact on it. Moreover, participants will not always fit like square pegs into the square holes of socially predetermined statuses or roles; the individual may help to create or, indeed, subvert a given situation.

Identity arises out of particular social interactions, which the participants themselves create in part. It is from the partial identities formed in specific interactions that broader versions of an individual's identity are synthesized. Each individual can therefore be seen as one of the authors of the partial identities that arise in particular social interactions, and as such is not merely a product of social forces but also a social force in himself.

Our approach will begin simply enough, but it will move toward complexity. The earlier chapters will look at the way simple metaphors structure the description of discrete worlds. As the argument develops we shall show the subtlety of interrelationships among partial identities, such as those based in gender, social class, kinship, religion, nationality, and ethnicity, while avoiding the reduction of any one of these identities to any of the others. We shall finally show why individuals do not usually see themselves or present themselves as having only fragmentary, partial identities, but believe that they remain the same person, no matter in how many frameworks their identity is defined.

3

History as Rhetoric

The Siege Metaphor

Journalists and others use the phrase "siege mentality" to speak of the views of Ulster Protestants. Protestants, it is alleged, believe they are besieged.

The expression has an obvious force. A glance at a map shows that the Irish Republic surrounds Northern Ireland to the south and west. Also, unionists make much of the Republic's claim to the territory of the North. The Protestant siege mentality is real enough.

In Ulster, however, the phrase "siege mentality" evokes more distant times. It refers to the most important symbolic event in Ulster Protestant history: the siege of Londonderry during the Williamite-Jacobite wars of the late seventeenth century.

The different versions of Irish history are well known to be entangled with ethnic and national identity. One version focuses on the story of the siege of Derry itself. There are also other narratives from the Williamite-Jacobite wars, notably that of the Battle of the Boyne. Another set of stories comes from traditional nationalist history. Yet another is a history now popular among Protestants: the history of the Cruthin (discussed below).

A feature of these different histories is that different groups of people, in different degrees, have appropriated them. Nationalist history, for example, is nowadays found in republican writings. Also, the banner paintings of the more moderate Catholic Ancient Order of Hibernians explore nationalist historical themes.

Popular histories of the seventeenth century in the Protestant tradition are still being written. This tradition, however, is most visible at seasonal festivities

Figure 4. Building an Eleventh Night bonfire. (Courtesy of the Ulster Folk and Transport Museum)

under the control of particular organizations. The loyalist Apprentice Boys of Derry hold demonstrations twice each year to celebrate the siege of Derry. The Orange Order has as its hero the figure of William III. Every year, on the Twelfth of July, it celebrates with processions his victory at the Boyne in 1690. This procession is often preceded, on the Eleventh Night, by drumming or bonfires. Together, Derry and the Boyne represent the victory of Protestantism over Catholicism in the late seventeenth century.

The author of the Cruthin hypothesis, Ian Adamson, is a moderate member of the Ulster Unionist Party, where his theories have some support. However, the paramilitary Ulster Defence Association early adopted the theory as an official doctrine.

All of the historical accounts cited in this chapter have a strong rhetorical element. They uphold the interests of one group against the other by describing past events in a well-selected frame. Another feature they all have is that the framing of the information is in each case partially structured by a common set of metaphors of invasion and siege.

One aim of this chapter will be to show how events gain their rhetorical

Figure 5. Eleventh Night bonfire. (Courtesy of the Ulster Folk and Transport Museum)

force by being placed in one frame and not another. Rarely in the conflict between rhetorical histories is there disagreement over facts. The disagreement, rather, is over the significance of the facts. What decides this significance is how the events are framed.

A second aim is to show that the siege metaphor is not at all the preserve of Ulster Protestants. Nor is it confined to ethnic questions. Longley (1990) has argued that unionism and nationalism are different *kinds* of ideology. We say, however, that ideas of siege and invasion underlie all of the versions of history described here, whether nationalist or unionist.

The chapter's last section will show that the siege metaphor is used widely in Western society to define good and evil. The siege metaphor is consistent with the idea of a sanctuary or temple. We shall show that the siege and the temple also define images of the human body and the self. This will allow us to claim later that descriptions of modern social institutions in Listymore are based on this same siege-and-temple imagery.

Despite the focus of this chapter and the next on rhetoric, two other points will arise. One is that history and other genres of description are not just matters

Figure 6. Wall painting of King William III. (Courtesy of the Ulster Folk and Transport Museum)

of persuasion. They may also act as operational models, or what Malinowski called "historical charters" (Bohannan 1954; Malinowski 1963). The second is that the very act of representing the past can be a way of dramatizing a social allegiance. This is true whether the representation is by means of a procession or through some type of narrative.

Nationalist History: The Invasion of Ireland

Nationalist perspectives have dominated academic and popular historical writing in Ireland from the last century to the present. Classically, such history portrays the opposition between Britain and Ireland, Planter and Gael, Protestant and Catholic as one between oppressor and oppressed. Scholarly nationalist histories have appeared throughout this century (e.g., Biggar 1910; Green 1908; O'Brian 1918). Thence their ideas have passed into school textbooks and the general consciousness. Modern historians (Bowen 1970; Connell 1968;

Connelly 1982; Stewart 1977) still think them important enough to be worth a systematic revision.[1] Even explicitly loyalist or Protestant histories can be regarded as refutations of the histories of nationalists.

The central theme of this nationalist history concerns invasions and the results of invasions. Invasions by the Danes in the ninth and tenth centuries led up to the Battle of Clontarf in 1014. Then came the Anglo-Normans, led by Henry II. And the invasions that had the most significance in modern times were those of the sixteenth and seventeenth centuries, called the Plantation.

The Plantation took place with great ferocity (Green 1908, 114), replacing Irish land ownership with British. The British removed the rights of tenants (Biggar 1910, 5–6; Green 1908, 118ff.). They disrupted Irish industry and trade (Green 1908, 123ff.; O'Brian 1918, 383ff.). They put Catholics under legal restraints. And England is ascribed the blame for the "decline" of Irish "culture," found in the Irish language, in ancient texts, and in folklore (Delargy 1945; Foster 1982; Kennedy 1891; O'Sullivan 1966).

Wrongs continued into the nineteenth century and beyond. Independence was the key, but even this was spoiled by the partition of Ireland and by the unjust laws and practices of the artificially created "majority" in the north. Scholars still hotly dispute the extent of these inequities (Hewitt 1981, 1983, 1985; O'Hearn 1983, 1985).

The rhetorical force of nationalist history comes from two sources. First, there is the reciprocity principle. For the "native Irish," the history contains a whole list of grievances awaiting satisfaction in the present: the British (or Planters) stole the land of Ireland, destroyed her trade, spoiled her culture, and suppressed her religion. Therefore, the argument goes, Irish people have the right to reclaim their land, reunify their island, and receive fair and equal treatment (see Boyce 1982, 306).

Second, however, the story's power lies in the idea of invasion itself. The whole point of the story arises from the idea that invasion is wrong. According to this formula, someone who lives inside his country — or inside his community, or inside his home — ought to be free from the threat of invasion. Those who approach from outside with rapacious intent are "bad," in contrast to those inside, who are "good."

Considered in this manner, one may quickly discover a range of oppositions, in the manner of classical structuralism. According to this view, those who are subjected to invasion — those living inside Ireland — are weak and powerless to defend their culture and religion. In this they differ from the evil, wealthy, and powerful invaders.

Inside	Outside
Defenders	Attackers
Good	Evil
Spiritual	Material
Poor	Rich
Weak	Powerful
Culture	Barbarity
Religion	Irreligion

The Siege of Derry

The siege of Londonderry has had major symbolic weight for Irish Protestants since soon after the siege itself. It is certainly still the most important of the loyalist historical stories (Stewart 1977, 52ff.).

The first accounts of the siege were written by its heroes. The civil governor of the city for much of the siege, George Walker, wrote an account of his experiences, based on his journal (Walker 1689). It sparked a massive sequence of polemical pamphlets at the time, and is still read today. One of the military governors of the city during the siege, John Michelburn, afterward wrote a play, *Ireland Preserved: Or the Siege of Londonderry* (1705), that depicted the siege. This was not, perhaps, a great work of literature. Still, it remained continuously in print for more than a century. Lord Macauley also gave a famous and swashbuckling account of the siege in his *History of England* (1855). Nowadays writers present avowedly Protestant accounts of the siege. One such was written by the Deputy Leader of the Democratic Unionist Party, Peter Robinson (1988). Robinson is well known as a fierce, outspoken upholder of the Protestant cause, and in the preface to his book he proclaims no intention of being "neutral in viewing such stirring events." Nevertheless, his account does not differ in substance from others whose aim is apparently more detached (Hippsley 1988; Lacy n.d.; McCartney 1988; Mitchell 1990).

Apart from the written accounts, the memory of the siege is kept alive by public demonstrations. The most important of these is the twice-yearly celebration of the siege by the Apprentice Boys of Derry. This consists largely of processions, formerly around the city walls but now, for security reasons, through the city center. In December there also takes place the burning of a gigantic effigy of Lundy the Traitor, a central figure in the tale.

The unionists' account of the siege closely echoes themes from nationalist histories. The broad outline of the story is as follows: During the Williamite-

Jacobite wars — in 1688–92 — the Catholic armies of James II besieged the city of Londonderry. The occasion of the siege was the advance of James's troops to garrison the city. Colonel Robert Lundy, the treacherous governor of the city, wavered with indecision, uncertain whether to support King James or King William, but his mind was made up for him when a group of apprentice boys shut the gates.

For many months, the loyal Protestants held out, enduring fierce deprivations. They were short of food and had only the crudest weapons, but somehow the Maiden City remained intact. Governor Lundy later escaped from the city by stealth. In consequence, the Apprentice Boys clubs burn his effigy as a traitor every December.

In the end, help for the city was at hand. The *Mountjoy*, a Williamite ship, burst the boom that had been set across the River Foyle. Then, following the arrival of William's army, the city was relieved, freeing the Protestants from the forces of oppression and Catholicism.

This version of the story provides a well-established metaphor for the relation between Catholic and Protestant, nationalist and unionist in the province. The frequently used loyalist slogans "No Surrender" and "Not an Inch" come directly from the siege narrative. Incidents from the siege recur as topics on the banners of loyalist organizations. Murals in loyalist areas sometimes declare that the population is "Still under Siege." Beyond this, details of the story also reflect long-standing hostilities based on class and ethnicity within Protestantism itself. Not least, there is a suspicion that the authorities (and English people) will fail to withstand Catholicism and nationalism. They may become traitors or "Lundys" (see chapters 4 and 7).

Robinson's account of the siege emphasizes the relevance of this distant event for the present. For example, he writes:

> The lessons to be learned from the siege are legion and the parallels to the present day are plain. There are many, even though in the service of the Crown, who profess to support the Unionist cause, yet their every action betrays the principle they claim to uphold. There are those like Major-General Kirke [whom Robinson condemns for failing to relieve the city], who, though they possess the power to take action that would relieve suffering and distress, hesitate, waiting on their own convenience, before engaging the enemy. But, thank God, there are many, like the brave thirteen [apprentice boys], like Baker, Michelburn and Murray [other heroes of the siege], who have that indomitable spirit which refuses to accept anything short of an honourable outcome. (Robinson 1988, 19)

Not all people, and not even all unionists, will agree that this story should be used as a model for community relations or for the politics of ethnicity in Ulster. Some unionists believe strongly that it is more appropriate to hold out the hand of friendship and effect a compromise. But this need not concern us here. The story needs to be seen as what it is: a landmark, a point of orientation for all who live in the society.

This unionist account of the siege and the nationalist account of the Plantation are the two most compelling myths of Northern Irish ethnicity. Although in some ways they are equal and opposed, in others they are remarkably similar. Both stories identify as cultured, spiritual, religious, and good the people who are on the inside, be they the Catholics who live inside Ireland or the Protestants who live inside Derry. Both stories reflect a conception of the people on the outside as wicked, irreligious, barbaric, and rich. Interestingly, both sometimes see the threatened structure as having a female gender. For the nationalist side it is "Mother Ireland," sometimes personified as the heroines Caitlín Ní hUallacháin or Róisín Dubh (Loftus 1990; Longley 1990, 18–19); for the unionists, it is Londonderry, "the Maiden City, wooed but never won."

Considering the two stories not as accounts of two separate historical events but as articulations of the same metaphor, the differences between the stories are remarkably few. In the story of the Plantation, the invaders were successful and the defenses were broken; in the account of the siege of Londonderry, the invaders were kept out and the defenses remained intact. Of course, it is also important that the identities of both the places and the people are different. Both stories, however, are stories of invasion, and both see the invaders as villainous oppressors and the invaded as virtuous victims.

The Cruthin

As rhetoric, Protestant stories of the Williamite-Jacobite wars, and especially of the siege of Londonderry, have always been flawed. (Indeed, for rhetorical purposes, modern unionist politicians rely more heavily on modern history. They argue that nationalists and especially republicans have failed to accept the democratic will of the Northern Irish people.) The basic problem with the story of the siege is that loyalist versions of the tale cannot always be kept in their frame. Accounts of the siege also form part of the narrative within the rhetorical framework of nationalist history. Considered within a nationalist frame, the encircled inhabitants of Derry may indeed be said to have had a difficult time, but the fault was their own: the Protestants of Derry themselves were invaders of a previously Catholic area and so should not have been in Derry in the first place.

In recent years a new historical framework, one that extends the narrative back into prehistory, has become popular as a response to this major flaw in Protestant historical rhetoric. The story of the Cruthin is set out in two books written by a Belfast doctor, Ian Adamson: *The Cruthin* (1974) and *The Identity of Ulster* (1982). Adamson's thesis is striking because it explicitly relates this ancient history to modern politics.

Adamson says that the first occupants of Ireland were not the Gaels, as nationalists assumed, but the Cruthin. The Cruthin were a people related to the Scottish Picts (Adamson 1974, 11). After the Cruthin, another people, the Fir Bolg, came to Ireland from Britain; other tribes followed from France. Only then did the Gaels arrive and establish hegemony all over Ireland, except in the northeast. There the Fir Bolg tribes of Dalriata and Ulaid formed with the Cruthin into an Ulster confederacy.

Adamson writes, "The descendants of the two races are the Ulster Scots" (1974, 12). He also adds that "through the kings of the Dalriata are all of the kings of Scotland descended, and through this line is descended the present Queen of the British Peoples" (1974, 13). By the fifth century, this mainly Cruthinic kingdom of Ulaid (later corrupted to Ulster) was pushed back into what is now Antrim and Down. Their defeat at the battle of Moira in 637 led to a gradual emigration of the Cruthin into lowland Scotland.

Adamson's attack is on three fronts. First, he questions the notion that all ancient Irish culture is Gaelic. He suggests that the Book of Darrow and the Book of Kells are "Pictish" or "Scottish Irish" (1974, 93ff.). More damning, he confiscates Cúchulainn, hero of the Gaelic-language epic *Táin Bó Cuailnge* (Kinsella 1969), and gives him to the Cruthin. Cúchulainn's statue stands in Dublin Central Post Office as a memorial to the nationalist dead of 1916, whose actions gave birth to Irish independence. Placed in the frame of Adamson's history, however, Cúchulainn clearly embodies the struggle of Ulster against the invading Gaels.

Second, Adamson appropriates St. Patrick to the Cruthin. "Patrick makes a clear distinction between the Scotti (Gaels) and the ordinary peoples, the Hibernians (Cruthin and Ulaid)" (1974, 42). It is the latter, he says, whom Patrick first converted. Thus, he argues, the Cruthin were responsible for spreading Christianity in Ireland.

Third, Adamson denies "the claim of the Gael to Ireland," which he says was made "by the sword only, and by the sword was it reclaimed in later years by the descendants of these Ancient peoples. . . . Of these two Ulster peoples, the paramount claim belongs to the Cruthin, last of the Picts" (Adamson 1974, 15).

In short, the Cruthin argument addresses the rhetorical challenge of Irish nationalist history. It claims that Ulster Protestants, and particularly those whose forebears came from Scotland, have at least as much right to live in Ireland as do Irish Catholics. It also takes from the nationalist heritage many of its treasured cultural traits, arguing their Cruthinic rather than Gaelic origins. And finally, it bends the historical linchpin of Irish nationalism, the Plantation of Ireland. The Plantation is no longer an invasion by an oppressive people. Instead, it is a reoccupation by a people who were once expelled.

When he wrote his first book, Adamson gave many lectures. Among his audiences were members of the paramilitary Ulster Defence Association. The UDA later officially adopted Adamson's ideas. The second printing of this book has a preface by Glen Barr, then an officer in the UDA. Barr later coordinated the general strike that destroyed the short-lived unionist-nationalist coalition government of Northern Ireland in 1974.

Adamson's books have had appeal elsewhere. In 1986, the junior wing of the largest unionist party, the Ulster Unionist Party, published a pamphlet that presents Adamson's views in a simplified form and uses them with much rhetorical effect; for example, they claim that "when the Plantation of Ulster got under way, in the 17th century, those Scots who come over from the Lowlands were in fact members of the Cruthin race returning to the land of their birthright" (UYUC 1986). Other books have been written popularizing his ideas (e.g., Hall 1986), and in at least one loyalist area of Belfast one can see a large mural depicting Cúchulainn as a defender of Ulster.

Perhaps it is surprising that these three accounts of Irish history — nationalist, loyalist, and Cruthinic — do not rebut each other in matter of fact, but differ only in the way events are framed. Nationalist history, of course, admits that the siege of Derry took place. And loyalists have never denied the fact of the Irish Plantation. However, the Cruthin argument has been subject to more criticism. One critic excitedly called the theory "nonsense" and declared that "Adamson has a brass neck in expounding it" (Morgan 1990). Despite this, Adamson's thesis is not particularly new (see O'Rahilly 1957), and for some it is not disreputable (Stewart 1977, 28ff.). Even nationalists cannot deny the relative lateness of the Gaelic invasions.

In any case, what is at stake in all these forms of history is not historical truth. What people find interesting is the way the facts are put into rhetorically useful frames, each partially structured by the siege metaphor but each defining a different rhetorical conclusion.

The arrival of the Cruthin argument has done much to discredit the whole enterprise of constructing Irish ethnic histories. The irony implied in cultural relativism (see chapter 2) is now a commonplace of political discourse. For example, a satirical local television program, *The Show*, famously mocked UDA men for claiming they were "Croûtons." Indeed, many people pour scorn on the different historical views. It is not that there is much dispute about the facts described. The scorn comes because the rhetorical aims that lie behind the histories are so transparent. It is plain to everyone that it is easy to build rhetoric from history: you just choose a strip of events that serve the purpose, and put them in an appropriate frame.

Before joining in the ridicule with too much glee, however, one should consider another possibility. This is that a people who can self-consciously make use of their history like this have at their disposal a useful tool. They can use their history for purposes other than the creation of mere social division. Chapters 12 and 13 will show how the reframing of history can also be used as an idiom to help a divided society heal its wounds.

The Siege Metaphor and Ideas of the Self

We said at the beginning of this chapter that the phrase "siege mentality" evokes the attitudes of Ulster Protestants. It particularly refers to attitudes about the siege of Derry. Already, however, we have shown that the main competing historical frame is very similar. Irish nationalist history is itself built on a similar image of invasion.

This final section will look more generally at the siege metaphor. This metaphor is far from being the preserve of Ulster's unionists, nor yet that of their nationalist rivals. It is very widely used in Western culture to define ideas of good and evil. It is also used to define general ideas about the self.

In Northern Ireland, as elsewhere, there is no one view about the nature of society. Similarly, there is no one vision of the self. There are ideas about body, soul, spirit, mind, feelings, thoughts, experiences, and the like. There are also some commonly used principles for putting such ideas together. When they are assembled, however, the result is often a mixture of inconsistent images of what the self is. The metaphors used to build generalized images of the self are also used in the description and understanding of social relationships and groups. It is useful, therefore, to draw attention to the recursive or circular nature of these metaphors.

Anthropologists and others have long known that ideas of the self, and particularly of the human body, are related to ideas about society (e.g., Buckley 1985; Douglas 1966; Leach 1958; see also Mead 1934). This relationship, however, can operate in two directions. As the self provides metaphors that define society, so too does society provide metaphors that define the self.

Later chapters will show that identities and social frameworks structured by body- or self-related metaphors can recursively provide structures for each other. Here we shall briefly examine some common beliefs about sexuality, illness, and the "inner life."

Sexuality and Invasion

Perhaps the most obvious area of life in which there are siegelike images concerns sexuality, and especially rape. Newspapers in the United Kingdom, including those widely read in Northern Ireland, are full of stories of rape. One survey (Heggassy and Webster 1990) showed that there were some four stories of rape reported each day in the national press. Of these stories, the vast majority were about rapes committed by strangers. The survey contrasted these newspaper reports with police crime figures. Acts of rape, it seems, comprise fewer than one percent of all reported crimes, and fewer than forty percent of rapes are committed by strangers.

Rape is, of course, a form of invasion, but recursively so. One may even see it as an archetype for violent territorial invasions. As the physical rape of a person can be said to be a form of "invasion" (a territorial metaphor), so the invasion of a city or a country can be described as "rape" (a physical image).

Rape is one of the most characteristic images of evil in Western society. It appears, however, to be something else as well. Rape, and particularly the rape of women by strangers, is also an image that is meaningful to people. Like the totemic animals that Lévi-Strauss (1964) describes, cases of rape are *bons à penser*.

Once can discern in the story of the siege of Derry a sexual imagery that recurs in many other manifestations of the siege metaphor. Not only is there an image of figurative rape (it is the Maiden City that is threatened with intrusion), but there is also an indication that the savior figure, in this case William III and his ship, the *Mountjoy*, is a more benign quasi-sexual intruder. The invasion by James's forces would have constituted a violation, but the intrusion of the Williamite ship was a salvation. It will be suggested later that in a variety of contexts the intrusion, by invitation, of a benevolent male figure is defined as the salvation of a beleaguered female.

We said earlier that Mother Ireland (sometimes in the form of Róisín Dubh or Caitlín Ní hUallacháin) was directly comparable to Londonderry, which is called the Maiden City. In both cases, a territory was subject to an invasion by the nasty, rough men who lurked outside. It is the metaphor of rape that gives these female images their rhetorical force.

Illness: The Body under Siege

Illness is also a familiar way in which a person is thought to be under siege. In this case, the metaphors of siege and invasion are operational, not rhetorical in character. They define practical responses to illness.

Lurking outside the body are countless bacteria and viruses, often lumped together as just plain "germs." They are in the water we drink, in the food we eat, and in the air we breathe. The siege metaphor is often used in talk about the way germs make us ill: someone may be "insufficiently on guard" against infection; the "natural defenses" of the body become weak; the microbes "invade" the body and "take over." In a similar vein, immunization, good nutrition, and exercise can "strengthen the body's defenses." Should we succumb to illness, we can use antiseptics and antibiotics to "fight off" the disease and "kill" the microbes that cause it.

It is perhaps worth underlining that this imagery is specific to Western culture. Yoruba herbalists in western Nigeria, for example (see Buckley 1985), also have a germ theory of disease; they speak of illness being caused by insects so small that they are invisible. Yoruba herbalists, however, do not see their patients as under siege. For them, the germs that cause illness are hidden away in the body in small bags, "where God has placed them." Germs fulfill a useful function in the body, aiding reproduction, digestion, and so on. The germs cause trouble only when a person indulges in immoderate behavior. Then the germs overflow their bags, spilling into the body and causing illness.

In speaking of modern Western germ theory as a siege or invasion theory, one should not oversimplify. European thought does not confine its vision of disease to the siegelike germ theory just outlined. There is a whole range of ailments, from fractures and sprains through genetic disorders and glandular imbalances to cancers, that do not fit this paradigm. There are also minority medicinal practices — homeopathy, acupuncture, and the like — that employ different paradigms. Many of these, however, also aim to "strengthen the body's natural defenses," employing from time to time another form of the siege metaphor. The point is not that the siege is the only metaphor through which Northern Irish and other people understand illness — only that it is very common.

The Inner Life

Apart from illness and sexuality, siege imagery also defines ideas about the inner life. The intellect, the mind, the emotions, the spirit, and the soul are all popularly differentiated from, and said to exist within, the body. In Northern Ireland, as elsewhere, there are to be found several versions of Descartes's "ghost in the machine," and these are informed by ideas of siege and, more especially, temples and sanctuaries.

When considering Northern Irish conceptions of a person and his inner life, one must see the siege metaphor as being often intertwined with another set of images: the sanctuary and the temple. There are important and subtle differences between the idea of a siege and that of a temple or a sanctuary. Unlike a besieged city, a sanctuary or a temple is a place where the holy is located and where it can be discovered. Nevertheless, there is much similarity between these different ideas. Feldman (1991), for example, self-consciously uses the image of the sanctuary in his discussion of Northern Irish violence. He says, for example, that his informants see the battle-torn working-class areas of Belfast as sanctuaries. Indeed, Feldman's use of the term *sanctuary* could be interchanged with the image of the siege as it is used in this volume. In both the siege image and the sanctuary image there is a goodness or spirituality that needs protection, and an evil or profanity that should be kept out. Although the term *temple* lacks the same emphasis on excluding evil, it translates readily into the same kind of language. Inside a temple is the sacred; outside is the profane.

One expression of this imagery, clearer than most, is that found in the Christian notion of the soul. The idea here is that the soul is contained in the body during life and is detached from it at death. In Ulster, where many people are churchgoers, this imagery is commonly used in the context of bereavement. It is consonant with the idea that the body is a place of habitation, occupied by the "real" self. One man, for example, overheard expressing his sympathy at the bereavement of another, said, "You only *live* in your body."

This widespread idiom defines the body as a place of residence, like a city or a home. Alternatively, it defines the self as a templelike container for a person's spiritual being (a real self) or for entities such as thoughts or feelings. According to such definitions, thoughts and feelings cease to be bodily activities. They become spiritual, part of one's "inner life."

This imagery can be quite elaborate. Since the body (more usually parts of it, such as the heart or the head) can "contain" such entities as thoughts and feelings, then it is possible to take these entities out of their container and send them elsewhere. Reddy discusses an elaboration of this imagery in his remarkable essay on the "conduit metaphor" (1979). He shows that ideas are often spoken of as though they were "things" inside the head. These things can be "put into words" and "sent" from person to person. The notion that ideas can be "transmitted" depends entirely on an image of the person as a container.

Also involved here is the question of the holy. That which belongs to a person's inner life is often thought to be sacred. Sometimes Christian thought in Ulster, as elsewhere, expresses this explicitly in the Pauline image of the body as a temple. Objections to drink and tobacco, for example, usually make explicit use of the idea that the body is a temple.

An extension of this image is the notion that we may allow Christ or the Holy Spirit to "come into our hearts." Here there is a benign invasion that helps save the individual from a more malign one (see chapters 4 and 6). Even when such religious imagery is absent, however, people speak of their "innermost" thoughts and feelings. They mean by this that certain experiences are precious to them.

Closely related to such notions is the idea that an individual may be vulnerable when certain topics are discussed. Some matters are precious to an individual. They belong to a person's inner life; they touch on his deepest feelings; they have a sacred quality. When gratuitously or lightheartedly revealed, they render a person vulnerable. For this reason, it is thought to be a gross breach of etiquette to condemn or make fun of the religious opinions of others, or to pry too deeply into those matters that belong in the home, or in the most intimate parts of the home. Attacks on the religious views of others tend, therefore, to be made in private, away from the ears of those who espouse such views.

It is useful again to note that these ideas are culture-specific. For Yoruba herbalists, the thoughts and feelings that are hidden within the body are not vulnerable to outside attack. Rather, thoughts and feelings — rather like germs, in Yoruba herbalists' ideas — are dangerous forms of power that need to be kept locked up (Buckley 1985).

For both Europeans and Yoruba, therefore, the sacred is typically hidden away and kept private. For Yoruba herbalists, however, the hiding is meant to prevent dangerous inner forces from overflowing and causing havoc (Buckley 1985). European hiding, in contrast, has the general purpose of safeguarding a person's most precious and vulnerable feelings for fear that they may be scorned or laughed into foolishness.

Although the siege, the sanctuary, and the temple provide important metaphors that allow individuals to describe aspects of the self, it is important to note that these are not the only images available to them. Northern Irish people sometimes belong to the worlds of the social sciences, psychology, philosophy, and so on. Some have therefore adopted behaviorist, Freudian, or some other psychology as part of their professional or personal lives. There are also adherents of Buddhism, Hinduism, and other minority religions, which have distinctive psychologies.

It would be a mistake to conclude that Western thought sees the inner life as only timid and fragile. A person's actions are the result of thoughts and feelings that can sometimes be very strong indeed. This inner influence can be good or bad: a person is sometimes said to be "filled with the Holy Spirit" or "filled with love," for example, but may also be described as filled with anger, passion, or lust, or even entered by Satan and his demons.

This kind of imagery is wholly compatible with the idea that the self is a container. And, indeed, it shows how highly flexible this kind of imagery can be. It translates into other metaphors relating to possession, and therefore has some obvious religious implications. It also exists in a common secularized form, mechanized into a metaphor of the self as a steam engine. This recast image suggests that emotions, like steam in a piston, are powerful, capable of "driving" a person to do whatever he does. Such a person can "come under pressure," and unless he can find a "safety valve" or some other way of "letting off steam" or "expressing" his feelings, he will "blow his top" or simply "explode."

Concluding Remarks

We do not claim that interrelated images of sieges, sanctuaries, and temples provide the only metaphors defining social institutions and individual identities in Ulster. These are only some of the more important ones. In later chapters we shall look at other metaphors that define ideas about social institutions, social relationships, and the self.

This chapter has considered various popular versions of Irish history, suggesting that they are all based upon ideas of invasion and siege and arguing that very similar ideas are the basis for more generally used images of good and evil. In the next two chapters we shall continue to look at manifestations of the siege metaphor. By so doing, we hope to establish its importance before moving on to more complex issues.

4

FIELDWORK BY A. D. BUCKLEY The
Siege
Metaphor
in
Listymore

The
Religious
and
the
Rough

Bringing the argument down to ethnographic earth, this chapter will look at descriptions of social life elicited during interviews held in the rural area of Listymore. They speak of a wide range of social institutions and relationships, or what we call "worlds." They include the worlds of fundamentalism, the Orange Order, the household, the farm, and Listymore itself. The interview is hardly a common genre of social interaction. Nevertheless, the opinions given here, and the form they take, are not very different from what might emerge in ordinary conversation.

In this chapter, as in the last, the descriptions have a rhetorical force that depends on the framework in which the events and objects are placed. One frame will define an individual or group as "good." In another frame, these same people are "bad." The central argument here is that although different descriptions convey rhetorically different or opposed messages, the structure of the framed descriptions is remarkably similar.

The last chapter showed that the siege metaphor defines different or opposed versions of both history and the self. In the same way, the siege metaphor is used in conversation to define different or opposed versions of everyday social institutions. Despite our concentration on the image of the siege, it will become apparent that other metaphors are also important. These and other complexities will be ignored as far as is possible here. The aim is to establish the bare bones of the discussion, leaving more difficult questions to later chapters.

Worlds in Listymore

The Orange and the Black

Important to the life of Listymore are several secret societies. The village of Long Stone has an Orange lodge, a Royal Arch Purple chapter, a Royal Black preceptory, and an Apprentice Boys club. The village of Killycarnon has its own Orange and Masonic lodges.

These different bodies are similar to one another in their organization and ritual practices. Indeed, it is widely supposed that the symbolism of the Orangemen, the Arch Purplemen, the Blackmen, and the Apprentice Boys derives directly from Freemasonry.

The Orange Order is a comparatively moderate organization devoted to upholding the Protestant religion against Catholicism. When it arose in 1795, it was only one of countless rural secret brotherhoods. Because it won the support of the gentry in its opposition to growing Catholic political power, it managed to achieve a position of some importance in Ireland. After the partition of Ireland in 1922, the local influence of the Order in Northern Ireland was considerable. It had a formal connection with the old Conservative and Unionist Party, which dominated Northern Irish politics until the early 1970s. This connection still persists in its continuing relationship with the Ulster Unionist Party. Though its influence has diminished since the early 1970s, the Order has provided an extraordinarily efficient channel through which Protestants could exercise influence over their elected representatives.

The Order is primarily made up of men, though there are women's lodges. Usually a man will enter a local Orange lodge and be initiated through two degrees, called Orange and Purple. Once he has been through these two degrees, he may then be admitted to another organization, the Royal Arch Purple Chapter, which is technically separate from the Orange Order. Then he may join yet another organization, the Royal Black Institution, which has eleven degrees.

Chapter 11 will discuss in more detail the practices and symbols of some of these groups. The aim here is to recount some comments of a member of the Royal Black Institution and to show how these comments are structured by the image of the siege.

Ken Wilson is a member of the Long Stone Orange lodge, and he is also a knight in the Royal Black preceptory encamped at Long Stone. Though he lives in Killycarnon, he attends church in the village of Long Stone and is active in the life of that village, running the Long Stone flute band. He is a member of a large Long Stone network of kin — a "connection" — and effectively he still occupies a leading place in Long Stone society.

Like other members of the Orange Order, Ken insists that the Order is principally a religious institution. For example, he told me that "a good Catholic would turn to an Orangeman if ever he was in need." This was because he would "know he could trust an Orangeman." Ken, however, knows that critics of the Orange Order complain of the drinking and rowdiness associated with it. "You do get a few that are a bit rougher," he said.

The Royal Black preceptory, he said, is a "higher order" of the Orange Order. The two organizations are separate, but "you have to go through the one in order to get to the other." In "the Black" there are eleven degrees, which "come out of the Bible." The Blackmen differ from the Orangemen in that "the roughest wouldn't get in."

I tried to probe Ken on the history of the Orange Order. I mentioned the eighteenth-century Hearts of Oak ("Oakboys") and Hearts of Steel ("Steelboys"), two of the more important of the agrarian secret societies that were the predecessors of the Orange Order (Biggar 1910; Donnelly 1978, 1981).

Ken did not really know much about the Oakboys or Steelboys. Nevertheless, he ventured the opinion that they were "like the things today" (I supposed that he meant modern paramilitary groups). He said the Orange Order was "a step above" these earlier bodies.

I repeated what I took to be his idea, saying that the Orangemen had put the Oakboys "on a higher level." He agreed, but said that they were "put onto a religious level." Orangemen could "keep these boys in order." The goal of the Order itself was "to keep trouble down, not to cause trouble."

It was perhaps unfair to try to discuss the Oakboys and Steelboys with Ken. There was no reason to suppose he would know much about them. But his comments demonstrate a pattern that I found elsewhere as well. The essence of this pattern is a distinction between the "religious" and the "rough." According to Ken's view, those inside the Orange Order are religious when compared with those outside it, who are rough.

The function of the Orange Order in the past, and present, is to "keep these boys in order," to "keep trouble down" in the wider society. Within the Orange Order, however, despite its religious nature, there are those who are "a bit rougher." These individuals are, it seems, kept in order by an especially religious element, the Blackmen, who do not allow the roughest into their organization. Both the Orange Order and the Royal Black Institution make a distinction, at least in principle, between the type of people they include and those whom they keep out. Broadly, the ones they include are "religious," or Protestant. Those they keep out are "rough," or Catholic.

This is, however, too simple. As I have indicated, within the Orange Order, there are two degrees: the Orange and the Purple. A third degree, the Royal Arch Purple degree, belongs to a separate organization, which is open only to Orangemen. In the Royal Black Institution, an order open only to Arch Purplemen, there are an additional eleven degrees.

Each degree, therefore, excludes men who have lesser degrees. And each degree is more religious than the last. In short, each social unit defined by the system contains a religious element that is enveloped by a rough exterior. Like Solomon's temple, which is a central metaphor in Freemasonry, each successive inward step is more sacred than the last, until, at the center, one reaches the Holy of Holies.

Ken's account uses an imagery based upon concepts of *inside* and *outside*. It also uses an opposition of *higher* and *lower*. The higher/lower distinction is an important one and will be considered more closely later. Here I shall simply note that items that a particular frame defines as inside are usually thought to be higher (in morality) than those that are outside.

It is important to note that not all Ulster Protestants, not all Orangemen, and not all inhabitants of Listymore share Ken Wilson's opinion of the Orange and Black institutions. Many Protestants decry the Orange Order. Some, for example, criticize the drinking evident at public Orange rallies. Others see Orange rites (as well as those of other brotherhoods) as unbiblical and even blasphemous. Yet others complain that the members of such organizations use their membership as a way of gaining unfair advantage in business. Even within the Orange Order, there are those who oppose the claims of the organizationally distinct Blackmen to have preeminence over the Orange Order.

Ken Wilson's remarks, however, imply a structure of concentric walls or boundaries. Each wall *excludes* those supposed to be relatively rough and *includes* those supposed to be relatively religious. The structure I have looked at here is one that appeals to Ken Wilson. Other people with different allegiances build other versions of the same temple.

The Saved

One network of people whose members often condemn secret societies and their rituals are those who say they are "saved" or, more contentiously, say they are "Christians" (see also chapter 6).

A small group of such Christians, the Long Stone Mission, meets for worship in a small, tin-roofed mission hall in the countryside between the two villages of Killycarnon and Long Stone. This group came into existence in the worldwide evangelical revival that took place after World War I, through the activity of a once-important group called Faith Mission. The group is not, in any valid sense of the term, a religious sect, for its members all belong to other denominations. There are Presbyterians, Anglicans, and Baptists among them, and one of its joint leaders is an Elim Pentecostalist. The group is interdenominational, but this interdenominationality does not extend to Catholics. Its theology is evangelical and fundamentalist.

One of its leaders, William Martin, saw the Long Stone Mission similarly to the way Ken Wilson saw the Orange Order. In most local church congregations, he said, there are groups of people who also attend the Mission. The Mission does not have a committee of elders or deacons to help with its government. In this, it differs from almost all of the smaller Protestant churches and religious groups in Ulster. If the assembly makes no division between members and elders, there is still a sharp line between members of the Mission and nonmembers. Once a month, the meetings of the Mission are open to the public for evangelism. For the remainder, meetings are private, for members only.

I mentioned to William Martin that I was interested in the great religious revival of 1859 (see Carson 1959; Gibson 1860; Gordon 1949; Orr 1949; Paisley 1959). This revival is widely regarded as the most important single event in modern Ulster's religious history.

William told me that the 1859 revival was also important for the political development of the province. He thought it was responsible for Northern Ireland's breaking away from the Irish Republic. The revival, he said, "kindled a spirit which is alive to this day." People who feel that "our kind of Christianity is the only sort" also feel that such groups are "a light burning in this island," which is "in danger of being swamped by Catholicism."

These ideas are clearly similar to those discussed above. By means of the Mission, those who have "let Jesus into their hearts" can separate themselves from those who have not, and are better able to influence the churches in which they remain members. In addition, William also thinks the separation of Northern Ireland from the Irish Republic is beneficial to the religious life of the province. It is even good for the whole island, since it permits Northern Ireland to act as a "light" for the Republic.

William and the other members of the Long Stone Mission are, at least in principle, far from decrying the work of the churches. Not only William but also other members of his group asked me whether I or my children went to church. When I said no, they greeted my reply with concern.

Like the rough element in Ken Wilson's picture of the Orange Order, the ordinary members of the churches have their place. It is better to be in the church than out of it, but it is better still to be saved. The Long Stone Mission provides a sanctuary that protects Christians from the influence of wicked people outside, like the walls of Derry. Or, to change the image, this is another version of Solomon's temple, in which the Holy of Holies is protected by multiple walls and veils.

William Martin's version of this temple is different from Ken Wilson's. This is because William is not an Orangeman, but runs the Mission; because Ken is not in the Mission, but is a leading Orangeman; and because each, when talking to me, wants to present his own organization in the best possible light.

Perils of the World

Mrs. Williamson is also a leading member of the Long Stone Mission. Her comments proved useful in clarifying the contrast between the inside and the outside, the religious and the rough.[1]

Like William Martin, she told me that the aim of the mission was not to remove people from their own church. On the other hand, "what most people call religion is not enough. Your religion alone does not save you," she said. "You have to make a decision."

Too many people, she thought, were interested only in the things of the world, and in making money. She referred obliquely to Ulster's "troubles" and complained of television. So much television, she said, is "unsuitable for children." Children are just "reared with the gun and the bullet."

I expressed sympathy for her point of view. She said, "Children need a brave grounding in the home." There is "far too much temptation about," she thought, and she mentioned drink and tobacco. It was better if one never started to smoke. Drink was also dangerous because one could become an alcoholic.

As she warmed to her subject she became emotional. "How do people get along without faith? What is this world, after all? You get money, a house, furniture, but you can't take it with you."

She laid so much emphasis upon the unimportance of money and material possessions that she feared I would misunderstand her. She did not mean, she stressed, that we should be lazy. "People should work hard to have a house and food, but they should not set too much store by these things."

Death, she thought, was an ever-present reality, and a danger for the un-saved soul. "Why should we not be afraid of death?" she asked. This life is only "a drop in the bucket" and "of little importance." On the same theme, she also commented: "In this world nothing is perfect, but in heaven everything is per-fect"; "The Devil is everywhere"; and "God has done all he can" (for example, through the Cross). Now it is up to man to make his own decision. Things are bad in the world, but in the Bible it says things will get worse (a reference to the tribulations at the Second Coming — see chapter 7). "When we go to heaven," she added, "we are going home."

Mrs. Williamson is unusually forthright in that she will tell a comparative stranger to give up drink and tobacco, and to send his children to church and Sunday school. She also makes special use of the term *religion*. By it, she means those formal religious observances that disguise a lack of genuine conviction.

Making allowance for this quirk of fundamentalist usage, her view sets out a widely accepted structure of ideas. This is that a rough person is one who drinks, smokes, and watches television, and is lazy, violent, and overconcerned with the accumulation of money. A religious person (or, in her case, a person who is a Christian) will, on the contrary, avoid these vices.

Beyond this, it is of interest that she speaks metaphorically of going to heaven as "going home" and that she associates roughness with the public house.

A Structure for the Home

There are, in fact, many people in Listymore who drink, smoke, and watch television. A minority even engage in shady dealings, petty crime, or violence. Most people are far from disowning the world in the sweeping manner advo-cated by Mrs. Williamson; in fact, what they have done is to concede that roughness is not all bad, and that it has a valued place in their lives.

The contrast between religion and roughness corresponds closely to that between the roles of the sexes, and to the dichotomy between parents and chil-dren. Broadly speaking, a man is "rougher" than his wife, and the children are "rougher" than the parents. It is the woman's role and the parents' role in these relationships to keep the men and the children in order, to stop them from smoking, drinking, and being rough.

So, the structure of the home may be expressed — as before — as a structure of concentric circles, with the polarity of inside and outside corresponding to the religious and the rough. A perceived function of the home is to protect its members from the evil influences without. In this model, the relationships show a similar structure to one described earlier:

Inside	Outside
Religious	Rough
Home	Outside world
Female	Male
Parent	Child
Old	Young

Talk about religion in Listymore usually turned into talk about young people and children. In these conversations, there was not much reference to the text "Suffer the little children to come unto me, for of such is the kingdom of heaven." On the contrary, conversations described the young mainly as latent wild people in need of control; and certainly religion's role as an agent of social control, as an important way for parents to control their children, is one of its many facets.

The Farm and the Village

Closely related to the home is the farm, because for many people in Listymore the home *is* the farm. Here too one finds siegelike or templelike imagery.

I spent a most informative evening with Jim Douglas, a young farmer, discussing the history of farming in the district. Jim owns what is, by Ulster standards, a large and thriving farm that belonged to his father and to his grandfather. He is a go-ahead businessman who does not at all wish to forgo the benefits of the modern industrial economy. When he discussed the history of farming in the area, however, he expressed concern that farming had "lost something" through modern improvements. In the old days, he said, it was "more what farming was all about."

As recently as fifteen years ago the Douglases made butter on their own farm. They grew their own potatoes and their own oats. They kept their own pigs. "You were self-sufficient in yourself," he said. "You grew what you needed and you sold the surplus." In making this point, Jim was most emphatic, and he was much less interested when I asked about other topics such as morrowing, in which neighboring farmers work together and share equipment (Bell 1978).

A little later in the evening, he returned obliquely to the topic of self-sufficiency. He told me of the various trades that had once been found in Listymore. There was the man who killed pigs (thus allowing people to cure their own bacon), a carpenter who made cart wheels, three blacksmiths, the man who caught and sold herrings, and the cooperative store in Killycarnon. By listing these occupations, he was clearly trying to make a point, but the conversation of others began to overwhelm him. So I jumped in. "You mean the area was self-contained?"

"That's the point I'm getting at," said Jim. "There was nearly everything you'd need within the village in the one area. . . . You didn't need to look outside for what you want." Finally he said, "Just like the farm was self-contained, so was the village." In saying all this, Jim was again emphatic, as though he was stating a major and significant truth about the past. Indeed, the same point is made (often with somewhat less clarity) elsewhere in the district. For example, people say that in the past, women might never go beyond the immediate area except perhaps once a year to buy such goods as blankets.

In speaking of the village and its past, Jim thus told me of a poverty-stricken life in which there was a self-contained farm in a self-contained village in a self-contained area. One could perhaps take this a step further and say that within his farm, the individual also should be self-contained. It is probable too that, like William Martin, Jim relishes a self-contained Northern Ireland.

Inclusion, Exclusion, and Penetration

A recurrent pattern emerges from the different accounts given above. It can be called "walls within walls" or, more simply, the siege metaphor. It is a pattern discernible in all the above descriptions of the province, community, village, farm, home, individual, church, mission, and different degrees of the lodge, chapter, and preceptory. Each of these social units is described as though it were insulated from the evil influences that threaten it from outside. Yet each also seeks to radiate a controlling influence of religion and virtue beyond its bounds.

If one were to look for a well-articulated image to explore this widespread principle of organization, the siege of Derry has obvious attractions. Here the Maiden City, to use the well-known epithet, is besieged by nasty, rough men. Perhaps, ideally, she should remain inviolate; but she is threatened with rape and the loss of her virtue. One man, aided by his army, is allowed to use his ship to break the boom across her river. Thus is she penetrated, and thus is her salvation effected.

From the Protestant point of view, then, these different images, of which the encircled city is but one example, all define several sets of people. One set includes a householder, a farmer, the loyal Ulsterman, and the beleaguered Christian within the walls of Derry (or the mission house).

A second set of people are the hosts of evil. There are "them boys," young, male, and rough; the drinkers in the public house; the television's salacious and violent influence; and the Republic of Ireland and the Catholic Church. All these evil forces are seeking to gain entrance, to overturn the established order, to bring destruction and perhaps death. In the last resort, they may condemn the soul to eternal fire.

A third category of people are the traitors. These are the ones who appear to be supporters (perhaps even leaders) of the loyal cause, but who are in reality turncoats, Judases, Lundys. These are the ones who would sacrifice fundamental Christianity to "modernism"; who are willing to engage in ecumenical dialogue with Catholics; who see little wrong in bargaining with the enemy; who would, indeed, leave open the city gates to the attacking hordes.

And finally there are the saviors, those who — like the Apprentice Boys, William III, and Christ Himself — come to the rescue of those in difficulties.

The different accounts here, of course, come from people who regard themselves as inside the walls of their respective social institutions. Their attitude to their various foes, however, is not one of mere enmity. On the contrary, their accounts are within a consciously Christian tradition. They even exhibit an element of compassion or charity: people who are in danger, whether inside or outside the walls, have the possibility of salvation.

Consider the plight of those who are outside the gate. In the case of the siege of Derry, it is clear enough that the besiegers are initially in a happier and healthier state than those within. Despite their apparent advantage, the ultimate outcome of the story is that they will be repulsed, scattered, and killed by the might of William III. The same pattern is found at the level of the individual. Whatever the immediate allure of drink, idleness, and sin, the evildoer will perish in hell when, at the last, he meets his Maker.

Despite the sinfulness of the diverse enemies defined by it, this paradigmatic structure allows for the inclusion of outsiders. Not only in the churches, but also in the Orange and Black lodges, there is a generalized invitation to come in. If one is willing to be Protestant and to profess loyalty to the Crown, then one can join the Orange Order. If one is willing to accept Christ as one's personal savior (and renounce the papacy), then one can become a Christian. And there is also room for a rough man and his rough children within the household. While there are obvious differences between entering a lodge, becoming a Christian, and getting married, there is nevertheless a remarkable similarity between the different processes by which someone is included in each of these institutions. Specifically, a person enters such a fold like a penitent.

According to the pattern here established, two individuals or two sets of individuals typically confront each other across a wall. The people outside the wall are deemed to be comparatively "rough." Those within may decide whether that rough person should or should not be admitted. If someone is admitted, he (or occasionally she) is subjected to an appropriate, often religious discipline.

All of the various social institutions discussed here are founded upon the decision of an insider to include or exclude comparatively rough outsiders. In such interactions of inclusion and exclusion, the insider is differentiated from the outsider in a systematic way, namely:

Inside	Outside
Female	Male
Parent	Child
Religious	Rough

The corporate groups into which people may be admitted, or from which they may be excluded, are often associated with femininity. This is most strikingly true of the Mother Lodge, the Mother Church, and the Maiden City.

By contrast, the rough outsiders who seek admission are usually male and young — in the local idiom, "them boys." In Listymore, descriptions of social life consistently emphasize the destructiveness, harmfulness, and even sinfulness of both youth and masculinity. The interactions that are here called inclusion and exclusion are the responses of godliness, femininity, parenthood, and authority to that presumed destructiveness.

To be let into the bounds of a social institution is not a simple matter, though. What is needed is a kind of transforming salvation. The nature of this salvation is of some interest, for it provides insight into another aspect of the male role.

Man as Savior

There are male individuals in the above accounts whose task is neither to be excluded from the social group on the grounds of their wickedness, nor to be weakly admitted in subjection to a religious discipline. These figures appear not as prodigal sons, but as saviors. These savior figures have a very special place in the frameworks generated by the siege metaphor. They also have a particular effect upon the definition of men in relation to women.

In the different savior figures there is often a significant ambiguity. All of them seem to have qualities associated with being both religious and rough. The apprentice boys in Derry, for example, slammed shut the gates of the city and took up an aggressive (rough) posture against the enemy. Their actions were not only pugnacious, but contrary to the wishes of a legally constituted authority. What they did, however, was not "bad." It was done to uphold religion and Protestantism.

William III also combines these same features. On the one hand, he is a champion of religion. Orange lodge banners, for example, often misinterpret his family motto, "Je maintenirai," to mean "I will maintain Protestantism." On the other hand, William is also a strictly military figure, a soldier.

There are, of course, directly comparable patterns in other, quite different contexts. There are nationalist heroes who, in the past, have taken up arms for their nation and their religion. And one can watch nightly the innumerable melodramas, generated by the producers of television programs and Hollywood films, in which worthy social institutions and virtuous women are regularly saved from destruction by rough, tough young men with hearts of gold. This is, of course, an ancient pattern. Its ancestry embraces the image of Mary Pickford tied to the railroad tracks, but it is at least as old as the tale of St. George and the dragon.

In all these tales, a savior is not merely, or even primarily, a destructive force. Nevertheless, both the creativeness and the destructiveness are vital. A savior is *constructively* destructive. His task is to step in and strengthen and reconstruct the body he has come to take charge of.

In the same way that the city was saved by heroic male action, so also is the individual. Here, the sinner "allows Jesus into his heart." Just as the bursting of the boom in the siege narrative was a traumatic penetration, so also is the process of admitting Jesus into one's heart. Jesus, rather like William III, can hardly be described as rough, but neither is He entirely meek and mild. In the fundamentalist world discussed here, God is not only loving, but also wrathful. Not only does God save people from sin, but He also casts those who reject Him into the darkness of the outside (see chapter 5).

Less obvious is the imagery of the Orange, Black, and Masonic lodges. Here too there is a strong emphasis upon the importance of death and rebirth.

When a candidate is admitted or "raised" to the degrees of these different institutions, he must undergo a *rite de passage*. At least for the more significant degrees, death and rebirth are a prime symbolic feature of these rites, with the male officials, acting on behalf of the lodge, undertaking the ritual destruction of the individual.

Finally, in an example closer to practical everyday life, when a man is married and submits to the discipline of wife and domesticity, he is similarly transformed by means of a *rite de passage*. Marriage, however, does not simply subordinate a man to his wife. Though by marrying, a man accepts regulation, he does not accept mere subordination. On the contrary, he becomes his wife's executive arm in his roles as breadwinner and parent. As in the story of the siege, where the sexuality is merely figurative, the man who engages in an act of (in this case actual) sexual penetration is transformed into a savior. The husband is the one who goes out into the world and provides for his family so that the wife can stay at home in a protected environment.

In every case, an individual, usually a man or youth or sinner, allows his destructive urges to be subordinated to discipline. He ceases to be merely destructive, and may achieve a heightened stature. He is no longer in need of control, his destructiveness having been placed in the service of a social institution. Thus is he transformed from a villain, sinner, or rebel into the loyal defender of his social group.

More than this, man, as savior, has ceased to stand in opposition to woman. Instead, the man now embodies and embraces both male and female principles. His strength embodies female virtues. He speaks and acts on behalf of both man and woman. Having both power and virtue, man the savior has authority.

The siege metaphor defines a wide range of different frameworks for people in Listymore, as elsewhere in the Western world. Crucially, however, it also defines in a generalized way the roles of women and men. Men are initially defined not only as physically strong, but also as wicked violators, while women, in contrast, are virtuous, weak potential victims in need of rescue.

The idea of the savior conceptually resolves this dichotomy. The savior has both strength and virtue, embracing the humanity of both the male and the female. Thus in the different variants of the siege metaphor there is a mediation between virtue and aggression, the religious and the rough, the male and the female. But this resolution takes the form of an affirmation of male authority.

Beginning with an image that pillories men as rapists, drunkards, and fools, then, the siege metaphor effects a remarkable transformation. In Ulster, as we shall continue to show, women always retain an important moral authority that contrasts with the inherent violence and roughness of men. And it will also be shown that in many relationships between the sexes, a woman will often act as a controlling "parent" to the man's "child." Despite this, the siege metaphor can also serve as a source of rhetorical frameworks that uphold male authority. From time to time, and in moments of crisis, the ordinary gender roles can seem to be reversed: women cease to be authority figures, and men cease to be childlike. In these moments of crisis, it is the man who assumes authority and comes to the support and rescue of the woman, and it is the woman who becomes helpless, like a little child.

Concluding Remarks

The tale of Derry's walls, in its local context, is a potent and compelling myth. It articulates a metaphor that defines a wide range of social roles by a simple pattern. It also touches upon issues of a more cosmic nature, including those of death, destruction, and rebirth. It identifies the forces of destruction with those of youthfulness and masculinity. But it also shows how these destructive forces may themselves be creative. The destructiveness of youth and masculinity may be what creates or saves the good order of society.

The frames presented here are not monolithic worldviews. On the contrary, the articulation of a metaphor into frames creates major discontinuities in experience. It is impossible for a person to describe all the objects in his or her universe entirely within any one of these frames. If a man is a churchgoer, for example, he may at another time be an Orangeman, a family man, an employee, or a golfer. In any given role, the metaphor must generate a distinct and relevant set of rhetorical frames within which the person may describe his experiences.

It is clear that the different descriptions given above are directly related to the social status of the speaker. The reasons for this may seem obvious, but are still worth stating. An individual's place in one rhetorical frame will often be quite different from his place in another. Thus, for example, the activities of an Orangeman may be represented in one frame as the upholding of law, order, and religion. When they are described in another frame, however, they may be seen as blasphemy, drunkenness, and rough behavior.

The same is also true of ethnic histories. When their stories are told by one side in Northern Irish society, events such as the siege of Derry carry with them rhetorical implications that favor only that side. The rhetorical significance of the events changes, however, when the frame is shifted.

A single metaphor generates countless discontinuous framed versions of the world in which both people and natural objects can be represented. Individuals will often define frameworks in which they, or their friends and allies, appear to be free of shame or guilt. They usually do this by shifting their descriptions of themselves and others from one frame to another.

There is a further point that later chapters will explore. This arises from the rhetorical nature of many representations of social life. Acts of representation, like other kinds of action, are also, in part, dramatizations. They exemplify or illustrate or signify the nature of the relationship between the actor and his audience.

McFarlane (1978), in a most useful study, argues that a prime purpose for engaging in conversation, including exchanges of descriptions of third parties in the form of news or gossip, is to establish allegiances. There is usually a tacit but real implication that the speaker and the listener are closer to each other than either of them is to the person being described.

One sees this, in Listymore, in conversations about drink. Some people, as a significant element in their friendships, complain about the people who drink. Others, as a part of *their* friendships, complain about the people who complain about the people who drink.

I was struck by a conversation with someone who explained to me that he did not drink. He said that he did not have any "moral objection" to drink, but felt it was bad for his health. The odd thing about this conversation is that *the* moral objection to drink is always its effect on health.

What my acquaintance meant was that, despite his own predilection, he did not want to be seen as one of those who complain about drink. Talking about the evils of drink was not, for him, a means of defining his friendships. He did not want to use not-drinking to define his identity.

If rhetorical conversations provide opportunities to dramatize one's identity, similar factors also apply to the celebration of historic events through parades, bonfires, pageants, and the like. These events similarly gather together participants and onlookers to affirm an identity that they all have in common.

In both conversation and historical commemoration, a listener or onlooker is effectively invited to agree with and support a version of events that has a rhetorical implication. To dissent from the conversation, or to decline to support the observance, is to withdraw support from the speaker or the demonstrator. It may also display support for the people against whom the rhetoric is directed.

There will be more discussion in later chapters of the rhetorical dramatization of framed social identities. The next chapter, however, will continue to pursue the image of the siege. It will show that the siege is important not only in conversational and historical rhetoric, but also in the way it frames violent action in the defense of urban territory.

5

FIELDWORK BY M. C. KENNEY Urban
Space,
Violence,
and
Identity
in
North
Belfast

We have shown that social institutions such as cities, countries, the family, the Orange Order, the church, and the community, and even the individual, can be described as though they were bounded entities, surrounded by external forces that might invade and destroy. A rescue from such a hostile force might in turn require invasion by a benign if harsh savior, who can cure the illness and repel the enemy. This characteristic image, which we call the siege metaphor, is particularly appropriate to the definition of physical territory.

In the cases examined in Listymore, the siege metaphor seldom defines territory. Later chapters will show that there is a certain territorial rivalry (based in social class rather than ethnicity) between the two villages of the area. Despite this, the importance of territory is muted. A home, church, or lodge will have its own bounded space, but it is only occasionally that the physical boundaries of that space are physically "invaded."

In Ardoyne in north Belfast, it is centrally *territory* that the siege metaphor defines. The external boundaries of Ardoyne are fenced off by metal and concrete to ward off the attacks of outsiders. Also, the occasional invasions of these outsiders ensure that homes, clubs, and other living spaces are practically and physically structured by the desire for physical protection.

The chapter will show, using Ardoyne as an example, how historical processes of settlement have shaped the pattern of violence and ethnicity in Northern Ireland. Belfast is more than a patchwork of working-class neighborhoods. It is an urban system that continually regenerates sectarian distinctions found in Northern Ireland as a whole.

Belfast, with its "frontiers in the city" (Boal and Livingstone 1984), functions as a major source of Protestant and Catholic ethnic identities. The city has been an engine of the troubles for two centuries. The violence that occurs on the borders of Belfast's neighborhoods reinforces Northern Ireland's version of what Sahlins calls "the oppositional character of ethnic identities and loyalties . . . found more generally in European society" (Sahlins 1989, 111).

Urban violence also defines ethnic identity in more peaceful areas. Rural Catholics and Protestants sometimes reject the sectarian hatreds found in the urban areas. They can maintain peaceful (even friendly) local patterns of social relations (Buckley 1982; Bufwack 1982; Harris 1972; Leyton 1975, 1976). But the fierce sectarianism of some of Belfast's working-class neighborhoods has a mythological force, influencing the construction of Protestant and Catholic identities throughout the province.

Darby (1986) has shown that sectarian intimidation, with the goal of maintaining the ethnic purity of neighborhoods, is common in Belfast. Boal (1982) describes Belfast as a "segmented city." He tells of a preoccupation with maintaining the boundaries of neighborhoods. This is expressed as fear of an invasion by communal enemies.

This spatial orientation in working-class neighborhoods is elaborated in a common view that geographically adjacent communities of the other religion are threatening. I have heard inhabitants of Protestant territories discuss Catholic enclaves as if those enclaves, as physical and social territories, are the natural hosts of an "infection" called the IRA. Republican districts are called "strongholds" or "dens" of the Provisional IRA. Many Protestants resent Catholic territorial "expansion" into formerly Protestant neighborhoods.

Catholics similarly fear the daily invasion of their areas by the British army, and by loyalist paramilitary groups bent on sectarian murder. This latter threat was for a long period very real. In the early 1990s random murders of Catholics by loyalist killers occurred with sickening frequency. Feldman (1991) has shown how paramilitary activists describe their own violent acts using images of (often sexual) invasion.

In Ardoyne, like anywhere else, one will hear much rhetorical description. Here, however, individuals *really believe* themselves and their territories to be under siege and subject to invasion. The fear of territorial invasion penetrates most of the worlds in which their lives are led. The population sees not only Ireland as a whole but also Ardoyne and the pubs, clubs, and homes of its inhabitants to be under threat. People in Ardoyne consequently find themselves supporting or acquiescing in the cruel activities of those who they hope may be their real saviors. Often this goes against the decency of their better judgment.

This chapter, therefore, will turn away from the subject of rhetoric and will look at the use of the siege metaphor in the structuring of operational models. The discussion will start with a historical discussion of territory in Belfast. It will then discuss riotous interactions on the boundaries of Ardoyne. Finally, it will consider local attitudes to the Provisional IRA and the republican movement.

Because Ardoyne has been so obviously under siege at various times during the nineteenth and twentieth centuries, it is easy to mythologize it. One can look to it for archetypes for bad people and good people, for aggressors, victims, and saviors. It is certainly in these terms that many in Ardoyne see their area, at least some of the time. In studying a beleaguered territory, in this case a Catholic area, one should not forget the existence of other worlds in Ulster. In particular, one should not forget that there are Protestant communities that are in a similar way terrorized by neighboring individuals, groups, and territories.

The problem is not to discover victims, villains, and heroes (there are plenty of these, depending on one's point of view), but to find solutions. The inhabitants of Ardoyne sometimes believe that their area is typical of Northern Ireland as a whole. They see it as a microcosm in which Irish history is acted out. Such a view should be treated with caution. One cannot deny that the urban territories of Belfast have potential as sources of mythology. But the world of Ardoyne is, in the last resort, only one world among many. From these other worlds, one can extract other stories.

Historical Dimensions of Urban Territory

Many working-class areas in Belfast — Ardoyne, Andersonstown, the Markets, Sandy Row, and others — were originally mill villages, built close to the great linen mills. Most were established as religiously homogeneous communities of migrants from the countryside.

The villages were surrounded, in the first instance, by farmers' fields (Milroy 1980). Later the city of Belfast expanded beyond the mills. The boundaries between the villages became filled with newer streets and housing developments (e.g., Ligoniel 1981), giving rise to the larger working-class areas such as the Falls Road and the Shankill Road.

From the first, these areas were ethnically homogenous. Nineteenth-century maps of Belfast (see the Ordnance Survey of Ireland 1837–44, sheets 60–65) reveal that many well-known "interfaces," where violence and confrontations occur today between Catholics and Protestants, are located where a rural border zone once existed between Catholic and Protestant industrial settlements (Kenney 1991).

Belfast lies on the eastern edge of Ulster, where Protestants have long been a majority. Catholic areas, therefore, first developed as islands within larger areas of Protestant population. To make matters more complex, however, small Protestant areas also grew up within the Catholic islands.

Given this territorial pattern, definitions of social groups — and especially of territory — based on inside/outside distinctions are crucial to everyday social life. The core working-class districts are well known as strongholds — or what Feldman (1991) calls "sanctuaries" — of the locally based paramilitary organizations on both sides. They are also sanctuaries to the ordinary population, fearful of the activities of their neighbors. These residential districts are conventionally described as republican and loyalist, to reflect their supposed political polarization and extremism.

Communal violence in Belfast (along with formally organized political violence) is a long-standing phenomenon. Bardon's history of Belfast (1982) gives accounts of Belfast riots in 1756, 1832, 1833, 1835, 1841, 1847, 1864, 1872, 1886, 1907, 1920, 1921, 1922, 1931, 1932, 1935, 1964, 1969, 1970, and 1971. These incidents, however, were only the fiercer ones.

Many of the biggest riots were closely related to the major political issues of the day. The activities of Daniel O'Connell and the different home rule bills, for example, provided occasions for riot. For all their association with major issues, however, the riots were often played out on very local stages and at predictable times of year. Belfast riots have tended to coincide with annual festivals and their accompanying demonstrations. The most famous of these have been the processions held by Orangemen on the Twelfth of July. The report on the causes of the 1864 riots stated, "Belfast is liable to periodic disturbances on occasions well known as the Orange anniversaries." It added, "If the celebration of these anniversaries be attended with such risk, we might well ask why any party should obstinately adhere to it" (quoted in Bardon 1982, 115).

Apart from the Twelfth of July, however, the biggest disruptions were associated with 15 August, the Feast of the Assumption. This was a religious festival, a holy day of obligation for Catholics. Beginning in the latter part of the nineteenth century, it was also celebrated, in much the same manner as the Twelfth of July for the Orangemen, by the processions of the Ancient Order of Hibernians. In 1872, for example, heavy rain flooded the Protestant area of Sandy Row on the Twelfth of July, and the occasion for the main riots was the large procession in the city on 15 August (Bardon 1982, 144–46).

Riots not only occurred at predictable times, but they also had a predictable form. They consisted largely of episodes of invasion and defense between Protestant and Catholic areas. In the nineteenth century, the most important (but not the only) areas were the Protestant Sandy Row and the Catholic Pound.

Such riots could also include incidents of what Darby (1986) calls "sectarian intimidation" but would now be called "ethnic cleansing." This is the eviction of Catholics living in Protestant areas and of Protestants living in Catholic areas (see, for example, Bardon 1982, 145–46, 197–98, and passim).

When the troubles erupted in 1969, and more so in the early 1970s, the same nineteenth-century patterns of riot were to be found. There was extensive conflict between adjacent neighborhoods of different ethnic composition.

Many "mixed" border streets, such as the streets between the Protestant Shankill and the Catholic Falls districts, were therefore blocked off by the construction of a "peace line." These fences, usually of concrete and corrugated metal, at first were built as an emergency measure by the army to separate rioting mobs of local Catholics and Protestants. They are now a permanent feature of the urban landscape (Boal and Livingstone 1984), though the Northern Ireland Housing Executive has gradually replaced them with more normal-looking brick walls that have the same function.

Since then, however, new borders have developed in Belfast. There has been something of a Protestant flight to the suburbs, and even to Britain and elsewhere. Correspondingly, Catholics have moved into parts of the old Protestant areas of the city with falling populations. In many of the remaining loyalist areas, there has been a paramilitarization of working-class Protestants, including those too poor or too stubborn to leave the old districts.

In the sixties and seventies, there were urban renewal plans similar to those in Britain described by Wilmott and Young (1957). These hastened the process of decline in the old Protestant areas. Modern buildings replaced the old terraces of small red brick houses and corner shops built before the Second World War.

The first of these developments included blocks of flats, shopping centers, and a multilane road built right through the middle of old west Belfast (Weiner 1980). More recently, highly intelligent public housing schemes have aimed to give residents their own front gardens and other "defensible spaces." The idea is that inhabitants can protect themselves and their homes against vandalism and worse (Brett 1986, 102).

The inhabitants of the old Catholic working-class districts have been affected by the same changes as the residents of the Protestant areas. Catholics, however, have experienced less upward social mobility. In the recent past (more so than today), they also tended to have more children than comparable Protestants. Catholics have not, in general, migrated to the suburbs in response to urban renewal and political violence. They have tended to stay in the inner city.

Populations from Catholic districts, suffering from housing shortages and domestic overcrowding, have expanded beyond old sectarian boundaries into formerly Protestant areas. Now riots, which continue to occur at certain times of the year and at well-established locations, also occur along the new sectarian interfaces created by Catholic population growth and by the building of new public housing.

The reality of much territorial "invasion" in Belfast is the occupation of houses on insecure urban frontiers. Usually this is by poor families (often, for demographic reasons, Catholics) who simply need housing. More deliberate action apparently occurs as well. Darby (1986) has shown, in one Belfast case study, that mobs can force residents "of the other sort" to flee their houses on sectarian borders. However, evidence of the direct coordination of these incidents by local paramilitary groups is difficult to come by. In general, though, Catholic expansion in the city reflects changes in the economy and in urban demographic patterns. It is probably only secondarily an attempt by Catholic paramilitarists to take over formerly Protestant parts of the city.

Nevertheless, there is a widespread Protestant belief that Catholic territorial expansion in Belfast has a *political* goal. A pamphlet produced by a small Protestant paramilitary group in the 1970s described this apprehension of Catholic territorial expansion very well, using the invasion metaphor:

> As always, almost unnoticed but with military precision, farm after farm, street after street, district after district was taken over. In a built-up area like Belfast, this is particularly noticeable. This is no haphazard operation, but a plan with a strategic military end in view! For future operations it was necessary that the enemy should dominate in three specific areas, Ormeau Park, Antrim Road and Oldpark. Once Protestant, these three areas are now in Catholic control. (Tara n.d.)

Ardoyne and Its Boundaries

Adjacent to Ardoyne are Woodvale and the Bone. Woodvale is a loyalist terri-tory that forms part of the much larger loyalist Shankill Road area. The Bone, like Ardoyne, is mainly Catholic in composition. The relations between the republican area of Ardoyne and the adjacent loyalist territory of Woodvale illus-trate the pattern of the development of rival neighborhoods, with resulting con-flict over the "ownership" of territory.

Ardoyne, Woodvale, and the Bone were originally built as physically dis-tinct villages. They provided religiously segregated industrial housing for the workers employed in the textile mills established on the Crumlin and Oldpark roads between 1830 and 1860.

Despite the erosion of the original village borders by the building of houses, the separate identities of these older settlements still exist. In the case of the Bone and Ardoyne, where the people in each area are almost all Catholic, the rivalries are friendly and muted. The physical boundary is known only to local people. Elsewhere, as with the stretch of the Crumlin Road separating the original Woodvale from old Ardoyne, the boundary has political importance. It has been the site of some of the most severe rioting of the present troubles.

The oral history of the locality conveys the impression that the current problems merely continue the similar problems of much earlier times. In par-ticular, there are vivid folk memories of the troubles of the early 1920s.

One elderly local historian of the communities of Ardoyne and the Bone (effectively what we have called a "curator") told me of the attacks of "the Or-angemen and the police" on the Bone of the 1920s. At that time, he said, "the people had no arms." On Easter Tuesday in 1922, "nine armored cars, with five or six men in each car," came into the area. They were "armed with rifles and a machine gun." They murdered, among others, Annie McCann, who was "shot in her front room while cleaning the grate." He also tells about the riots of the 1930s, when crowds of rioters from the nearby Protestant area of Tiger Bay "came in and did the shooting."

During the same period there were also sectarian incidents across a part of the main Crumlin Road. This, for some distance, is the effective boundary between Ardoyne and Woodvale. The two areas were, around the turn of the century, residential areas of about the same size.

During the relative peace in Belfast between the troubles of the 1930s and the beginning of the present conflict in 1969, many Catholics came to live on the Woodvale side of the Crumlin Road. They lived near Ardoyne's parish church, Holy Cross, which happens to be on the Protestant side of the road, in Woodvale. But the looseness that had crept into the definition of the territorial boundary between Woodvale and Ardoyne since the 1930s was removed in the riots of 1969. On the eve of these riots, the larger issue was the campaign to improve the civil rights of Catholics. This campaign was run by several organizations: the Northern Irish Civil Rights Association, People's Democracy, and others, all of them much resented by large numbers of Protestants. Then, as now, major political issues were acted out on local stages, at predictable places and at predictable times.

The riots in 1969 in Ardoyne began in the period before the Twelfth of July. At that time, Orangemen and their supporters throughout Northern Ireland annually make preparations for their festivities. They put out flags and bunting, and build arches across the streets.

In their official report on the riots of 1969, Scarman and his colleagues (1972) wrote:

> On 9 July there had been a new development. It had been the incessant habit of a Mrs Gilmour, an elderly Protestant living in the predominantly Catholic Chatham Street, to display a Union Jack at about this time of year. This had caused irritation in the past and extra police attention had had to be given. In 1969 tension was greater. On 9 July the flag was torn down and much damage was done to Mrs Gilmour's house. This incident received much publicity. On 11 July a crowd gathered outside the house in Hooker Street of Mrs Gilmour's daughter [Minnie Baillie] and chanted threats such as "burn Minnie Baillie out" and "get Minnie Baillie out." . . . Mrs Gilmour's house was petrol bombed on 26 July but the bulk of the intimidation in July was practised on Catholics and a good many families felt it necessary to move. (Scarman et al. 1972, 6:25, 6:33)

Trouble flared again, once more at a predictable time, in the approach to 15 August. In 1969, 14 August in Ardoyne was a time for the building of bonfires, to be followed by demonstrations on the next day. On 15 August, a mob from Woodvale invaded Ardoyne across the Crumlin Road, shooting two Catholic men dead, wounding thirteen others, and burning a number of pubs, shops, and houses.

According to the official report, the nights preceding the deaths and destruction of 14–15 August 1969 had been marked by the building of barricades, the gathering of mobs in Woodvale and Ardoyne, and rioting on the Crumlin Road. This is a description of the scene on 14 August at 10:45 P.M.:

> By this time all four corner buildings at the Hooker Street/Crumlin Road junction were ablaze as well as two houses on the Hooker side of the Crumlin Road itself. The roadway was littered with bricks and broken bottles. Youths from both Disraeli Street and Hooker Street were fighting in the middle of Crumlin Road and the fighting stretched into Hooker Street as far as the junction with Chatham Street. (Scarman et al. 1972, 22:23)

These incidents echoed what was happening in other parts of the city. In consequence of what the report calls this "invasion" (Scarman et al. 1972, 2:10), the Catholics who were living among the Protestants of Woodvale, and the Protestants who lived in streets south of Ardoyne, had to leave their homes. They fled to find sanctuary in areas where their own side was in a clear majority. The somewhat fuzzy boundary zone between Woodvale and Ardoyne, therefore, hardened to the line that it is today.

On 27 August 1969 the army arrived in Ardoyne. There it has remained, its presence and operations becoming part of daily life. The army built a peace line along both sides of the Crumlin Road that stretched a quarter mile from the Brookfield Mill to Holy Cross Monastery, sealing off most of the side streets that provided access into both Ardoyne and Woodvale from the main Crumlin Road. Corrugated metal walls shielded the two neighborhoods from sight and sound of each other and hindered movement across the sectarian border.

It is a cliché of the troubles (one that is nevertheless true) that the army came to protect the Catholics and stayed to fight the IRA. The republicans of the early 1970s came to see their role to be as much harassing the British out of Ireland as protecting local populations against their Protestant neighbors.

This growing opposition reached a famous crisis on 9 August 1971, when, in an operation beginning at 4:15 A.M., men (republicans, loyalists, and allegedly those with no involvement) were dragged from their homes by the army and held in prison without trial.

This event, which has come to be known as Internment, led to the biggest spate of forcible evictions Belfast has seen. All over Belfast, people were intimidated by riot or the fear of riot. According to a well-informed estimate, one percent of the households in Belfast left their homes and went to live elsewhere (Black et al. 1975).

This series of events was particularly traumatic to people in and around Ardoyne, both Catholics and Protestants. Ardoyne became famous as a stronghold of the Provisional IRA. By the 1980s, when I came to live in Ardoyne, conflict between the army and the IRA was daily evident. On the one side, there were soldiers' foot patrols, the apparently random firing of plastic bullets from military and police vehicles, and raids on houses in search of arms or IRA suspects. On the other, there were riots, shooting, bombings, and ambushes.

Residents of Ardoyne long ago stopped seeing the army as a protective force. This was mainly because of Internment, but also because of a more general deterioration in relations. Now residents see the army as intruders.

On an average day in the mid-1980s, one could see the security forces stop and question youths, who would then be spread-eagled against the side of an army Land Rover. You might walk up a front path to knock on the door of a friend. Suddenly a soldier would appear in full battle gear, poised at the corner of the house or crouched behind the hedge. Squads of four or five soldiers typically patrolled in single file along the pavements of Ardoyne, carrying their semiautomatic rifles at the ready. They pointed their guns this way and that, alert for snipers.

For a time in the 1970s, this state of siege was formalized. There was a general movement in republican areas to exclude not only Protestant terrorists but also the security forces. Such a "no-go area" was established in Ardoyne. Woodvale's Ulster Defence Association reacted by setting up its own no-go area. It too blocked the police and army from entering its own neighborhood. Finally the army responded. It used bulldozers in a show of force, breaking down all barricades. It has made a point of its ability to patrol in all of the different areas of Northern Ireland, but this situation is changing as a result of the ceasefire of 1994 and the subsequent negotiations. The army no longer patrols in this highly visible and aggressive manner.

At the Border

Despite, and in part because of, the peace line, the sense of being besieged in Ardoyne continues. During my main period of fieldwork (1984–86), there continued to be regular confrontations on the border between Ardoyne and Woodvale.

Two of the original side streets off the Crumlin Road, built in the 1860s — Flax Street in Ardoyne and Leopold Street in Woodvale — are directly opposite each other. Both remained open to traffic long after other such streets were closed. In 1990, Leopold Street was finally closed. Before then, the two streets permitted sight between and access to the two areas, even after the erection of the peace line along the Crumlin Road. This corridor also allowed groups from both sides — usually bands of stone-throwing children and youths — to confront each other and even to encroach upon each other's territory.

Many of the confrontations of the kind I witnessed here did not have any serious aim of taking territory or producing any political or other obvious outcome. They usually consisted of one side attacking the perceived territory of the other, or else defending their own. The riots were primarily recreational acts, with a strong element of enjoyment or fun for the participants. Usually the security forces were involved, too, in some way. These events also had a ritual or dramatic quality (see chapter 10).

Despite their playful and ritual nature, such actions have quite serious consequences. First, it is out of this kind of violence that more serious aggression arises, involving eviction, burning people out of their homes or businesses, vandalism, injury, and death. Second, the fact that Ardoyne, during my stay there, was perpetually on the edge of such recreational violence contributed to the chronic sense of being under threat.

The following account is of violent forms of interaction that took place on 9 August 1986. Although loyalists as well as republicans were interned on this date in 1971, 9 August is now a republican festival celebrating this anniversary. In 1972, this anniversary superseded the Feast of the Assumption as an occasion for demonstrations in Ardoyne. An elderly republican explained this change to me. "The priests up there," he said, gesturing with a tilt of his head toward the church overlooking Ardoyne, "never did like the bonfires being associated with the Feast of the Assumption on August fifteenth. You know, they never did like it being associated with a feast of the Church. So the summer after Internment, the people decided that it would be better to have the bonfires to commemorate Internment, and they did it that way." No doubt the republican movement was pleased to have, at this time of year, an anniversary that was peculiarly its own.

The Ancient Order of Hibernians formerly organized the demonstrations on 15 August, and it still does in some rural areas. While roughly a Catholic equivalent of the Orange Order, the Hibernians do not have the same unifying role that Wiener (1980, 77) attributes to the Orange Order. At the beginning of the twentieth century, the Hibernians became strong in Belfast. They were then, as now, identified with moderate nationalist politics, opposed to republicanism. Their significance had declined by the 1970s. Even in Catholic rural areas, the Hibernians now lack the support and political impact of their Orange counterparts. The shift of this major Ardoyne festival from 15 August to 9 August had perhaps a largely symbolic effect, removing any impression that the Hibernians controlled this important occasion for demonstrating.

Figure 7. Demonstration by members of the Ancient Order of Hibernians. (Courtesy of the Ulster Folk and Transport Museum)

The events described below took place against a background of confrontations (to be examined more closely in chapter 10) at the bonfires of the previous night.

9 *August 1986, 2:30 P.M.*: A convoy of army trucks and a bulldozer was under way up the Crumlin Road. The convoy turned into Flax Street and went on into Ardoyne. A few minutes later, the army was busy demolishing a meter-high cement wall that had materialized across Flax Street, blocking the way to the main Crumlin Road and to Woodvale. The IRA had built an identical street barricade at that spot a few days before, and the army had removed it just as quickly.

Opposite the entrance to Flax Street, in Woodvale, Protestant children had gathered at the end of Leopold Street (a terrace of old housing that stretches to the Crumlin Road). Near their Land Rover, three policemen faced a group of boys. One policeman was holding a gun for firing plastic bullets. All of the children were twelve years old and younger.

One boy threw a stone at a passing bus driving up the Crumlin Road. A policeman shouted at him, then lectured the group, threatening to "put a boot up your backsides" if they caused any trouble.

Returning to the area a few hours later, I saw the same group of boys at the same spot, stoning the police Land Rover. The policemen were inside, with the riot screens down, and were driving in a circle. Some boys, as young as eight years old, were running close alongside the vehicle, within three meters, heaving broken bricks.

I was on the Woodvale side at this time. I was walking toward the scene when a girl about eleven years old spoke to me. "Sorry, missus," she said politely, "you can't get through there." I asked what was going on. She said, "They're bricking the peelers."

Another Land Rover drove suddenly into Leopold Street, and the mob of children stoning the police scattered. I watched two boys slowing to a trot after their mad dash away from the police. "One of them had his plastic-bullet gun out, the fucking bastard!" said one boy angrily. The other responded, "Are you going home now for your tea?"

I returned to the scene in the early evening. This time, the children, including some teenage girls, were running from Woodvale across the Crumlin Road into Flax Street. One or two at a time, they would dash down Flax Street with a piece of brick in their hands. Then they would race, moments later, back to Leopold Street. It was impossible to see exactly what they were doing. So I asked a boy, "Are those Woodvale kids running over to Flax Street to fight with Ardoyne kids?" The boy replied, "Yes, they are going halfway down." He then explained, in a wistful tone, while continuing to gaze toward Flax Street, "I'm on parole. I can't go down there. If I go down there, I'm away."

11 *August 1986:* During the night there was more throwing of bricks, this time in the opposite direction, by adults from Ardoyne, attacking Woodvale Protestants across the Crumlin Road.

I was now with a woman called Tracy, with whom I did community work. She told me that she had seen this rioting because she had been in a club until 2 A.M. Then, when the bars closed, the crowd belonging to the club had been standing around with nothing to do. A line of police vehicles had been blocking Flax Street, at the location of the former IRA-constructed barricade. Tracy said the crowd had started milling around, shouting and trying to put out the streetlamps. She described the mood as "just a happy bunch of people." Stones and bottles had been thrown at the police.

All of a sudden, she had seen a machine gun being fired from behind the line of police vehicles. She had also heard something "that sounded like a shotgun." She thought that all the gunfire had come from the direction of the police and not from inside Ardoyne.

A major consequence of interactions such as these in the 1980s was to

Figure 8. Catholic teenagers watching the St. Patrick's Day parade. Lower Falls Road, Belfast, March 17, 1985. (Courtesy of Mary C. Kenney)

make the border with Woodvale more ominous. The violence might be recreational and ritualized, but the bricks and guns were real enough.

Due to the intermittent rioting over a long period, the boundary between Woodvale and Ardoyne deteriorated. It acquired a derelict and indeed threatening appearance. Near the rubble-strewn peace line, houses were left empty and condemned. This was made worse by the propensity of children to break in and light fires. One section in particular was totally empty; riots in 1969 had destroyed all of the buildings there, and they were later torn down. Looking from Ardoyne toward this particular section of Woodvale, one could see only a lone baker's shop beyond the gray metal and barbed wire of the peace line. Elsewhere, graffiti celebrating the paramilitary groups covered available walls in Woodvale visible from Ardoyne. These were updated according to the current political issues of concern to loyalists.

The end site on Leopold Street in Woodvale was an empty space, where a commercial building once stood; it was burned down during the disturbances of 1969. In the vacant lot, gangs of children and teenagers gathered to throw

Figure 9. Loyalist paramilitary mural, Crumlin Road, Belfast, 1990. (Courtesy of Mary C. Kenney)

Figure 10. Flax Street, near the road dividing Protestant from Catholic territory in North Belfast. Flax Street is one of the few unblocked roads into Ardoyne. Belfast, 1990. (Courtesy of Mary C. Kenney)

Figure 11. Republican mural commemorating Bobby Sands, the leader of the 1979 hunger strike. Falls Road, Belfast, August 1990. (Courtesy of Mary C. Kenney)

stones. A section of the wall of the demolished building still stood and was visible from the Crumlin Road as a kind of graffiti board. It showed the slogans "UVF" and "UDA" and "This Is Free Woodvale" that mark the edge of Protestant territory and announce that the inhabitants of Woodvale are prepared to defy the state.

Beyond the vacant site, away from the main road, ropes of red, white, and blue pennants are strung between the rows of houses and draped over the narrow street. Curbs in Leopold Street are painted red, white, and blue. From the vantage point of Ardoyne, the combined effect is like looking down a hostile loyalist tunnel.

Things have changed since the late 1980s, when these observations were made. The Northern Ireland Housing Executive, in a characteristic gesture, arranged for an attractive, ornamental brick wall to be placed at the end of Leopold Street, sealing it off from the Crumlin Road and Ardoyne.

This solution to a problem of perennial rioting is one that has been successful all over Belfast. Unfortunately, as everybody knows, its longer-term effect is only to seal off the ethnic groups more effectively from each other, to shut each side into its own area and to shut everybody else out.

Figure 12. Anonymous graffito, Joy Street, Belfast, 1985. This graffito, in a Catholic area, incorporates a weapon, a heart with rays (a common image in Catholic Ireland), and images of crucifixion, and is perhaps a comment on the ambiguous relation between the Catholic church and republican paramilitary organizations in Northern Ireland. (Courtesy of Mary C. Kenney)

The Republicans

The provisional republican movement embraces both the political party Sinn Féin and the paramilitary IRA. Everyone in Ardoyne knows that the provisional republican movement has a major, if not dominant, place in Ardoyne society.

Ethnographers of republican districts in Belfast (Burton 1978; Sluka 1989) have stressed the high level of passive popular support for the paramilitary groups that operate within these districts. They assume the basis for this support to be political, reflecting a commitment to the broad goals of Irish nationalism. No doubt it is the case that most people in Ardoyne would assent to the nationalist view of history described in chapter 3, which has a hoped-for denouement in the reunification of Ireland. Their support for the IRA, however, rests on a more solid foundation than historical rhetoric. It results from what is widely accepted as a proven need for protection against the police, army, loyalist mobs, vigilantes, and random sectarian killers. The perceived need is for an armed militia that will, when necessary, repel those outsiders who may come into the area to do them harm.

Occasional comments reveal this general tolerance of paramilitarism. One middle-class Catholic woman from outside the district explained to me that some measure of nationalism was essential if she was to be "accepted" into the social life of Ardoyne: "You don't have to be pro-IRA, but you do have to be anti-Brit." Another woman, an Ardoyne native, said simply, "They [the IRA] protect the people."

There are, however, many dissenting voices. In Ardoyne, the main alternative view to republicanism comes from the Roman Catholic Church, represented locally by the Holy Cross parish church. In all of its official pronouncements, the Church holds that the violent activities of the Provisional IRA are wicked. For example, while it will bury the dead of the IRA, it will not countenance the bringing of IRA insignia into its churches. When he visited Ireland, the Pope succinctly expressed the view of the Catholic hierarchy on the matter: "Murder," he said, "is murder."

The parish church influences the life of every person living in Ardoyne. Holy Cross monastery, of which the parish church forms part, is run by the Passionist Order. Built on the Woodvale side of the Crumlin Road in 1902, the massive, imposing church buildings stand on the crest of the hill. Their twin Romanesque towers loom over the district. There are seven well-attended masses each Sunday, and ten priests minister to the religious and social needs of the people of Ardoyne.

As in other Catholic areas, all the primary and secondary schools located in the district are parochial schools. These, to use an expression familiar to Ulster's educationalists, have tried to provide "oases of calm" (see chapter 13) in a troubled district. Teaching nuns in Ardoyne have an authority similar to that of the priests. Both exert a considerable influence over local people's personal lives, as they do elsewhere in Catholic Ireland.

Both the Church and the republican movement are empowered with the historical role of defining Irish identity. In the territorial microcosm of Ardoyne, there is an important sense in which the Catholic Church and the republican movement, therefore, represent rival powers.

This struggle between advocates of physical force and the Church has been a recurring theme in Irish nationalism since early in the last century. It is an especially stark version of the contrast, found in Listymore, between "religion" and "rough behavior." In the recent troubles, the Church has continued this long-standing tradition of opposition to political violence.

The Church, like the republican movement, can lay claim to being a custodian or curator of a major aspect of distinctively Irish culture. Its role in this regard is defined by the framework of nationalist history outlined in chapter 3. The Church is widely seen to have been the principal ally of the Irish peasantry during the eighteenth and nineteenth centuries against the oppression of English landowners. Part of the suppression of Irish culture in the past is seen to have been the attempt to proselytize Catholics and otherwise suppress Catholicism. More generally, Irish nationality and ethnicity is unambiguously associated with the Catholic religion. Certainly nearly everybody in Ardoyne, including many priests, nuns, and active churchgoers, is sympathetic to the idea of a united Ireland.

The republican movement does not seriously dispute the place of the Church in Irish life. Though disagreeing with the Church's expressed political views, its members are mostly loyal Catholics. Indeed, Catholicism is part of the heritage of Ireland, which the republican movement seeks to uphold. Republicanism, however, is the heir to another nationalist tradition, that of armed revolt against Britain. Therefore republicanism too is a custodian or curator of aspects of specifically nationalist culture.

The social and cultural division between the republican movement and the Church finds a Meadian echo (Mead 1934) in the minds and activities of individuals in Ardoyne. Many Ardoynians are straightforwardly opposed to the republican movement. Others, with equal simplicity, give active or tacit support to the "armed struggle." Many are more ambiguous. These people condone the activity of the IRA in specific instances, but demur in others. Above all, they regret the situation that has brought the armed struggle into existence, and regret too the consequences of the violence.

Throughout the period of the troubles, there has been some considerable opposition among urban Catholics to the Provisional IRA. The Social Democratic and Labour Party has steadfastly opposed the use of force. The Official IRA, from which the Provisional IRA broke away in the 1960s, is now represented in the Workers' Party. This Marxist group eschews both violence and sectarianism, and has supporters throughout Catholic Belfast and elsewhere. The Peace People, an organization set up in the 1970s in opposition to paramilitary and other violence, was also well represented in republican areas of Belfast. And after the ceasefire, there have been outspoken Catholic objections to the continuation of the "punishments" (notably the breaking of limbs with iron bars) continuing in Catholic neighborhoods.

One common kind of objection is to the fundraising activities of the Provisionals, which some people allege often involve robbery and racketeering. One man said, with some pride, that the social club of which his father had been a leading member did *not* make payments to the IRA: "My dad started this club and he fought hard to keep the IRA out. They tried to bring their [pinball] machines in here [to provide a source of revenue] but he wouldn't let them. I know everyone on the board of [the club] and they aren't IRA."

Another common view is that many active members of the IRA are psychopaths or are otherwise crazy. Jim, a construction worker, had lived for a time outside Ardoyne. He wryly commented, "They [the working-class people in Northern Ireland] take men who in any other society would be considered nuts, and allow them to take over responsibility and leadership in both communities."

People also complain that the Provisionals' operations contribute to a general state of lawlessness in Catholic areas. They are blamed too for the breakdown of communal and familial forms of social control.

There is some truth in these allegations. Rioting and the lighting of fires are said to be *ordered* by the IRA. Ordinary people in Ardoyne are therefore hesitant to control the aggressive and destructive actions of the young. This is undoubtedly bad for the peace of the neighborhood. According to informants, the local IRA also has brutally punished local people who have interfered with their operations. In consequence, people fear reporting suspicious or even openly criminal events to the police.

In contrast to these rather negative opinions, republicans present themselves, and are widely seen, as the saviors of the local people. The Royal Ulster Constabulary (the Northern Irish police) can scarcely carry out routine police functions within Ardoyne. The IRA, therefore, lays claim to being an unofficial police force and judiciary. It punishes not only informers and traitors within their own ranks, but also joy-riders, hooligans, and criminals. It is known to hold quasi-judicial "courts." Punishments, often brutal, have included beatings, kneecappings (shooting people in the knee), and death.

Sinn Féin has increasingly taken pains to present itself as socially responsible. In retrospect, one can see in this growing respectability a tendency that led to the declaration in 1994 of a ceasefire. No doubt Sinn Féin was also concerned that the activities of young delinquents might give republicanism a bad name. Whether or not the IRA does order specific acts of rioting, as has been alleged, Sinn Féin has come to disapprove of the impromptu riots that are associated with demonstrations and the building of bonfires.

When I returned to Ardoyne briefly in 1990, Sinn Féin had begun a campaign to restrict the building of bonfires, starting in another republican area, the Falls Road. A member of Sinn Féin explained to me that the organization was trying to substitute open-air concerts and other events for young people for the bonfires in Catholic districts.

For many people, the change was popular. One woman said to me, "There's great crack [conversation, camaraderie] over on the Falls tonight. They're having free music and street parties to keep the kids away from the violence."

The Sinn Féin member explained that there were (in 1990) no Internment Eve bonfires on the Falls. Sinn Féin was now working to eliminate the practice in Ardoyne. He said:

> I suppose the kids want to have the bonfires because the Protestants have theirs. We want to change it because it's just license, you know. It's an excuse to get drunk and steal cars. It's the atmosphere. That's the night that everybody goes crazy. It's been changed now on the Falls Road for a couple of years, and we are trying to get rid of the bonfires in this district too.
>
> It's bad enough stealing and burning the cars of Protestants, but the Falls Road stopped it because they were going into middle-class Catholic areas and stealing and burning *their* cars. We have been trying to only have one bonfire in the district. There used to be a bonfire in every street. Some of the parents objected. They wanted their kids to have their own bonfire. But this year we just had the one, down there [he nodded in the direction of Flax Street].
>
> The police don't drive through here anymore on the anniversary of Internment anyway. They stay beyond the boundaries of the district. It was just a provocation. They fired plastic bullets at kids. You know, some of the police had a few [drinks] themselves that night.

An important social institution in Ardoyne is the Advice Centre run by Sinn Féin. Everything in Ardoyne operates against a background of poverty. Despite a superficial atmosphere of cheerfulness in the streets and clubs, the condition of the area is poor. There is material poverty and undeniable psychological stress. This is caused not only by the interactions of the IRA with the soldiers, but also by poor housing and general deprivation. The unemployment rate is over fifty percent, typical of Catholic areas of Northern Ireland. However, many Ardoyne men "do the double," earning money from unofficial, temporary employment while collecting unemployment pay (Howe 1990).

One local woman told me, however, that unemployment statistics were misleading. They counted only one wage-earner for each household although, in the past, women were usually also employed. "The women kept these districts going" with their work in the mills, she claimed. Unemployment in north Belfast, she implied, has been even more devastating than officially recognized, since the statistics ignore women's loss of jobs and income.

Unemployment and living in public housing have the perhaps inevitable result of entangling people with officialdom. The Sinn Féin Advice Centre helps people in a practical and businesslike way with the problems of unemployment pay, rent, housing, legal matters, and the like.

Sinn Féin's Advice Centre in Ardoyne is a house converted into an office. It is protected with security screens and video cameras. Sinn Féin is technically distinct from the IRA to ensure its legality as a political party, but the connection between the two is well recognized. For example, a group of teenage boys in Ardoyne playfully asked, "Are you from America? Are you going over to the Advice Centre to join up?" (This comment was also an oblique allusion to what can be called "political tourism" by Irish Americans who like to visit Belfast.)

The gable end of the row of houses that includes the Advice Centre is the site of a shrine built to commemorate republicans from the district killed in the current troubles. Republican marches and rallies gather at this shrine to hear speeches denouncing the British troops, who observe the scene from a distance.

It is not, however, the Advice Centre or Sinn Féin's community work that provides the basis for the passive support for the IRA. Rather, it is the sense of permanent threat. One aspect of this is the way that the need for security constrains quite harmless activity.

There are, for example, seven social and drinking clubs in Ardoyne. Most of them were opened after the pubs burned down in 1969. They play a central role in the social, political, and economic life of the district. Partly to promote security, and partly for legal reasons, these social and drinking clubs are technically for members and their guests only. In practice, all Ardoyne residents are admitted. The "crack" (fun, conversation, and camaraderie) to be enjoyed in these clubs is equal to any to be found in Ireland. Of the seven clubs, only one has a generally recognized identification with the Provisional IRA.

Pubs and clubs in Belfast have long been easy targets for random killers, who use both bombs and bullets. Cages of heavy steel mesh, designed to deflect bombs, cover the doors of the clubs. The door of the cage is kept locked. When the bell is rung, a doorman, usually an old man, emerges to scrutinize the person seeking entry. Any stranger who fails to convince him that he or she has local friends waiting inside will not be admitted. Closed-circuit video cameras over the entrances, heavy screens covering doors and windows, and loops of barbed wire strung around the roofs are reminders that these clubs are targets for loyalist paramilitarists.

Inside, however, there is no sign of danger. Most of the clubs have a traditional men-only bar with darts and snooker tables. Here the old men of the district spend much of their time. There is also at least one lounge bar for younger people of both sexes. Some have a large disco with DJs, live bands, and large screens for rock videos.

In a narrowly territorial and practical sense, they reflect what was earlier called "walls within walls." These social clubs, including the one controlled by the paramilitarists, have become the main focus of social life in Ardoyne. They represent both the constriction and what Harris called the "intensification" of neighborhood community life (Harris 1972, xiii) brought about by a quarter of a century of continuous political violence. Within their walls can be found "good crack" and community spirit. This exists, however, because it is enclosed by the steel at the doors and windows. It exists too because the neighborhood is itself closed off by a peace line made of concrete and iron.

One woman's domestic experience illustrates the central issue. The story begins in 1971, when Ardoyne was still mixed, with Protestants living primarily in a northern area, in the streets farthest away from Woodvale. In the evictions and removals that followed Internment in 1971, many Protestants fled their homes in this area. Some of them even set fire to the houses so that Catholics could not move in. As a result of these disturbances, the army erected a peace line, dividing most of the new part of Ardoyne from a smaller area of streets inhabited mainly by Protestants.

Despite the peace line, this small Protestant area, inhabited by about a thousand people in the mid-1980s, retained easy access to the main part of Ardoyne. It lacked its own shops and churches and had only a new community-center building, where local groups met and where a loyalist flute band could hold its practice sessions. Until the Housing Executive built an extra wall in 1989, Protestant women crossed the peace line every day, walking through a door in the metal fence to buy food and use a nearby post office.

Kate is a community worker who is very familiar with Ardoyne. She shared with two friends a house on the Catholic side near this peace line. For some time, this house was subject to occasional intimidation from the other side of the peaceline.

Then, on Eleventh Night in 1987 (that is, 11 July, when loyalists have their midnight bonfires in anticipation of the Twelfth), "a crowd from the other side dismantled the peace line" and attacked their home.

First they wrecked my car by bashing it with cricket bats and beer cans. I found sixteen full cans of beer in my car the next morning! Then they tried to come in the house. Before, we only had windows broken, but this time they were trying to get in and kill us. We tried to hold the door shut, and I phoned the police.

It took too long because they kept asking me to spell my last name. Can you imagine? A mob is coming in the front door, and the police keep asking me, how do I spell my name?

The IRA waited, because they must have known that we would call the police, but it became obvious that the police wouldn't get there in time. We decided that we had to get out, because they really wanted to murder us.

On the way out the back, I saw two men in the garden. "Get back in, love, and lie on the floor," one of them said. We did, and the IRA shot two of the rioters dead.

The two that the IRA shot weren't even from the other side [of the peace line]. They were from the Shankill — foreign rioters!

I don't like the IRA, but the police wouldn't have come in time. . . . I had to testify in court, and the other side claimed that the IRA had been shooting at the barricade first.

Without wishing to take sides or to attribute blame in this or other cases, it is not difficult to see how even quite detached people such as Kate can find themselves, in specific circumstances, regarding the IRA as an ally and a savior.

Concluding Remarks

In the recent history of Ardoyne, the population has been subject to violent attacks. Some have been driven from their homes; many have been killed or injured. Riotous situations still occur on a regular basis, dramatizing the fact that their small territory is under threat. The pattern of this recent local history is one that has been repeated countless times during the last two centuries. It also echoes events in other parts of Belfast and other parts of Northern Ireland.

This feeling of being besieged makes sense of the nationalist histories that provide the basis for republican ideologies. In Ardoyne, the idea that one's land was invaded in the seventeenth century merely reinforces a direct experience of having one's local area invaded in the twentieth. And the fact of being under siege in one's own locality lends an immediate credibility to narratives of invasion in the distant past.

The possibility of a united Ireland seems to offer Ardoyne's residents salvation from the area's chronically bad social situation. A united Ireland would include Northern Ireland's Catholics in a countrywide Catholic majority, and, it is hoped, would provide them with protection from the British army and from the loyalists. It is this salvation, as well as more immediate protection, that the people of Ardoyne seek — ambiguously — from the Provisional IRA. Unfortunately, by turning to a paramilitary solution, the population of Ardoyne has compounded the problems it has with local loyalists, and found itself in direct confrontation with the police and the British army. In consequence, they have found themselves invaded by these, as well as by the loyalist gunmen. This British invasion has been experienced in an actual, everyday sense, not only the mythic and historical sense in which it is experienced by those of their supporters who live elsewhere.

The plight of the people of Ardoyne has undoubtedly been hard. Ardoyne seems fated to remain a stressful place to live despite the new sense of safety brought by the ceasefire. No matter what nation they belong to, residents will probably continue to suffer from extremely high rates of unemployment and from the multitude of social problems characteristic of urban poverty in Western countries.

None of this, however, need necessarily convince anyone to take their side against the people on the other side of the Crumlin Road, for on the Protestant side too there has been a comparable loss of life and a similar history of invasions and mayhem. The inherently similar experience of inner-city Protestants gives credence to the siege-structured histories of Protestants in exactly the same way as inner-city Catholic experience validates nationalist histories.

The violent incidents described here are rooted in the close proximity of territories that provide sanctuaries for members of the two endogamous groups. Members of each group can readily define their situation as a state of siege, each being subject to the attacks of their neighbors. So the siege metaphor that defines these circumstances is not *merely* a metaphor. On the contrary, it defines what is, for the people concerned, a very real set of events. It also defines a set of actions for dealing with the perceived invasion of communal space.

Metaphors, we have argued, can be "metaphors we live by" (Lakoff and Johnson 1980). They can structure the operational models by which people define their lives, even in the most deadly of social interactions. The siege metaphor is a major aspect of group and individual identities in Northern Ireland, and — though it admits of different emphases — is part of the shared cultural tradition of both Catholics and Protestants in Northern Ireland. Individuals on both sides in the conflict define themselves, their ethnic groups, and their communities as under siege and subject to invasion. Seeing their lives in this framework, they sometimes turn to political violence.

In the next chapter, the argument will leave behind the siege metaphor. Returning again to the comparative peace of Listymore, we shall examine the role played by another set of metaphors. These define people as not merely "inside" or "outside," but as "superior" or "inferior."

6

FIELDWORK BY A. D. BUCKLEY Interlocking
Identities

Bad
Boys
and
Little
Old
Ladies

They were those whom the local populace always referred to as "the boys" — Whiteboys,
Oakboys, Steelboys, Rightboys . . . Peep o' Day Boys, Orange Boys. To this day in Ireland
a local reference to "the boys" will generally be taken to mean the IRA (or whatever terrorist
group is supported in the area). The Irish meaning of "boy" thus retained something of its
Elizabethan connotation as a swaggerer, a warrior, an armed man. (Stewart 1977, 116)

Identities translate into one another. The preceding three chapters showed
how quite disparate definitions of a person's identity could be partially structured by the same metaphor. Descriptions of particular events or institutions or
activities were placed in a framework and organized, in the cases presented
above, according to the siege metaphor. This meant that some people and objects belonged to a menacing "outside," and others to a vulnerable "inside."
Despite the likeness that can exist between frameworks, different definitions of
a person's identity may carry distinctive, even opposed rhetorical messages.
Most especially, in one framework a person may be defined as good; in another,
the same person may be redefined as wicked.

There are in fact many metaphors available for the definition of identity,
and while the siege is an important metaphor, it is not the only one. Indeed, it is
the ability to switch not only between frameworks but also between the metaphors used to structure frameworks that enables people to make subtle and
complex judgments about themselves and others.

Here we shall consider another important set of images. These define social relationships according to whether the participants are "superior" or "infe-

rior" to each other. Such relationships usually also contain asymmetrical forms of social control, with the superior element seeking to control the inferior.

There are, of course, many relationships in which there is an asymmetry of social control. We shall lay particular stress on the relation of parent and child, which has a major metaphorical significance, but there are others. In the villages of Killycarnon and Long Stone, which together make up Listymore, I came to see these asymmetrical relationships as summed up by two prototypical figures: little old ladies and bad boys. One prototype, that of the little old lady, typifies the kind of person deemed locally to be in authority. The other, the bad boy, epitomizes those in rebellion against authority.

In an earlier chapter, it was shown that the siege metaphor was used not only to define social relationships and groups, but also to define aspects of the individual self. Sexuality, illness, and the inner life were shown to be defined by means of this same image.

In introducing this new set of metaphors, it is appropriate also to suggest that notions of superiority and inferiority, which have a widespread application in defining social groups and relationships, are similarly employed to define aspects of the individual self. In the same way as there are higher and lower elements in society or in specific social relationships, so too are there higher and lower elements in the self.

The higher and lower faculties of the individual human being correspond to the head and the genitals, respectively. The higher faculties are supposed to be rational and cerebral. In contrast, the lower ones are passionate, irrational, and erotic. This popular opposition is inherently similar to the more technical distinction between the *Überich* (superego) and the *Es* (id) employed by Freud. The opposition assumes that the baser emotions can lead a person into libidinous or rebellious behavior, erratic as well as erotic. The controlling, cerebral judgment of the head, on the contrary, guides the individual into paths of self-control.

The idea that there are superior and inferior elements in the individual self is not, of course, peculiar to Northern Ireland. Here we are pointing to conventional assumptions that are found throughout Western society; indeed, they have biblical roots. Similar oppositions can also be found in other parts of the world. Willis, for example, shows how an East African people, the Fipa, use these same bodily images of the head and the loins in much the same way as people in Listymore do, as a key metaphor in defining their social lives (Willis 1967, 1972, 1978).

The opposition between the head and the loins is perhaps not used as often as the siege metaphor to define the structure of the individual self. A person's illnesses, his thoughts, emotions, feelings, spirit, and immortal soul —

even his carnality — are all given clearest definition by means of temple and siege metaphors. By contrast, the head/loins distinction has lesser importance.

However, as this chapter will now start to show, the opposition between the higher and the lower is very important as a metaphor for framing social relationships. Self-control, therefore, rapidly translates into social control. As the head tries to control the libidinous loins, so do the superior parts of society try to control the inferior. And so too, in a direct reflection of Freud, does the parent seek to control the rebellious child (see Berne 1975, chapter 2). It is to this social definition of the higher and lower in society that the discussion now turns.

Bad Boys and Little Old Ladies

There are to be found in Listymore many stories about eccentric upper-class old ladies. In contrast, there are few stories about other categories of woman or old person. There is also much standardized gossip about delinquent bad boys. Few people, however, tell stories about good boys or about girls, whether good, bad, or otherwise.

The plural terms "the boys" or "them boys" in Listymore, as elsewhere in Northern Ireland, carry with them a moral ambiguity. They do not always refer to members of paramilitary groups. Nevertheless, they imply the Elizabethan swagger noted in the quotation by Stewart at the beginning of this chapter. It is a half-admiring term directed toward men who are prickly, dangerous, or difficult.

Feldman, for example, notes that in republican areas of Belfast, there is a connection between membership in the IRA and the role of the criminally aggressive and dangerous figures known as "hard men." He notes that the hard men of the past, in contrast to the paramilitarists of the present, are romanticized as rough and tough characters who nevertheless had a code of honor and recognized the rules of a fair fight (Feldman 1991, 46–52). In the north of Ireland generally, to be addressed as "boy" (which is fairly common) is to be received, perhaps provisionally, into a rather manly and aggressive camaraderie.

A like ambiguity exists in descriptions of the elderly gentlewomen known as little old ladies. People sometimes criticize these women, but they may also be treated with esteem and even awe.

Oddly, the badness of the bad boys is often explained by their having too much money. It is, however, plain to see that it is the little old ladies who are, on balance, the richer.

The question to be raised here is why, in Listymore, old ladies and bad boys are singled out as topics of conversation. Part of the answer is that in Listymore they are good examples of two much broader types of people. One of these types is deemed to be too judgmental or authoritarian. The other is said to be too rebellious or rough. Old ladies and bad boys, therefore, encapsulate a whole range of quite disparate identities. These are all interlocked by virtue of their perceived similarity to one another.

When taken together, little old ladies and bad boys also provide a curiously elastic rhetoric. In Listymore people will occasionally adopt the sort of attitudes associated with old ladies. At such moments they may condemn others for being "rough," an epithet that contains not only moral censure but also implications that the behavior in question is of the lower classes. They may, however, resist attempts to employ the same values if those values imply censure of themselves. In such a case, the resistance to moral authority may include a complaint that the critic is being "snooty." And people of all ages, classes, and genders will justify their own aggressive, manipulative, rebellious, or otherwise rough behavior. Yet in the same breath they can condemn bad boys for actions that are inherently similar.

The ambiguities in the images of old ladies and bad boys arise in part from the relation of these prototypes to idealizations of other social statuses. They also arise out of practical interrelationships. These include, notably, the often ill-defined conflict between those people in Listymore who condemn their opponents for being rough and those who, using a different framework, say their opponents are snooty. Above all, the ambiguities arise from a need for a pliant rhetoric through which high ideals can be used, when needed, to justify bad behavior.

Killycarnon Village and the Old-Lady Ideal

Old ladies came to my attention because of two locally well known stories. They refer specifically to old ladies of the gentry or upper middle class (cf. Shanks 1988), and they are related to the idea that until recently Killycarnon was a village for the wealthy and retired. One story goes as follows: Two old ladies arrived at the station in Londonderry just as the train was leaving. The man in the ticket office quickly handed them two tickets for Killycarnon. "How did you know we were going to Killycarnon?" demanded one of the old ladies. "All the old ladies go to Killycarnon," said the man. ("That," explained my informant, "is how Killycarnon used to be.")

The other story concerns the driver of a horse-drawn vehicle. He was driving one day past a flax dam, an artificial pool where flax is left to ferment ("ret"), a process notorious for giving off an evil smell. One of his elderly female passengers turned to the other and commented upon the stench. Her companion silenced her. "I think it's the driver," she said in a whisper.

Killycarnon grew up in the last century, after the building of the railway. According to a well-known folk history, the landowner placed a lower limit on the size of houses. He thereby restricted the village's early social composition to only the wealthy.

There is an important ambiguity in the stories that refer to upper-class old ladies. On the one hand, they are told in a mildly deprecating way, for old ladies of this type represent in Listymore a "stuck-up" snobbishness that sometimes goads other inhabitants to rebellion. On the other hand, the ideal of Killycarnon as a village where gentlefolk, and especially old ladies, end their days in serenity can be attractive to its inhabitants. Killycarnon, people say, is "a quiet place."

The main reason why the image of old ladies is a local prototype is that it embodies a wide range of idealized statuses identified in Listymore with moral authority. The first of these statuses is, of course, old age. The distinction between the old and the young is precisely parallel to that between parent and child. This is usually the first and most formative context in which an individual's actions are regulated by another person.

A second reason is femininity. It was suggested in chapter 4, and also in an earlier work (Buckley 1982), that in Northern Ireland women typically adopt attitudes of regulative morality in relation to their menfolk. In Ardoyne, Kenney has noticed that older women play a similar role as guardians of public order and enforcers of good behavior in relation to Catholic men and youth (see Kenney 1991). With the exception of barmen and bouncers, only women in Ardoyne typically interfere publicly with the bad behavior of children, teenagers, and men. Throughout Northern Ireland, a significant feature of the role of women in relation to men consists of attempting to regulate men's untidiness and drinking, and generally to treat them "like children."[1]

The third element is Englishness. Old ladies in Listymore are typically "English." Most people seem to believe that they actually come from England. In reality, it is more correct to say that they speak with a dialect close to that of the English upper-middle classes. This dialect is still associated, both in Britain and in Ireland, with wealth, education, culture, and power.

Shanks's study of the gentry of Northern Ireland (1988) shows that this "English" accent comes not from ancestral origins in England. It arises, rather, from the fact that many upper-class people went, as children, to public (i.e., private) schools in England. Despite the popular view to the contrary, most of the so-called English people (including the old ladies) of this class were born in Ireland. If asked, they will cheerfully concede the fact.

It is well known that there is a close bond between accent or dialect and social class. This extends, however, to other kinds of social status. Douglas has made a most useful contribution to this in a study set in a village near Killycarnon (Douglas 1975). Apart from the gentry, where the evidence is clear-cut and striking, certain other types of people in the village also have a more English accent than their fellows. Douglas shows that people of high status and high ambition, and also women and the old, differ significantly from people of low status and low ambition, and men and the young. The former types tend to use several phonological variables close to Received Pronunciation, giving them a more "English" accent. The latter tend to have an indisputably Ulster accent (Douglas 1975).

A more English accent	An Ulster accent
Authority	Lack of authority
Higher class	Lower class
Ambitious people	Less ambitious people
Women	Men
Old people	Young people

The image of the old lady is one of someone who has an English accent; is upper-class, female, cultured, and old; and lives predominantly in the "snooty" middle-class village of Killycarnon. As a result, the image intersects with most of the major social categories that locally typify authority. The stereotype thus translates a wide range of diverse social statuses into one another. Another important feature is that it also calls up a widely shared vision of Killycarnon as a village from which a strict authority keeps out the rough element (see chapters 3 and 4 above).

"Too Much Money"

Bad Boys

If the clearest image of authority in Listymore is that of the old lady, rebellion against authority is most emphatically typified in the image of the bad boy. Here are two of many examples.

A group of farmers sitting in the house of Jack Stewart were complaining to one another about a gang of bad boys. The boys had recently broken a window at a youth club. In consequence, the minister of the Killycarnon Presbyterian church had banned them from the club. The boys had gone on to break other windows on their way home to Long Stone. They were, said Jack, a gang of skinheads. They carried around a costly portable television-cum-radio, a gift from a parent; "they got that, when they should have got a kick up the arse." The murmured consensus was "too much money."

In the second example, a wealthy farmer has an adopted son who, people say, has "gone wild." His misdeeds are credited to his having too much money. Three people told me separately that because the son was adopted, his adoptive father gave him more money than was good for him.

In obvious ways, the image of the bad boy contrasts with that of the old lady. She is female, while he is male; she is old, while he is young; she is cultured, while he is rough; she represents moral authority, while he is bad; her accent is that of upper-class England, while his is of lower-class Ulster; and she typically lives in the village of Killycarnon, while he lives in Long Stone.

One effect of the gossip about these stereotyped individuals is to focus attention on only a narrow range of human traits. Just as the old lady stands at the intersection of categories that typify authority, so the bad boy stands at a similar intersection. He stands between those categories of person — male, lower-class, Long Stone–living, rough, young, and with a broad Ulster dialect — who are thought to be in rebellion.

Real people, of course, seldom correspond precisely to stereotypes, but even in idealized form, identities based upon ethnicity, gender, or age are highly complex. The idea of an English person, even in the abstract, is not a simple idea; nor is the idea of a woman, or a young person. By fixing discussion upon bad boys or old ladies, however, these complexities are distilled away; the residue provides a much narrower focus on the contrast between moral authority and rebelliousness.

The contrast between old ladies and bad boys, however, seems to break down when one considers why the youths are accused of having too much money. Although young people in Listymore often have money, they can seldom be described as rich. There are many people, including many old ladies, who are visibly better off than most of the teenagers described as bad.

A question that arises, therefore, is why "too much money" is the most readily available explanation for bad behavior among the young. The answer to this may be found in the structure of the social classes in the area, for it is this that gives the contrast between age groups its clearest relevance.

Snooty People

The bad boys in the above examples were being criticized for their rough behavior from a perspective of moral (and implicitly religious) authority. The descriptions were being framed by metaphors similar to the ones described in chapter 4. "We," according to such frameworks, are good, law-abiding people, living our lives according to tenets that have their roots in religion. "They," the bad boys, act in a rough manner, breaking the law and being disruptive.

This familiar contrast between religious (or moral) and rough behavior is not, however, the only framework used in Listymore for criticizing others. Another common epithet, used especially by the comparatively poor to describe the well-to-do, is "snooty." The same term is also used in a general sort of way to describe the village of Killycarnon. And indeed, the upper-class little old ladies who so typify moral authority might also be described as "snooty." The word *snooty* is not a term used to criticize the disruptive activities identified with the lower classes and the young. It is used in frameworks that indicate an attitude of rebelliousness against the rich, the educated, and the powerful.

Few people in Listymore are either bad boys or upper-class old ladies. In addition, although there are many degrees of wealth, education, and other indicators of prestige, few Listymore inhabitants would admit to being either "snooty" or "rough." Snootiness and roughness do not belong in the same framework. To say somebody is snooty is not to imply that one is oneself rough, nor vice versa. Snootiness and roughness are rhetorical devices that point to the unacceptable extremes of the moral and social spectrum. Poorer people may sense with dismay that they are seen by the snooty to be rough. But even high-status people sometimes look upon wealthy, educated, and forthrightly English old ladies with suspicion. Evidence of the common hostility to people of high prestige in present-day Listymore is apparent in the stories people tell of the past.

Overlooking Listymore is a ruined castle. This, in living memory, was the home of the local landowner, Sir Charlesworth Beck (Buckley 1979–80). In the century before World War I there was a succession of baronets, of whom all but one had the name Sir Charlesworth Beck. More so than all others in the area, Sir Charlesworth was someone who had too much money.

The Becks had three estates, of which the one in Listymore, with its sumptuous castle, was the biggest. One of the other estates was also in Ulster; the other was in the English midlands. To these the family would travel each year "like royalty" for the different shooting seasons. Gentry would also come to the castle, both for the game and to consume food and drink.

To many local eyes the castle was a place of excess, even depravity. Some-one told me of a butler who sought to elope with Lady Beck, and who subse-quently was murdered on the orders of Sir Charlesworth. The butler's ghost is said still to walk. Tales are also told of shooting "accidents" and mysterious suicides.

In contrast to such goings-on, the lives of the poor, and especially the ten-ant farmers, were very hard. "They [the Becks] kept us poor," said one aged farmer. "We were like slaves." A widow could be expelled from her farm if it had become inefficient. And if Sir Charlesworth spied a thistle in a field, the tenant could find his field taken from him and let to a neighbor.

This view of Listymore's past is of a starkly stratified society in which the upper classes looked down on the needy. The poor tried to find an income where they could; these impoverished people, whether children sent to caddy on the golf course for pennies for the household budget, farmers nervously digging thistles from their fields, or serving maids working long hours in the Killycarnon boarding houses, described their plight as "slavery."

This folk history reflects a muted but real conflict between the social classes in the Listymore of today. Chapter 9 will show some of the ways that individuals playfully challenge figures of authority. Beyond this, different pro-fessional people told me they have felt themselves overtly harassed by farmers and working-class people of all ages.

Here, a crucial element is often the assertion of a *loyalist* identity. Wallis et al. (1986) correctly claim that the poor are especially jealous of the self-esteem or "honor" that they garner through membership in an ethnic group. This sense of ethnic honor belongs peculiarly to men and especially young men. Unlike many other forms of self-esteem that are available only to the rich or the educated, the prestige due to ethnicity is available to all. It is this honor or prestige that is demanded through the ethnic group's rhetorical histories, its demonstrations, and more generally its culture.

In Listymore, the rebelliousness of masculine youth most commonly takes the form of vandalism. Very occasionally, this vandalism is mere destruc-tiveness. More commonly, it takes the significant form of painted political slo-gans. These advertise the different loyalist paramilitary organizations, which, however, exist only nominally in the area.

Mrs. Park is a Killycarnon boarding-house owner, and, incidentally, a Protestant. She told me how her ordinarily immaculate garden walls have been targets for painted political slogans. She complained particularly about one incident during the Protestant Twelfth of July festival. It seems some Catholics drove round and round the circular road where she lives. Several Protestant youths stood in her garden pelting the car with ornamental stones that she had recently bought for her garden at great expense.

As in many other cases, there was multivocality in these activities. The aim was indeed to assert a Protestant ethnic identity against Catholicism. Simultaneously, however, it asserted the importance of the loyalist lower classes by tilting against the snooty respectability alleged to exist predominantly among Killycarnon residents (see also chapter 12).

Killycarnon does not take such activities lying down. The Killycarnon Community Association is a voluntary body that holds occasional meetings open to all village residents. Its elected committee (of which Mrs. Park is a member) makes a substantial claim to speak for the village.

This committee leads a campaign against vandalism. It has also concerned itself with related questions of caravan sites and amusement arcades. These, if developed in Killycarnon, would attract both lower-class people and the unsupervised young. Jamie McLiesh, the longtime chairman of the association, told me how he resisted the growth of caravan sites and amusement arcades.

Some years ago, he said, a man acquired land to sell to a caravan-site developer. The proposed development would have produced a continuous line of caravans encircling the village. Jamie explained to me that he had not joined in the controversy. Instead, he had privately found another buyer willing to build a housing estate. Thus, Killycarnon escaped being enveloped by caravans.

By a similar coup, Jamie resisted attempts to bring amusements to the village. With a site available, and a developer willing to purchase, Jamie organized a group to raise money to buy the ten-year lease. The land would be used for a cricket club. People spent long hours leveling the ground, sometimes on winter evenings by the light of car headlights. The cricket club was a failure; Killycarnon people, it turned out, were not interested in playing cricket. But the enterprise was successful in its main purpose: it had kept away amusement arcades and the rough people they might attract.

It will be noted that in defense of their quiet way of life, the association is willing to resort to quite robust tactics. These are scarcely consonant with the image of Killycarnon as a quiet place occupied by old ladies. Mrs. Park, for example, would have dealt very firmly with any vandal she found decorating her walls. In the local idiom, she would have been very rough. And Jamie McLiesh is here describing quite complex maneuverings that are manipulative rather than violent, but which undoubtedly have a dubious propriety. But in conversation these people strove to win my support, justifying their actions because they helped keep Killycarnon a quiet place.

Here there is a parallel with the activities of younger, poorer men of Long Stone. The main activities for which bad boys are criticized are, effectively, assaults upon the snooty residents of Killycarnon. These, however, often take the ostensible form of defending the high ideals of Protestantism. What we see, then, is people of high and low status, males and females, and the young, old, and middle-aged employing rough techniques to defend supposedly high moral ideals against their opponents.

Concluding Remarks

There is an important sense in which the images of the little old lady and the bad boy typify the opposition between unacceptable extremes of moral authority and rebelliousness. In Listymore, however, there are considerable ambiguities in social practice. Few people utterly reject the values locally associated with the image of the old lady. Yet all are willing to condone rough tactics more suitable for bad boys in order to defend these or similar ideals.

This chapter began with a quote from Stewart to the effect that people described as "the boys" were members of paramilitary organizations. It is generally the case that most Northern Irish people will state in conversation that the activities of paramilitary groups are wicked. Chapter 5, however, showed that in practice, even occupants of the more battle-torn areas of the province see paramilitary organizations more ambiguously, as a necessary evil. This chapter has shown that peaceful Listymore too regards more modest bad behavior with ambiguity.

Badness is peculiarly associated with the roles of masculinity and youth. It is justifiable when employed in a worthwhile cause. Oddly enough, even goodness can sometimes be suspect, when it is found in too great an abundance.

In real life, the bad boys of Listymore are typically not small children but adolescents. There is an important sense in which their rebelliousness is thought to be unavoidable. Throwing off parents' authority is seen to be part of the life cycle. It leads to the creation of new conjugal households. Because of this, adults who condemn present-day youth may sometimes slip into a different kind of frame when they speak of their own teenage pranks (even violent ones) and of their early experiments with alcohol, tobacco, and sex.

Many conflicts found in Listymore can be portrayed by participants as resistance to either snooty or rough behavior (or to both at the same time). In reality, the boundary between the wealthier and poorer groups in Listymore society is not very clearly drawn. Sometimes a person will oppose himself to what he believes to be the social superiority and high moral tone — the snootiness — of others. At other times, the same person will condemn others for being rough — for having lower-class attitudes that offend against some moral or religious code. The conflict here has its root in differences of wealth and education, and in the quest for prestige and self-respect. It is this quest that relates the prototypes of youth and old age to the wide range of other identities found in Listymore society.

The two extremes of rebellious, masculine youth and of authoritarian, feminine old age have, in principle, little in common. The notion that rebellious lower-class youth have too much money, however, provides something of a bridge between them. Scarcely anybody in Listymore thinks himself or herself to have too much money. This expression, therefore, is a useful rhetorical device. It allows the censure of virtually any type of person or any type of action.

But these opposed prototypes are united in a different sense. One occasion on which it is legitimate to break normal moral rules in a manner appropriate to bad boys is when someone acts in defense of the ideals embodied by the old ladies. Thus, by a paradox, the quiet, peaceful life of Killycarnon and Listymore is generally thought to be worth fighting for. So, too, when someone refers to a person as one of "them boys," or even addresses someone as "boy," he is unlikely to intend an insult.

In Listymore, both the high ideals associated with old ladies and the rough, Elizabethan swagger typical of "them boys" have their place in popular rhetoric. Either, however, may be set aside or condemned when it is not required.

7

FIELDWORK BY A. D. BUCKLEY

Being Saved

A Change of Identity

Religious identity has a special place in Northern Irish life, not least because of its link to ethnic identity. Nowhere is the link more clear than among Protestant fundamentalists, who make a particularly explicit connection between their religion and the political aims of their ethnic group. This chapter and the next look at religious identity among fundamentalists, concentrating particularly upon Pentecostalists in north Belfast and south Antrim. It will explore how, when someone is "saved," he or she changes his or her identity.

The aim of this chapter is to look at some of the complexity in what is called "getting saved." Converting to fundamentalist Christianity is usually more involved than, say, joining a dramatic society or a cricket club. The person will experience a profound change of identity that in some cases can be painful. The process of getting saved is one that is structured by narrative and example — and, therefore, structured by metaphor.

Among the metaphors to be encountered here is the siege metaphor, but we shall also find metaphors drawn from family life and from the courtroom. These will be shown in the next chapter to have even greater complexity. Here we shall look at the way a person can abandon the rhetoric that shores up a past identity so that he or she can lead "a new life."

We shall also see how this new identity finds an echo in concerns that are related to more narrowly ethnic identities. It has been shown that religious groups recruit from only one side of the ethnic divide. But there is also an intellectual link between religion and ethnicity. An important point is that, even for Ulster's fundamentalists, religious identity cannot be reduced to ethnicity, nor vice versa. Rather, the relation between the two is one of translation.

Religious Affiliation

It would be a mistake to see religious identity as merely a social identity. Identity is not reducible to a mere web of particular in-groups, each related to its out-group by siegelike imagery. There is more to identity (and to religious identity in particular) than the siege metaphor or even "boundary maintenance" (Barth 1969). Identity is also a practical way of life. Despite this, one cannot ignore Northern Ireland's innumerable in-groups defined by means of religious labels, doctrines, and practices.

One set of these in-groups comprises the different denominations found in Northern Ireland. There are the so-called mainline churches — the Roman Catholic church, the Presbyterian church, the Church of Ireland, and the Methodist church. And there are very many smaller denominations, of which the Baptists, the Brethren, the Congregationalists, the Free Presbyterians, and the Elim Church are among the biggest.

Cross-cutting the denominations are other allegiances. Of these, an important group is the fundamentalists. Fundamentalism is present in all of the mainline Protestant churches, occasionally dominating particular congregations, and it provides the *raison d'être* for most of the smaller ones. Fundamentalists sometimes visit each other's churches to hear particular preachers, or they attend meetings in mission halls. Fundamentalists are also firmly and openly opposed to the Roman Catholic church.

Another major grouping is the ecumenical movement. It is found in the mainline churches and a few of the smaller churches. As with the fundamentalists, but less often, members of the ecumenical movement can dominate whole congregations. Their aim is to cultivate links among the denominations, and particularly between Catholics and Protestants.

There are also two sets of people who place special emphasis upon the so-called Gifts of the Spirit (of which more later). The Pentecostalists, who are fundamentalist in their theology, have their own separate churches, of which the Elim Church and the Church of God are the most important. The other group is the charismatics, who are found in all of the mainline churches but who are best represented in the Roman Catholic church. Charismatic theology is similar in many ways to that of the Pentecostalist fundamentalists, but its ethos is ecumenical.

In many congregations, there is a further division, not always clearly defined, between conservatives and liberals. The conservatives strictly and strongly uphold the particular doctrines and traditions of their church. The liberals want to allow individual interpretation of these traditions.

In Catholicism, conservatism looks back to the 1950s and earlier. This conservatism is most publicly known for upholding strict views on contraception, abortion, and divorce. It also embraces an active resistance to the liturgical reforms of the Second Vatican Council, and looks back with fondness to the Tridentine mass and to devotional practices that the modern Church has discouraged or suppressed. I have noted that many conservative Catholics, as well as liberal ones, harbor a suspicion of the Vatican and the Church's hierarchy.

Conservatism in the mainstream Protestant churches often takes the form of evangelicalism — the doctrine of which fundamentalism can be described as an extreme or dogmatic form. Like fundamentalism, evangelicalism emphasizes the need for an individual to have a direct personal encounter with God.

Presbyterians identify their conservatism with Calvin. Sometimes this Calvinism is seen as a form of evangelicalism; sometimes it is not. Some conservative Presbyterians quietly resist evangelicalism, seeing it as the Arminianism to which Calvinists were opposed centuries ago. ("Evangelicalism?" said one conservative Presbyterian with a smile. "That's Methodism, isn't it?")

In many cases, religious conservatism can be linked to a desire to maintain the symbolic boundaries that set apart Protestant from Roman Catholic doctrines and practices. It is, therefore, related to the desire to maintain ethnic boundaries.

In many churches there is a fuzzy division between the enthusiasts and the mere participants. The most enthusiastic churchgoers are to an extent curators (see chapter 1) of their religious tradition: the religious word is *stewardship*. They enable the less enthusiastic to dip or plunge into the world of religion when they need to. Some of the occasional churchgoers see religion as a marginal part of their lives. Others are genuinely interested in religion, but feel no desire to identify closely with one or another faction.

Despite the existence of a bewilderingly large number of diverse religious allegiances, organized in both formal and informal groups, it is important not to regard religious identity as merely a matter of allegiance. While identity is indeed partly a matter of allegiance to social groupings composed of people judged to be similar to oneself, allegiance does not constitute the whole of religious identity, or indeed any other form of identity. More than this, it is important not to see beliefs, liturgies, dogmas, and so forth entirely as diacritical markers used only to define social boundaries.

This chapter will take as an example a small group of fundamentalist Christians with whom I worked for several months. These people, who live in north Belfast and south Antrim, are members of three Pentecostalist congregations.

Perhaps with the single exception of Catholicism, fundamentalism, more than any other major form of Christianity, has attracted the hostile attention of "cultured despisers." In my research I was pleased to find it a remarkably robust form of religion. It has a rich intellectual tradition that one can respect, and it addresses the real lives of its members in a very direct way. Although I do not personally share the views of fundamentalism, I was impressed by the sincerity, profundity, and even wisdom of many of the people associated with it. Indeed, it is its very liveliness and intellectual vigor that makes it a subject worth studying.

In approaching such a small group, one becomes immediately aware of the more complex aspects of identity. More especially, fundamentalists do not just say that they *are* Christians. They also say they have *become* Christians. They have been through the process that they call being saved. As such, therefore, they have undergone (to a greater or lesser extent, depending on the individual) a change of identity.

Becoming a Christian: A Change of Identity

When describing their religious identity, the most common term used by fundamentalists, and also by charismatics and some evangelicals, is "Christian." To a considerable degree, the use of the term in this manner is contentious or even offensive. People who call themselves Christians use the term to differentiate themselves from non-Christians. Among the latter, they include not only Hindus, Buddhists, and atheists, but also Jehovah's Witnesses, Mormons, and Roman Catholics.

Fundamentalists may also describe as non-Christian other ordinary Protestant churchgoers. Even members of the Christian's own congregation may be disparaged as merely "religious." Others, even worse, may have "liberal" or "modern" opinions, perhaps even questioning the historical validity of parts of the Bible. The merely religious and the modernists may also think that by attending church and by trying to be good, they may aspire to everlasting life; but fundamentalists strongly reject such a view as contrary to biblical teaching.

The people who are thus defined as non-Christian do not always accept this designation graciously. It can, indeed, be a source of annoyance. A Catholic woman once accompanied me to an interview with a Christian informant. She was quite startled and upset to find that he regarded her as a non-Christian. For Christians themselves, however, this usage is quite simple. To be a Christian, a person must be "born again"; he must have "accepted Christ as his personal Savior"; he must be "saved."

Stories of how a person is saved are called, in Northern Ireland, *testimonies*. The testimony will therefore provide a focus for this chapter. When somebody tells his testimony, he does so by explaining details of his past life within a well-defined framework that is innately similar to those that define other people's testimonies (see Clements 1982).

The particular actions and events that a testimony describes are certainly selected because they find a place in this narrative structure. While it is possible for somebody to fabricate or "fake" a testimony, it is probably rare that the teller of the story intends to mislead. Thus the events told in the stories may usually be treated as true.

Following are the outlines of two testimonies. Because of their very great length — up to half an hour each — it is not possible to quote them in full.

Willie's Testimony

Willie left school with no qualifications, having "done everything that usually a bad boy in school does." In particular, he enjoyed "fighting" and "beating people up." When he got work in a garage, he started to steal. He began with small objects, but soon had a shed packed with stolen goods. His girlfriend became pregnant and he married her, but the marriage ended in divorce, largely because of his drinking. The drinking increased, and he borrowed money from his friends to pay for his social life.

Then, at the insistence of a friend who had lent him some money, he attended a church service. During the service the pastor made an appeal for non-Christians to raise their hands as a sign that they wanted to be saved. When this happened, Willie felt "electrocuted." "I knew I should have been saved, but oh no, Willie wanted the drink, and Willie wanted to enjoy himself. So I went out and I said, 'Ach, they're a load of old headers in there.'"

Willie returned to his life of drinking and fighting: "I enjoyed beating people up. I liked seeing the blood flying." But he was again urged by his friend to go to church. And again he felt the need to be saved. Instead, however, he approached a psychiatrist for help to reduce his drinking. It did not work, for at one point Willie found himself sitting in a bar, knowing that he ought to be saved.

Later, when the pastor again made his appeal for people to commit themselves, Willie felt a strong impulse and raised his hand, feeling as though a bag of coal had been lifted from his shoulders. When he went home, he broke all the whisky bottles he found there, and from that day on did not take another drink. Soon he had a regular job as a bus driver.

Helen's Testimony

The transformation of Helen's life began with a car accident in which all her family, but particularly her son, Sammy, were injured. The incident, and especially her son's suffering, deeply shocked Helen. She suffered a "nervous breakdown." Despite medical and psychiatric treatment, she eventually found herself staying at home, dejected, unwilling to meet her friends or even to leave her house. "I came home absolutely helpless, and John [her husband] used to plead with me not to take my own life."

One day, after several years of depression, she happened to meet a neighbor in the backyard. "She's a Christian, and I didn't like her. She was a hypocrite as far as I was concerned." The woman was excited, eager to tell Helen that her daughter had been recently saved. Returning indoors after the conversation, Helen sat down and cursed her neighbor. She thought what the woman had said was "the stupidest thing I had ever heard." Despite this, Helen saw her past flow before her eyes "like a drowning man." "And I thought of what I had come to. I was in the gutter, I couldn't have went any further. And there was nobody could help me. And I didn't want to live anymore."

Suddenly wondering if there was a God, she prayed angrily, "God, if you exist . . . prove it to me and . . . give me back the life I've lost, all those years I have lost — you give them back to me." All of a sudden she felt peace. "Peace flooded through me. And not only peace, but a realization that He existed . . . and I got off my knees singing."

Helen, who had been virtually housebound for four years, left the house and visited her mother. The mother, when she heard the story, thought Helen had finally gone mad. Soon Helen found a church and began attending services there. And within a short time she had, by her example, persuaded her husband and many of their relatives to be saved also.

The Purpose of Telling a Testimony

This chapter deals centrally with the *events* described in the testimony, not with the narrative. Nevertheless, it is useful to outline the way the testimony is typically used during social interaction. Most of the testimonies I recorded were told to satisfy the curiosity of a passing anthropologist. There are, however, some more common purposes for telling a testimony, and all of them contribute to the practical creation of an identity.

Testimonies are told, first of all, to define the speaker as a member of a social category — a Christian. In many cases, this is a fairly ordinary self-definition, comparable to other forms of narrative. By the end of the story, the speaker is defined as someone who has a positive value.

In other cases, this self-definition may have a more formal aspect. A person may have to tell his testimony to a pastor or an elder before he can join a particular congregation. Many denominations and mission halls have this requirement. If the story is judged to reflect a genuine experience, then the individual is admitted.

A testimony may also be offered to others as an operational model, a model for action; it invites other people to change their identities. The commonest time to hear a testimony is in a church service where non-Christians (or at least "backsliders") will be present. Sunday evening church services, for example, are often advertised in the local press, and some Protestants will visit churches where they are not members to sample the sermons of other ministers. Churches also occasionally organize missions aimed at non-Christians. On such occasions, members of the congregation will give their testimonies. The idea is that non-Christians or backsliders will recognize the similarity of their own situation to that of the speaker, and perhaps follow the speaker's example and become saved themselves.

Reframing a Past Identity

One reason why the testimony is of interest is that it involves rhetoric. The testimony broadly describes two processes. In the first, the individual suddenly perceives that his or her habitual actions (prototypically drinking, but also smoking, theft, wife-beating, and the like) are sinful. Using Goffman's language, we may say that the individual redefines or reframes these past actions. Sometimes, as with Willie, the wickedness of the action can be quite considerable. In other stories, the evil is barely perceptible, except to the individual himself. For example, Helen's husband, John, told me how he was suddenly and sincerely ashamed of his regular Sunday game of golf and subsequently of his smoking. Sometimes, too, as with Helen herself, the wickedness consists less of specific actions and more of a general turmoil that afflicts other people.

Whatever the nature of the guilty actions, the testimony tells how the actions came to be deprived of the rhetorical support that excused them and made them seem above criticism. Consequently, they were reframed and redefined as unequivocally evil.

The second process described in the testimony is the practical transformation of actions. This allows the individual to begin a new life of sobriety, frugality, hard work, and clean living.

In principle, as we have seen, individuals frequently and readily shift between frames. Everyday life involves a continuing process of framing and reframing specific situations, whether for pragmatic purposes or for rhetorical ones. The reframing involved in religious conversion, however, is usually more painful.

The reason for this trauma is not easy to grasp. Religious conversion may be painful because of its quasi-political and practical implications. The reframing or redefinition of one's habitual actions is sometimes a quasi-political victory for somebody else's vision of one's actions. Also, testimonies often tell of friends or relatives who have unambiguously told the "sinner" about the evil or folly of his ways. To admit one's faults in such a context is to admit the truth of another's criticisms, to give way to that person's demands. Still another factor seems to be the sheer upheaval involved in changing one's routines. The discovery that one's habitual actions are wicked or foolish or otherwise unworthy invites changes that are not always easy to make.

The conflict between what one does and what one thinks one should do can lead to a form of self-deception. In a telling phrase, Fingarette (1969, 39) describes self-deception as a failure or unwillingness to "spell out" a particular set of information. Sometimes the person fails to spell out the information reflexively to himself. Commonly, however, as Haight (1980, 108ff.) claims, self-deception also involves deceiving other people. Several of the people whose testimonies I heard dimly knew that their lives were unsatisfactory. Often this was because friends and relations told them so. Instead, however, of spelling out what they knew to be a reasonable description of their actions, the person placed their actions into an implausible rhetorical framework — an excuse.

Even a flimsy rhetoric of self-approbation, Fingarette suggests, can have the positive effect of allowing an individual to function when that individual is in a state of anxiety (which he defines as an inability to act, caused by a strong emotion, such as guilt), though this functioning may be ultimately self-destructive (Fingarette 1965, 76ff.).

However, reorganizing one's life requires thought, reflection, planning, and a renegotiation of one's relationships. The self-deception that helps an anxious person to function can therefore also inhibit a practical reframing of his situation; it can stop him from changing his life. A person who fears that abandoning his excuses will lead to guilt, anxiety, and impotence can be trapped by his own rhetoric in a self-imposed "double bind" (Bateson et al. 1956).

A testimony describes how somebody nevertheless abandons a rickety rhetoric, recounting the well-known events of his life in a new frame. No doubt this new frame will already have haunted him for some time; other people may long have been offering it to him. This new frame defines aspects of his past life as foolish or wicked. In consequence, he now discovers himself to be guilty and worthy of punishment.

Doctrinal Definition of Being Saved

Fundamentalist doctrines of salvation address themselves directly to this double bind: to the desire to change, and to the impotence of guilt and anxiety. The following (edited) extract of an interview with a pastor in the Church of the Nazarene describes the church's doctrines on the subject of redemption. It is a weighty statement based upon passages from Paul's epistle to the Romans, but it also provides a succinct exegesis of the testimony and of the experience of being saved.

> Man is born with a twofold sin. There's a sinful nature in mankind, which was given to our race when Adam sinned. This manifests itself in actual sins as we grow up. We believe that the necessity is laid upon man to turn from his evil ways. And Jesus came that he might deliver his people from their sins, so we preach that there is a better quality of life, a higher quality of living available to all who will turn and who will live this higher way. And people will then come, by the grace of God in their lives, and say, "Yes, I want to live that life."
>
> And at that point in time, the first thing that's uppermost in their mind is the guilt of sin: guilt for the things which they had done wrong, where they've displeased the Lord. The Lord offers forgiveness for those acts which are wrong, and we would encourage the penitent to seek forgiveness.
>
> When he has the assurance that he has the forgiveness of God, then he goes out into the new life in Christ. You're not very long living in that new relationship until you realize that there's something warring against you. St. Paul depicts it as a war between the flesh and the spirit. "The good that I would, I do not, and the evil that I would not, that I do." "Who shall deliver me from the body of this death?" The picture he uses is the picture of the murderer who has the corpse tied to his body and he carries that around until eventually the putrefaction of that spreads into his own body and kills him.

> And then, "I thank God through Christ Jesus there is a way of deliverance." So you come and ask God to cleanse you from inward sin, this depravity, and to fill you with the spirit and equip you for service and to give you victory.

This statement clearly supports the interpretation that the failure of the individual to act in harmony with his own wishes is much more important than mere wrongdoing.

It was mentioned earlier that one of my informants, John, had suddenly felt an urgent distress at being unable to give up smoking. John told me that his pastor voiced the problem of smoking thus: "If you stop smoking, do you believe that this will get you into heaven? Of course not. It's only because you want to be a Christian and you have a certain standard within yourself that you want to stop this." This surely is the nub of the issue. A person feels bad when he fails to act in harmony with his own ideals. But when he continues to act badly, contrary to his own wishes, he feels doubly helpless.

The Sense of Helplessness: Family and Judicial Metaphors

A central image defining a fundamentalist identity is the sense of helplessness. This sense of helplessness, however, is only a part of a more general imagery, and it would be a mistake to regard helplessness as somehow restricted to fundamentalism, or indeed to religion. On the contrary, helplessness is commonplace. It is a universal human experience on which other, more culturally specific experience is built.

The main metaphor that a testimony elaborates is the family relationship mentioned in the last chapter, that of parent and child. This is augmented with images drawn from judicial processes.

In earliest childhood, no child can alone satisfy the needs that will allow him or her to survive. It is only because adults feel a strong impulse to provide the necessities of life to the helpless child that the human species can perpetuate itself at all. A sense of helplessness is thus a moment in a symbiotic social relationship. Its other half is the desire to give "nurture" (Berne 1975, 118ff.). The desire to give to those in need is not mere sentiment. Humanity's survival has depended on it. Its prototype is the relationship of parent and child. This desire is found not just in philanthropy, but in all intimate relationships (Midgley 1979).

The symbiosis of helplessness and nurturing contrasts sharply with the other main aspect of the relationship between parent and child, described in the last chapter: the asymmetry of control. Here, the nurturing or punishment of the child is conditional upon the child doing good or evil actions.

Both these aspects of the relation of parent and child are explicit in the theology of fundamentalist Christianity. On the one hand, God is a father and also a judge. In this guise, God's task is to point to the wickedness of the sinner and to damn him to hell's fire. In contrast, God also appears as Jesus, the advocate. As mediator and advocate, Jesus has the function, in the judicial metaphors of fundamentalist theology, of recommending to the judge not judgment and punishment, but mercy and forgiveness. Or, to use the contrast evoked by Berne (1975), Jesus, the advocate, represents the unconditional giving of the nurturing parent that supplants the criticisms and punishments of the judgmental parent.

These ideas of advocate and judge are, of course, images taken from the courtroom, but they also contain an imagery derived from family life. In relation to God the Father, Jesus is Son. In relation to man, however, Jesus is God and therefore a parental figure. In Lévi-Strauss's sense (1961), but also in a biblical and hence a judicial one, Jesus is a mediator between God and man, being Himself both God and man.

In this imagery there is again an interpenetration of metaphors — in this case, images of family life merge with those of the courtroom. Because all images are multifaceted, a specific aspect of any one set of images can be evoked only by translating them into another set. Thus, the translation of family-based images into those of the courtroom reveals parenthood in its judgmental and merciful aspects. And it reveals childhood to be divided between guilty rebellion or virtuous compliance and mere helplessness. All these images become metaphors for the relation between God and man.

The Second Coming and Ethnic Rhetoric

It would appear at first sight that fundamentalism has little to do with ethnicity. On the evidence given so far, one could conclude that fundamentalism was a form of religious psychiatry. In fact, however, fundamentalism is closely tied to a radical form of ethnic Protestantism.

One should perhaps note that the fundamentalists of Ulster do not usually share in the kind of right-wing conservatism with which fundamentalism is identified in the United States. Also, although there has been a form of connection between the Ulster Unionists and the British Conservatives in the past, most fundamentalists in Ulster are out of sympathy with the free-market conservatism associated with the name of Margaret Thatcher. Matters such as these are not, in any case, important issues in Northern Ireland.

The connection between fundamentalism and ethnicity in Northern Ireland is in part a matter of recruitment, for fundamentalists are mainly lower-class Protestants, who often feel a strong sense of ethnic allegiance. We have suggested, following Wallis et al. (1986), that working-class people often attach particular importance to specifically ethnic definitions of themselves because other avenues to prestige and self-esteem are closed to them.

The connection between religion and ethnicity is also metaphorical and rhetorical. In adopting a new identity, the people who now call themselves Christians discover a ready-made rhetoric that is relevant to Northern Ireland and to its ethnic conflict. This rhetoric comes from biblical prophecies, and speaks of Christ's second coming.

Chapter 4 showed that fundamentalists can distinguish themselves from outsiders on the basis of their spirituality. In this, they prove to be similar to countless other people who also think their institutions (and they themselves) have a spiritual essence. Fundamentalism, however, goes further. It takes the division between good insiders and bad outsiders and projects it into cosmic history.

Fundamentalist views on the subject of the second coming do vary. Many ministers take care not to be too specific in their opinions on the subject. They seem to fear stirring up theological trouble among their members, who may espouse differing views. The most widely held belief among fundamentalists, however, is a form of premillenialism. This asserts that Christians will be "taken up," or "raptured," to meet Jesus in the air—some say in the "heavenlies"—before the tribulations that herald the thousand years of Christ's rule. But this opinion is not the only one to be found. Others—particularly but not exclusively members of the ecumenical charismatic movement—incline to the opinion that Christians too must go through the period of tribulations. Both these opinions agree that the tribulations will be a time when the earth will be ruled by the Antichrist (or the Beast, or the False Prophet). They also agree that the number of the Beast, 666 (see Rev. 13:18), will be branded on those compelled to serve him.

The stories of the last days are based upon the enigmatic prophecies in such books of the Bible as Daniel, Ezekiel, and, above all, Revelation. A common view in Northern Ireland in the early 1980s was that the ten-horned beast of Revelation (Rev. 13:1) represented the feet of the statue (with ten toes) in Nebuchadnezzar's dream (Dan. 2:31–35) and the fourth beast in Daniel's own vision. These images, I was told, referred to the last Roman empire — the European Community, founded by the Treaty of Rome, which at that particular time comprised ten nations.

There is a significant difference between most charismatic accounts of the Last Days and those of Protestant fundamentalists. For the charismatics, whose meetings include both Protestants and Roman Catholics, the Antichrist or Beast will soon be revealed to be a Jew. Noncharismatic, nonecumenical fundamentalism, however, adopts the view (a version of which is found in the Presbyterian Westminster Confession, for example) that the Antichrist is the Pope.

There are rhetorical implications in a view that identifies the Antichrist as the Pope. This opinion divides the world between those who have found God's favor and those who have not. On the one hand are the Christians, whom God motivates and approves of; on the other, there are the Roman Catholics, who are not only non-Christian but also — wittingly or not — servants of the Antichrist.

Whichever of the different versions of prophetic theory a person may adopt, the overall frame is structured by means of a familiar metaphor. As in the testimonies, this metaphor defines a Christian as predominantly embattled and helpless, but ultimately safe because of his belief. For those few people who believe that Christians must go through the tribulations, the prophecies also show that God will protect them. Such a person may refuse to be branded with the mark of the Beast during the tribulations. He or she can still live by faith and rely on God for safekeeping.

The majority fundamentalist view also foresees disaster in the world. For them too, however, salvation is at hand. They look forward to being taken up to be with Jesus in the air, while the tribulations go on beneath.

Concluding Remarks

Fundamentalism is well known in Northern Ireland to be an exuberantly loyalist form of Christianity. Its prime focus, however, is not on ethnicity or politics at all. Instead, it fastens on the sense of helplessness that individuals experience in their daily lives.

The emphasis upon individual helplessness may perhaps reflect a genuine fragility in the real lives of many fundamentalists. Many seem to have found in their faith a radical solution to pressing personal difficulties. Many, too, are working-class people or the owners of small businesses striving to sustain a precarious, respectable style of life with few resources. For those with such troubles, the familial and judicial metaphors of fundamentalism can structure a genuine sense of helplessness within frameworks that point to regeneration and to hope.

This same pattern of helplessness and salvation — rooted in metaphors of childish helplessness and parental nurturing — is also used in relation to the broader context of Ulster politics and ethnic conflict. The identification of spirituality with helplessness is one that is entirely consonant with the siege metaphor described earlier. The story of the siege of Derry, for example, tells not only of the heroism of the defenders, but also of the extreme hopelessness of their situation.

It is worth restating that the religious identity of even these, the most loyal of Ulster's Protestants, cannot be reduced entirely to ethnicity. Nevertheless, their religious identity can readily be translated into an ethnic one. When, then, fundamentalism's central theme of helplessness, sin, and the need for salvation and redemption is translated into the long-standing Bible-based religious traditions that identify the Antichrist with the Pope, it is easy to see the parallels to Protestants' political hopes: As the final battle approaches between the Antichrist, who is the Pope, and the God who is their savior, Christians hope to find protection. Then, they say, when victory is finally theirs, all will be peace and joy.

8

FIELDWORK BY A. D. BUCKLEY   Dramatizing
Identity

Playful
Ritual

The definition of a person's identity is often very messy. A person may, in principle, be a husband, a bus driver, good fun, very religious, or whatever. He need not, however, always *appear* to have any of these identities. So from time to time, either informally or in set-piece interactions such as rituals, he will dramatize his identities through different genres of social drama (Turner 1982).

This chapter will look at such a genre, a typical church service found among Pentecostalists, calling it *playful ritual*. The ritual is structured by means of two metaphors that have already been discussed. In some ways, the ideas that spring from these metaphors seem at first to be inconsistent, even contradicting each other. The first metaphor is that of the relationship of parent and child. Here the Christian acts playfully beneath the indulgent eye of his God, in much the same way as a playful child might act, watched over by an approving parent. The second metaphor is the temple or siege. Here the Holy Spirit enters the individual, whose actions are thereby motivated by an indwelling God.

The chapter argues that Pentecostal church services are social dramas that spell out individual identity. This identity is then available as a framework, to be used by the individual to understand actions and events in his or her daily life. These more ordinary actions and events are often the product of quite arbitrary circumstances. They can, however, be understood and made meaningful within the rhetorically satisfactory frame that the ritual provides.

Play in Pentecostal Ritual

To my great surprise, when I stepped into the street after attending my first Pentecostal service, I had to stop myself from dancing. Later, as I sat in my office performing the ordinarily tiresome task of transcribing tape, I found that I was singing along with the words of the Pentecostal chorus I was transcribing, banging out the rhythm on my desk.

To one whose childhood Sundays were spent in the subdued Church of England, the rites of Pentecostalists are unusual. What is most unusual about them is that they are fun. Pentecostal ritual is playful ritual.

The playful activities in question include the so-called Gifts of the Spirit. These include speaking in tongues, interpretation, and prophesying. There are other ecstatic activities visible in Pentecostal services as well. And there is also much clapping, calling out, and singing.

The term *play* is fitting here because a striking feature of Pentecostal worship is that it is enjoyable. One cannot call playful *all* the activity that takes place in the ritual. Play, however, exists in the frame that the ritual provides. Just as the occasional comic elements in *King Lear* do not detract from that play's tragedy, so the fact that Pentecostal services are playful does not detract from their serious ritual nature (see also Manning 1976, 1977).

Play arises out of the flexibility of social control over actions. When I punch someone, I deserve punishment and I may feel guilty; I am subject to judgment. When I punch someone playfully, however, I do not feel guilty; I am surprised or annoyed if I am punished. Play is a major part of everyday existence. Even animals play (Bateson 1955), and play is important in the processes of learning. Play takes place when the social control or self-control exerted over action has been relaxed.

The prototypical frames within which play takes place occur in the relation between parent and child in childhood. A parent ordinarily exercises control over a child's actions. However, the parent may sometimes relax this control, allowing the child to become playful. It is not that the indulgent parent has abandoned control; rather, that control is relaxed. If the child behaves sufficiently badly, parental authority will reveal itself still to exist.

In the Pentecostal service are to be found some obvious examples of religious play, with a relaxation of social control over action. This account of a Pentecostal service begins, however, not with my own description, but with that of Margaret, a member of a Pentecostal church.

Here, Margaret describes the service she had attended the previous day. It was the last service to be held in an old church building before the congregation moved to larger premises. She starts by describing her response to testimonies given during the service by some young men. Her account is filled with emotion, and this is why I chose it. She illustrates how a central feature of the Pentecostal experience is the experience of love.

> These three of them had served their own sentences in Long Kesh [the Maze Prison for terrorists near Lisburn]. And I mean some of them were real characters. It was just so down to earth, nothing fancy. One or two of them had a strange experience, and some didn't.
>
> But it was the love I had — I couldn't understand it when I looked at them. I thought to myself, "How could I love these people, the way I love them?" It really mystifies me, that, truly mystifies me. I come out loving everybody. "It's like a soft glow round me," I thought to myself. I didn't want to leave. It was the strangest thing.
>
> I, sort of, was distant from the Lord, generally cold — well, we say "cold," you know what I mean — [I] found it difficult to pray. And about two minutes before I went to church, I prayed and I just asked the Lord to let me be able to get into the spirit of things and to really feel at one with the people.
>
> But you see, when I walked in that place, I mean, the Lord really takes your breath away, some of the things he does. I walked in and it was incredible, my heart nearly leapt out of me. And the most unexpected thing was, yesterday — I'm crying even thinking about it, yesterday — it was as if it was the day I came back to the Lord all over again.
>
> So there was six testimonies. And there was six souls saved, and there was one young fellow saved yesterday morning, and one of the fellows that came past me at the end. He brought back memories. He had on all his leather gear. And I says, "About a year ago, a fellow just dressed the same as you," I says, "walked past me," I says, "on his way into that wee room and he is still going on with the Lord and he's lovely." He said to me, "Aye, I've come back to the Lord tonight." I couldn't get over it.
>
> You could talk and talk and talk the whole night to express what you feel in your heart. You wish you had the words to try and say all that He is and what He means to you. You know, even when you're cold. I think it's just the realization that the Lord loves you even when you are not nice, you know. He loves you just the way you are really. [Momentarily shy] So there you are now.

The tone of Margaret's remarks is very similar to that of other Pentecostalists speaking of their religious experience. She begins by saying how she felt "cold." She felt distant, unloving, uninterested, apathetic. Then she prayed to God to allow her to "get into the spirit of things." When she walked into the church, she found herself filled with joy and love both for God and for her fellow worshipers.

It is important to note that the silent act of feeling love and joy in this manner is itself an unconventional way of acting in a public place. Still less conventional are acts of expressing these feelings, verbally or through other representations, whether at a service or elsewhere to strangers such as myself. In Pentecostal services, it is quite the accepted thing for members of a congregation to express their emotions by gesture or speech. During the service, members of the congregation will interject with such remarks as "Halleluja!" or "Praise the Lord!" or "Amen!" This can occur during prayers, hymns, or choruses, or even in the sermon or ministry.

Less commonly, an individual will stand and prophesy or speak in tongues. Episodes of speaking in tongues are followed by an interpretation given by the minister or by another member of the congregation.

In addition, some individuals will stand or sit with closed eyes and uplifted face, raising one or both hands heavenward to show some deeply felt emotion. At appropriate moments, an individual may call out the name of a particular chorus or hymn — or simply begin singing. The congregation will then join in, the organist scrambling to find the right key. During the singing, others will clap their hands or sway in their seats.

The emphasis in all this is on the spontaneous expression of emotion of a kind that would be forbidden in ordinary intercourse. In Ulster people do not ordinarily express their love toward virtual strangers. Nor do they sit or stand in postures of even mildly ecstatic emotion. To do so in private would induce embarrassment in some individuals. To do so publicly is even more difficult. But in Pentecostal services, the individual gradually learns to join in the fun, to sway, to close his eyes, to clap, to sing loudly, to lift his face and hands to heaven. Thus he loosens his self-control and becomes playful.

As though to illustrate Durkheim's (1977) opinion of religion, Pentecostal services draw individuals together in a collective simultaneity. An almost immediate impulse on entering such a service is to join in — and this is as true for the skeptical anthropologist as it is for the believer.

Once inside, it seems churlish not to clap or sing the choruses. Choruses are a simple form of verse set to music, and are usually repeated a dozen or more times. Often they are quite charming little songs, and by the end of several repetitions even a complete outsider can join in with ease. The temptation to imitate, to behave similarly in a "mechanical" solidarity (Durkheim 1933) with other members of the congregation (using the actions of the other members, of course, as operational models) is almost irresistible. All is joy, spontaneity, love, happiness, fun.

Gifts of the Spirit

Apart from this mildly ecstatic activity, Pentecostal services also include Gifts of the Spirit. This expression refers to the gifts listed by St. Paul (1 Cor. 12:8–10) of wisdom, faith, healing, miracles, prophesying, discerning of spirits, speaking in tongues, and interpretation of tongues. In principle, Pentecostalists give equal weight to all these gifts. I know of only one congregation, however, in which discerning of spirits is common. Here I shall look at prophesying, speaking in tongues, and the interpretation of tongues, which have a significant part in all Pentecostal congregations.

Of the various Gifts of the Spirit, prophesying is perhaps the simplest to understand and especially so if it is contrasted with preaching.

Ordinarily, when a preacher wishes to give his ministry, he will prepare it in advance. He will select a text from the Bible that he regards as especially interesting and instructive. He will set out to explain the circumstances in which the text was written, the meaning of its more difficult passages, and its lesson for the members of the congregation.

During his preparation, the minister will, like a teacher or lecturer, engage in a form of dialectical reasoning. He will construct his argument beneath his own critical gaze. If he is especially competent, he will take care to structure his argument carefully, to use rhetorical devices and so forth.

Thus at each of several levels of organization, the preacher will carefully and precisely organize and control his talk. Having prepared it, he will deliver it with rehearsed skill, alternating humor, exposition, and passion in considered proportions.

Prophesying is quite different. Here, the individual may feel himself "burdened" with something to say. He may simply stand up on impulse. But he will not have prepared his speech with written notes. On the contrary, he will stand up and merely say what he has to say. He may later say that the words were put into his mouth by God. Such prophesying done during a church service is seen as inherently similar to that practiced by the Old Testament prophets. These began their pronouncements using the prophetic formula, "Thus saith the Lord."

Speaking in tongues is more difficult to understand. A useful approach is to recognize that actions, including speech, are organized simultaneously at several different levels (Goldman 1970).

Pentecostalists say that speaking in tongues is a way in which God transmits messages through the individual to a congregation. They also claim that the language spoken can be a genuine foreign tongue, as in the account of the first outburst by the apostles (Acts 2).

Be this as it may, one study of this phenomenon shows tongues are usually spoken in the phonemes of the speaker's native language (Samarin 1972, 44, 125ff.). It seems that "words" are generated from these phonemes and are constructed into patterns that resemble sentences. These sentences sometimes have a verselike form. Tongues differ from the native language of the speaker in that in tongues, the words do not correspond to known words, nor relate directly to known objects. The speaker has thus relaxed control over his speech at some levels (especially the lexical) but not at others.

After an act of speaking in tongues, it is customary for someone who has the gift of interpretation to stand up immediately and translate the communication. Interpretation, like prophesying, is spoken spontaneously and without preparation. Often the translated message is also difficult to understand.

These three kinds of communication all emphasize a loss of control. In prophesying and interpretation, a person will stand up and address a crowd — perhaps hundreds of people — without even thinking about what he will say. In tongues, he will utter what, in a different frame, would appear to be nonsensical phrases. These utterances are such that if they were spoken in any other frame — for example, before unsympathetic observers — they might induce ridicule.

When someone thus employs the Gifts of the Spirit, he commits himself publicly to lose some control over his actions. His control, however, is not completely lost. It is merely relaxed. Also, this control is lost only at certain levels, and not at others. What the individual learns is that activities performed beneath a looser form of self-control or social control can be safe from condemnation. Effectively, he is learning, or perhaps relearning, how to play.

Controlling and Being Controlled

When describing Pentecostal experience, or indeed when participating in it, people frame their activities using two entirely different sets of metaphors. One comes from the images of parent and child discussed in the last chapter. The other harks back to the siege metaphor, and particularly to the image of the human body as a temple.

First, it is reasonable to describe the relationship between congregation and pastor — and also that between congregation and God — as similar to that of a playful child and a watchful, indulgent, nurturing parent.

In the Pentecostal church service, the minister stands in his pulpit or on the platform, sometimes with elders or fellow ministers. Rather like the conductor of an orchestra, he oversees the activity. The chaos of events is only an apparent chaos. A distinction is drawn between acceptable and unacceptable behavior, and seldom (never, in my own experience) is the line between them overstepped.

In all Pentecostal churches, the Gifts of the Spirit are subject to regulations and guidelines. These are laid down in St. Paul's lengthy discussion of the subject (1 Cor. 12–14). One rule concerns the number of instances of tongues and prophesying to be uttered on any given occasion (two or three). Another is that no one should speak in tongues without an interpreter (1 Cor. 14:27–29). The injunction for women to be silent in this context (1 Cor. 14:34–35) is not generally observed.

People who use the Gifts of the Spirit, or who more generally engage in ecstatic activity, do so subject to the control of the minister. He, in turn, can justify his regulation with reference to the Pauline injunctions.

A minister can readily resume direct control by several devices. He may himself choose a chorus or a hymn. He may invite the congregation to have silent prayer. He may direct the prayers himself. The minister's direction of events is gentle, but in the last resort it is firm. In any case, the prime source of control comes from the individual members of the congregation. These people prevent their own playfulness from overstepping the mark into deviance by a self-control within bounds that ultimately the minister sets.

In this manner, the church service is a dramatization of a social relationship. The members of the congregation act beneath the eye of an indulgent minister and an indulgent God. They raise their hands in praise and thanksgiving; they speak in tongues; and they prophesy. All takes place within the bounds set by the minister and by God's Word. They therefore demonstrate that they are indeed Christians, children of a loving, nurturing and forgiving God whose representative, in this context, is the minister.

Unfortunately the matter is not so simple. Members of Pentecostal congregations do not only see themselves as acting *beneath* God's tolerant and forgiving eye. They also see God as acting *through* their actions. When speaking in tongues or prophesying, but also when taking part in a service or merely going about their everyday business, Christians may regard their actions as the actions of God Himself.

This second kind of imagery can be separated quite easily from the first. Theologically speaking, the first kind of imagery is bound up with the first two Persons of the Trinity, the Father and the Son. Thus the Father, as the last chapter showed, is predominantly a judgmental figure, whose role, but for the intercession of His Son, is to condemn. The second kind of imagery also occasionally involves Jesus (one can therefore "let Jesus come into one's heart"). More carefully, however, Pentecostalists will also say that they are "filled with the Holy Spirit."

Frames that mention the Holy Spirit generally abandon the metaphor of parent and child in favor of a siegelike or templelike imagery. In these cases, the body is a house or temple or other edifice that can be entered by God.

It is recognized, however, that not only God but also Satan can enter a person. There are ways to distinguish whether a spiritual penetration is by God or by a more malevolent force, though. A general opinion is that when the Holy Spirit enters a person, that person can, at will, resume control over what he is doing.

I have never heard Pentecostalists make explicit here the parallel with sexuality. It is not difficult, however, to do so oneself. One could say, for example, that the difference between being possessed by Satan and being filled by the Holy Spirit is that between being raped and being loved. Here is how Margaret puts it.

> The Lord doesn't control you like a robot. Paul tells you that the prophet is in control of the prophecy. In other words, I can choose and I can control this. You know, you get some people who say, "Oh, I can't control this. This has took over me."
>
> I mean, it's only Satan that possesses. I mean, the Lord never ever does. You choose whether or not you come to Him. You choose whether or not you want to do certain things, and as you choose, you also learn. You learn how to handle it. You learn more about it, and you learn how to test it, how to make out where it's from and all the rest of it.

In the following extract, another informant, Cecil, tells of his first experience with tongues. He also speaks of the self-control that he maintained as he nevertheless allowed his body to utter strange words. It is clear, too, that in this he received direct help from the social control exercised by the pastor. Indeed, it seems Cecil was being taught how to participate in this ecstatic experience (see Becker 1953; Preston 1981).

> It was about the early part of March. There was an evangelist from America, Richard Edgar. I always remember him — what he said that night. He said, "Look, if any of us wants to receive the baptism of the Holy Ghost [an expression for speaking in tongues], put your hand up." He said, "Don't be afraid."

He said, "Look," he says, "the Holy Spirit is a perfect gentleman. He'll never embarrass anyone."

And I put up my hand that night. And there was quite a lot, I would say maybe thirty, in that line that night stood up in church, you know. I was away at the end of the line — the far end of the line from Brother Richard Edgar. And while they were praying for the ones at the far end, I was praising the Lord.

And you know, I really felt myself getting filled and I started speaking in the prayer language. And you know, I don't know still to this day — it seemed like Arabic or something that was coming out of me. I was just lifted, really like floating, like separated from my own body. And anyhow, when [my own pastor] got to my end of the line, I was just praising the Lord in my own language again. So anyhow, [the pastor] came up to me and he put his hands round me and the next thing, I am away again. And he said, "That's it, Cecil."

It shows you how this Holy Spirit can work through a person, like, if you're willing. And you've got to empty your mind of everything, your thoughts and everything, let the Spirit take over. That's just it. Empty your mind of all thoughts. Instead of saying to yourself, "Well, I wonder, will I get it? I wonder, will I be embarrassed?" or "I wonder, will I have to come away from here this night without getting it, and all?"

And that's what kept me from going in the line time and time again. I wouldn't have went up for the fear of being embarrassed, of others getting it and me not getting it. But you really have to empty your mind.

It's not really an emptying of the mind, but thinking thoughts towards God, you know, like, letting God be the center of your thoughts and the center of your whole being. And that's when the Holy Spirit will take over, because that's what happened at Pentecost.

Cecil's experience of tongues is unusual in one sense. He seems to have been one of a large number speaking in tongues on a single occasion. Apart from this, the experience is very typical. His description is also typical in that it uses two apparently inconsistent metaphors.

On the one hand, Cecil sees himself as the actor. As such, he acts subject to a parentlike judgment. The judgment here is not primarily that of God, but rather that of the congregation. He explains that he fears embarrassment. He may fail to speak in the approved manner or, once speaking, he may lose complete control and speak in an emotional outburst.

On the other hand, when he does speak in tongues, he says he is "filled with the Holy Spirit." Having first "emptied his mind," he allows the Spirit to enter and "take over."

He is encouraged by several things. One is the well-known Pentecostal adage, "The Holy Spirit is a perfect gentleman." Another is the immediate support and encouragement of those around him. This provides a gentle and firm frame within which this letting-go can take place. As he acts, the speaker feels that his actions are approved and supported both by God himself and, more immediately, by the pastors and congregation.

A Christian Identity

I have argued that a Pentecostal service provides a context or framework within which a person can dramatize a particular identity. Once a person has taken on such an identity (by being saved, by participating in such services, and so forth) this identity provides a framework for interpreting events and actions in daily life. Ordinary actions and events that otherwise would be comparatively unstructured, meaningless, or arbitrary now acquire heightened meaning and value.

One of my informants, John, told me that before a service we both had attended, he had asked the pastor to pray for the bereaved. The conversation and the service had taken place in the same week that a prominent fundamentalist Member of Parliament, the Reverend Robert Bradford, had been shot by terrorists.

> Maybe you remember [in the course of the service] the pastor saying about praying for bereaved people? Well, normally of a Sunday morning, we spend the time in worship. It's a sort of standing, accepted rule that we don't petition on a Sunday morning. It's all spent in praise and worship.
>
> I was the instigation of that [the prayer for the bereaved]. I felt so overwhelmed with this urge, and something inside me saying there was somebody who definitely stood in need of prayer. And normally I wouldn't do it, like, and I asked the pastor, could we take a moment? I didn't know.
>
> I felt at the time, naturally, that it was because of what had happened at the weekend [the death of Bradford]. But even while he [the pastor] was praying, I suddenly became aware that there was somebody there in the church who had lost a loved one. I don't know who it was. I suddenly became aware it was them who stood in need.
>
> [My wife] and I have learned, as two individuals, to move as God motivates us. Now, that doesn't prevent us from having preconceived [i.e., incorrect] ideas of what God's going to do.

John's point, that God can move a person to do His will, is a common one. What they may see at first as an intentional action can often be reinterpreted post hoc as the outcome of some previously unknown divine purpose.

Norma, another of my informants and an owner of an unprofitable business, told me how she was unable to sell her ailing small shop. She therefore began to wonder if she had been placed in the shop by God for a purpose.

> I find God has me in the shop, and I can talk. I can meet people and I can talk to them and comfort them. And everybody seems to be going through things that I went through these past years myself. You can help the person because you've been there yourself.

Norma says that even her misfortunes were given to her by God so they would help her to help others. When her unmarried shop assistant had a baby, for example, she was able to give her necessary advice.

> She'd sort of a depression, a nervous state, what people would think and all. So I've had this problem with one of my own girls. And so I was there before her. So I was able to step in on this, and so this young girl's coming to church. She brought the baby [to the church] this morning. We had the baby dedicated, and nobody's looking down their nose at her.

For Norma, as for John, the vicissitudes of life are often meaningless at the time. Even their impulses and actions may seem undirected and trivial. Later, however, especially since they are constantly on the lookout to do some good, they can reinterpret such events and actions as "God's work."

A major feature of Pentecostalism, then, consists of spelling out one's guilt and anxiety and putting one's trust in God. This God, like a good parent, will hate the sin but love the sinner. He will save the sinner from the consequences of his bad actions, and impel him to act in accord with what are seen as His own purposes.

Spontaneity and Morality: Some General Points

Emerging from this brief discussion of Pentecostal ritual are two contrasting types of framework. They both have a special place in Northern Irish culture. In the first, a strict, parentlike morality is seen as an important way of controlling childlike bad behavior. Second, however, a childlike (sometimes Holy Spirit–inspired) spontaneity is seen as a source of joy and of love.

It is important to note that these two kinds of frame are not peculiar to Pentecostalists. They are very widespread. Many different groups are willing to use them to contrast themselves with outsiders. And these outsiders will frequently do much the same.

An earlier study (Buckley 1982) showed that inhabitants of the Upper Tullagh placed great emphasis on good neighborliness. The people there spoke of a great willingness to help the sick, the aged, and the bereaved. They thought it important to give to others when there was a need.

Good neighborliness, in this context, was seldom conceived of as a solemn duty, undertaken because of an obligation to be good. On the contrary, Upper Tullagh people understood good neighborliness as part of what they called a "rich community life." In this community life, play had a significant role.

Apart from "good neighborliness," community life ideally consisted of storytelling, dancing, music, practical jokes, and game-playing. Good neighborliness, in short, arose in a broader frame in which a dominant feature was recreational play.

Though this loving, neighborly community life is still present today, Upper Tullagh people see it as belonging to the past. It belonged prototypically to the poverty-stricken life of poorer farmers and laborers. Neighborliness arose out of a "genuine morality" consisting of openness and friendliness, but also of fun.

In oral history, the good neighborliness of the poor in the past is contrasted with the more independent lifestyles of wealthier farmers. The richer farmers allegedly led rather pinched lives of self-seeking and devotion to money. They "kept themselves to themselves." These farmers, usually Presbyterians, also had a religion that forbade such pleasures as drink and cigarettes. This strict religion prohibited any sort of amusement or even work on a Sunday. In the Upper Tullagh, therefore, a strict form of morality was identified with a lack of neighborliness.

Most of the good neighborliness found in the Upper Tullagh is undoubtedly thought of as having a secular character. One cannot, however, ignore its religious connotations. In particular, the expression "good neighbor" conjures up the biblical image of the Good Samaritan. He, spontaneously and out of pure good fellowship, went to the aid of a stranger who was in need.

Good neighborliness and spontaneous good fun are not just a matter of rhetoric in Northern Ireland. They are very real practical phenomena. Nevertheless, the idea of a good neighbor and the notion of spontaneous love have a major part in rhetorical definitions of identity in Northern Ireland. This is true in the Upper Tullagh, but it is also the case more generally. For the mainly Catholic people of the Upper Tullagh, good neighborliness is a quality of the poor, of the powerless, of country people, and of people living in Ireland. It is also, by implication, a Catholic virtue. Especially, they say, it is a quality of the people living in the Upper Tullagh. It is, in short, a virtue that they claim for themselves.

For the Pentecostalists, of course, the same is broadly true. Pentecostalists claim that a loving approach to strangers and to those in need is a feature of people filled by love and by the Holy Spirit. In short, it is a virtue possessed by Pentecostalists.

What we have here is a variation upon the theme explored in the chapter on bad boys and little old ladies. On the one hand, individuals see themselves as subordinate to a legitimate authority. And they will, of course, take the side of that authority if the circumstances seem right. On the other hand, they also feel that too much control is unacceptable.

Obeying and enforcing authority, whether parental, divine, moral, or legal, can be part of an operational strategy or a rhetorical self-image. But so too can be variants upon the opposite. Childlike spontaneity, and both the playful and more serious forms of rule breaking, can be valued for their own sake, and for their practical effects.

Any stranger to Northern Ireland is likely to be told of the openness and friendliness, the "good crack" (conversation and camaraderie), the fun, and the kindliness of the local population. In different circumstances, both obedience to authority and also spontaneity, kindliness, and fun are characteristics of "us" and not "them." And this is the case, whoever "we" or "they" happen to be.

Pentecostalism: Some Conclusions

The identity of Pentecostalists consists not only of being a Christian, but also of having become one. A past identity, therefore, provides a frame for a present identity. Indeed, many of the frames that together structure Pentecostal identity and experience can be thought of as moments in a larger structured sequence.

First, a person acts in a way contrary to what a parentlike Other regards as good. The guilt of this bad behavior, however, is hidden beneath a tissue of rhetoric. Second, the rhetoric is cast away, and the individual confronts the parental Other and knows himself to be bad. Third, throwing himself on the Other's mercy, he finds himself forgiven, rescued from a guilty anxiety. Fourth, he internalizes the values of the Other, and allows the Other to come into his heart. And finally, filled with the Spirit of the Other, he is motivated to act by these now internal values, often not knowing that this is what moves him.

The term *internalize* is, of course, much used by sociologists. In studies of socialization, or in the sociology of knowledge, it refers to the acquisition by the individual of the values, norms, beliefs, or knowledge of someone else. Berger and Luckman (1966, 149ff.), for example, use the term, and they also speak of "externalization."

One can see this sociological usage as a transformation of an older Christian imagery. With some writers, this has been explicit. Feuerbach saw God as a disguised form of man; Freud thought God was a father; and Durkheim saw God as society. Whatever its form, much sociology still shares with the Pentecostalists the siegelike (or templelike) ghost-in-the-machine psychology associated with the name of Descartes. In each case, the individual can be penetrated (metaphorically or otherwise) by spiritual entities.

This volume has avoided Cartesian metaphors in its analyses. We have avoided analytical definitions of the individual that assume an inside and an outside. Instead, we have preferred pictorial and dramaturgical metaphors, arguing that in being saved, an individual reframes his description of his past actions and then declares some new allegiances, dramatizing them in, for example, the playful ritual of the Pentecostal church service. In the framework of this new identity, even the more commonplace events of the individual's life can be given a rhetorically useful meaning. Within this new frame, the individual can understand himself and present himself to others with new self-respect.

9

FIELDWORK BY A. D. BUCKLEY　Dramatizing
Identity

Playful
Rebellion

"You want to watch out for them boys," said a colleague good-humoredly to me. "They'll
never miss a chance. There's nothing they'll enjoy more than wrong-footing you."

I raised an eyebrow.

"They'll try to get you on the wrong foot," he explained cheerfully, "just out of
badness."

Few studies of Northern Ireland mention the humor of the place. Ask inhabitants why they like to live in Northern Ireland and they will probably say that
they would miss the "crack" — the fun, the witty conversation — if they lived
elsewhere. Fun is an important feature of life in Ulster, and it is odd that so
many social scientists should ignore it altogether.

More than this, playful genres of social interaction often provide a means
of dramatizing the existence of social relationships and identities. The dramatized relationships, however, are not always as loving or as friendly as those
defined in the playful rites of the Pentecostalists.

"Them boys," to whom my colleague referred, live in the villages of Long
Stone and Killycarnon in the district of Listymore. The playful activity that I
saw there contained varying degrees of aggression. It was used to dramatize the
existence of a range of different kinds of social identities, some of them
antagonistic.

The idea here is not to classify the different genres of playful interaction.
There is no need for a taxonomy of forms. Rather, there is a spectrum of different genres built from a range of different symbolic devices variously exploited
(see Heald 1990, 386).

Wrong-footing is not a term much used in Listymore. It is retained here because it is so apt. In Listymore, the commonest epithet for the wrong-footer and his activity is "tricky." Aggressive kinds of play are also called "winding somebody up" or "keeping them going." Playful people and playful acts are also described as "crazy," "mad," "wicked," "wild," "idiot," "sinful," "a nut case," and so forth. Many such expressions come from the vocabulary of deviance. They are usually uttered with a smile to show that, like the activity described, the expression is not seriously meant.

The relationships defined in play are often both antagonistic and amicable. Sometimes the drama shows no more than the trivial fact that participants are different from nonparticipants. In other cases, however, the differentiation is more pointed. Here there may be some people who are decisively in on the joke, while there are others, equally decisively, whom the play defines as outsiders.

The operational model for play, the last chapter argued, is the relation of parent to child. This framework is based upon an asymmetry of social control. During a day, a child will perform various actions. He may sit decorously, read a story, break a vase, climb a tall tree, tease the cat, kneel in prayer, and so on. The parent will tell him which of these types of action are permitted and which are not. Where an action is known to be forbidden, the child has the option either of complying with the parent's regulation or of rebelling against it. It is uncommon, at least with young children and their parents, to find these stratagems of social control reversed. Seldom will a child comment upon his parents' actions. When a child does speak in such a manner, his parents usually try to establish a rule forbidding such criticism. A child's method of social control is generally restricted to evading, ignoring, or disobeying the parents' verbal regulations.

There is a pattern of two contrasting stratagems of social control here, a pattern that is found not only in Listymore but in the Western world more generally. Let them, in the manner of Eric Berne (1975), be called *parent stratagems* and *child stratagems*. Their interrelationship may be broken down into three discrete moments.

1. The child acts (or is deemed likely to act) in a particular manner.
2. The parent, who witnesses the act, either permits it or tells the child that actions of that type are forbidden. Such a prohibition may be reinforced with action.
3. The child either complies with the precepts embodied in the parent's definition of the situation or rebels against them.

Chapter 4 argued that people in Listymore saw a wide range of different social relationships as similar to the asymmetrical relationship between parent and child. These relationships were summed up in the images of the little old lady and the bad boy. Here are some of the relationships that these images evoked, together with others more widely thought in Ulster to have the same asymmetry (see also Buckley 1982).

Parent	Child
Female	Male
Old	Young
Wealthy	Poor
English	Ulster
Killycarnon people	Long Stone people
Employers	Employees
Protestants	Catholics
Officials	Non-officials

The playfulness described in the last chapter took place within a ritual framework and had a decidedly nonrebellious character. There, the authority figure who witnessed the act (whether God, other members of the congregation, or the pastor) set the bounds of the playfulness. The congregation then kept dutifully within them. Other kinds of playfulness, however, consist of the deliberate breaking of such quasi-parental bounds.

With the breaking of rules comes risk. There are some risky nonsocial forms of play, such as mountaineering or ocean-going solo yachting. In such activities it is the physical environment — the mountains or the sea — that threatens the actor with punishment. Most forms of play, however, are social. In social play, individuals can use their skill playfully to evade a socially imposed punishment. Play, indeed, is often merely bad behavior that has been provisionally sanctioned by a sympathetic authority figure.

This chapter, then, is concerned with play, wrong-footing, and social drama, but it will also examine relationships involving figures of authority. The relationships in question are those between men and women, and those between Northern Irish people and the people described as "English."

Men and Women in Listymore

The psychologist Jay Haley (1959a, 1959b) argues that in all relationships there is a continuous interplay of social control. A person acts, and the other, who witnesses it, either permits or strives to prohibit that type of action. Searching for a good example, Haley chooses a familiar kind of interaction between men and women.

> When two people meet for the first time and begin to establish a relationship a wide range of behaviour is possible between them. They may exchange compliments, insults, sexual advances, statements that one is superior to the other, and so on. As the two people define their relationship to each other, they work out what sort of communicative behaviour is to take place in this relationship. From all the possible messages, they select certain kinds and reach agreement that these rather than others should be included. . . . If a young man puts his arm around a girl, he is indicating that amorous behaviour is to be included in their relationship. If the girls says, "No, no," and withdraws from him, she is indicating that amorous behaviour is to be excluded. The relationship they have together, whether amorous or platonic, is defined by the kinds of messages which are mutually agreed shall be acceptable between them. The agreement is never permanently worked out, but is constantly in process as one or the other proposes a new message or as the environmental situation changes and provokes changes in their behaviour. (Haley 1959a, 153)

People in Listymore make frequent reference to the social control exercised over men by women. Everyone is, of course, aware of the considerable body of opinion, given expression in newspapers and television, that regards women as unduly subject to the authority of men and in need of liberation. This view is sometimes expressed directly in Listymore. However, it is found most usually among those who are outsiders to the core community.

The majority seem to express two somewhat contradictory views. One is that women have a potential to "nag" or "henpeck" their menfolk, keeping them under too-strict supervision. When this is the case, a man is said to be justified in resisting the woman's authority. The other viewpoint is that certain men are too "wild" or "rough" and that "them boys" need to be kept under control. I have never heard it said or implied by any member of the core community that specific men, or men in general, keep too close a control over women, nor that women are out of control and need close regulation.

To place this idea into some sort of relief, it might be useful to contrast this vision of Listymore with Ardener's (1975) comments upon male-regulated societies. The instance he specifies is the Bakweri of Cameroon. Here men constantly complain about their ill-disciplined womenfolk. He writes:

> Ethnographers report that women cannot be reached so easily as men: they giggle when young, snort when old, reject the question, laugh at the topic, and

the like. The male members of the society frequently see the ethnographer's difficulties as simply a caricature of their own daily case. (Ardener 1975, 2)

This ethnographer found broadly the same contrast in Listymore, only the other way around. Men were often shy and reticent or truculent and prickly. They were capable of ignoring my questions and of making fun of me and my task. Women, on the contrary, were open, direct, and willing to discuss ethnographic topics with great intelligence and interest. Not infrequently, they expressed sympathy with whatever difficulties they suspected I might have in learning anything of interest from men. In contrast to the Bakweri, perhaps Listymore should be regarded as a female-regulated society.

This last statement, of course, requires some qualification. It is true only within those frameworks in which the female/male distinction is relevant, as, for example, in the relationship of wife/husband, sister/brother, mother/son, and even in certain cases daughter/father. In short, it is true in the comparatively intimate relationships of the family.

I should perhaps also make clear that there is here no claim that the women of Listymore have more (or less) power in the family than men. The suggestion is merely that in relation to men, women tend to use the distinctive stratagem of social control that I have called the parent stratagem. Men are commonly either compliant or rebellious in relation to this parental control.[1]

It is also the case that not all interactions between men and women have this clear formal structure. Some individuals and some relationships between men and women seem preoccupied with issues relating to social control. Other relationships are more easygoing, and questions of social control come up only infrequently, the couple devoting themselves to more interesting matters.

Female social control over men takes place most obviously in set-piece situations. One such is that described by Haley above, which it is tempting to call "courtship ritual." Another, closely related, is the flirtation that occurs between those individuals who are unlikely ever to become attached. Flirtation in Ulster is a social drama almost entirely focused on female control over male sexuality.

Another area is female control over male drinking, for in Listymore, as elsewhere in Ireland, drink has major symbolic significance. Masculine drinking has a close correspondence to childlike behavior: in the same way as a child goes out to play and thus evades the restrictions of his parents or teachers, so adult men will go out to the pub. It is widely accepted that women should and do exercise control over the way their men spend their spare time. Beyond drink, women strive to exercise social control more over the generally rough and tricky tendencies of men.

Play is an articulation of this kind of structured relationship based upon an asymmetry of social control. In childhood, play is distinguished from seriousness first of all by the relaxation of the parents' social control. This is not to say that in play parents exercise no social control; rather, the child is allowed to break many of those rules that, in a serious frame, the parent would impose. It is not surprising that a child's play often takes place in a physical setting from which the parent or parent figure has withdrawn. In schools, this is exemplified by the physical distinction between the classroom, which maintains strict standards, and the (nevertheless walled) playground, where rules are more lax.

Here we are concerned with the interactions of men and women in play. In Listymore, in serious frames, it is an important aspect of the male role to rebel against the excessive regulations of women. So also, in playful relations between men and women, do men attempt to disrupt and challenge female regulations. A few examples will illustrate this.

The first concerns Saturday night in Long Stone Lounge. On Saturday nights, many men take their wives or girlfriends to the normally all-male Long Stone Lounge to drink, dance, and listen to the musical entertainment. On one such occasion I was sitting at a table, armed with a tape recorder, in order to record some music. At my table were two young couples, and there were similar groups at the other tables around the room.

Standing at the bar were a number of bachelors, who were visibly drunk and becoming drunker. Throughout the evening, these men leaned against the bar, talking and engaging in horseplay. Occasionally one of them would break away from the group, wandering from table to table to chat to those sitting there. Whenever the music stopped, they engaged in banter with the lounge's owner, who doubled as master of ceremonies.

Throughout the evening, their demeanor teetered on the seemingly narrow line that divides acceptable from unacceptable behavior. The owner, a nervous man by disposition, looked especially anxious that night. Although he was able to joke with these men, he whispered with concern to a muscular relative whenever events seemed to be getting out of hand.

At my own table the young couples were in a relaxed and cheerful mood. The men had their own conversation and the women theirs. Much of the men's dialogue, though to a lesser degree than was the case with the bachelors, took the form of joking insults to each other. There were also playful threats reinforced by occasional light punches. For the most part, the women ignored their husbands, being engrossed in their own, apparently more serious, conversation. From time to time, however, one or the other of the wives would indicate by a glance or a quietly disapproving remark that her husband was becoming too exuberant.

The behavior of both of the husbands at my table and of the bachelors at the bar was playful. There were many regulating glances and remarks transmitted by the owner and the women. Nevertheless, the regulations imposed were certainly more relaxed than would be the case in a serious frame. On this occasion, there was a much greater challenge to the limits of order than is normal when women are not present in the bar.

In the next example of playfulness, between a man and his wife, there was no overt attempt by the wife to exercise control over her husband. Instead, there was almost a conspiracy between them to define the husband's behavior as playful rebellion.

On the evening in question I arrived at the house of Jack Stewart, having made an appointment to see him. His wife told me that this was his regular night out with two friends. He had left word that I was to meet them at the pub. I said I would walk down to the pub and that I might meet them on the way back. Smilingly, she said I was unlikely to meet them on their way home. She conveyed the firm impression that the men were out for a hard night's drinking. When I met up with them, someone bought me a drink. I was, however, unable to repay the courtesy because the three men had no wish to drink beyond a very strict limit.

When we all returned to Jack's house, I was surprised to see that Jack, who most emphatically was not drunk, behaved as though he were. He talked volubly, lolled in his seat, and leaned affectionately over the people he was sitting close to. His wife, far from disapproving, regarded him with deepest affection. Presumably a man may in his own home playfully break the rules made by his own wife. The others behaved with quite normal propriety.

Female regulation of male activity is not confined to drinking, nor to relationships involving husband and wife. The next example is of a married daughter whose attempt to limit male untidiness was flouted by her father.

When I visited the farmhouse of the Gordon family, Mrs. Gordon's father happened to call. During our conversation, it became apparent that he was rather ostentatiously dropping cigarette ash onto her neat kitchen floor. I had the suspicion, as I had had with Jack Stewart, that this was done, in part, for my benefit. I am easily identifiable as both English and educated. Because of this, people often presume that I have a desire to impose high moral standards upon the people of Northern Ireland. Occasionally, they may challenge my supposed morality.

In any event, while I was given an ashtray, he was not, and he commented on the fact. "It" (the clearing up), he said, "gives the women something to do."

When he said this I glanced at his daughter, whose task it would be to sweep up the mess. Far from being annoyed, she was beaming at her father's undoubted misbehavior.

In all of these cases, the playful mode allowed an exaggeration, and hence a dramatization, of the ordinary relationships that exist between men and women. It is a significant part of the male role to override playfully a woman's regulations. Also, it seems, artificially strict rules are sometimes invented so that they may be playfully overridden. As with the Pentecostal ritual, a kind of relationship supposed to exist more generally is dramatized in a heightened and exaggerated form.

Paradoxical Play: Wrong-footing the English

In my discussion so far of cases of playful behavior, there has been no need to introduce the concept of paradox. This point has some consequence, for Bateson (1955) has argued that all play is paradoxical. The essence of Bateson's argument is that to indicate by means of a direct metamessage (or social context or whatever) that "this message is play" is effectively to negate the normal meaning of the message.

Here is one of my own examples, close to Bateson's own. When one of the husbands in the lounge punched his neighbor, he first qualified it by a metamessage (in this case provided by the general context). This metamessage defined it as play. Had he not thus defined it, the punch might have been taken seriously, and might even have been interpreted as downright aggression.

Bateson argues, however, that because the metamessage "This is play" negates the truth value of the playful messages, it also creates a paradoxical frame such as the one given below.

> All the messages
> within this frame are untrue
>
> I am attacking you

Here not only is the primary message, "I am attacking you," negated; so also is the metamessage itself. "All the messages within this frame are untrue" is, therefore, identified as untrue.

In contrast to Bateson's argument, I wish to claim that although paradox can have an important place in playful behavior, there is no particular reason to suppose that *all* play is paradoxical.

As I watched the two men amiably insulting and punching each other, neither I nor they had any difficulty in regarding their activities as play. The reason for this is simply that the metamessage "This is play" is not itself expressed within a playful frame.

Indeed, if anyone were to misinterpret the situation and call into question the meaning of their actions, the men would probably respond by saying, "We are only fooling around." This message would be delivered with great seriousness from outside the playful frame.

Play is never paradoxical in structure when it is "honest play," in which the definition of a message or action as playful is clear and shared by all relevant people. And play need not be paradoxical, because it is possible to establish a hierarchy between the serious metamessage "This is play" and the playful messages themselves, viz.:

All the messages
within the frame are untrue

I am attacking you

Once this hierarchy is established, the (untrue) attack, the playful punches, and the threats can become a metaphor. They can exemplify the mildly rebellious, rough and tough kind of person that the participants claim to be in real life.

It was suggested above that the English stand in relation to Ulster people in the role of parent to child in much the same manner as do women to men. This needs some qualification, for in their attitudes toward the English, people in Listymore manifest some ambiguity.

Let me put this more carefully. When a member of the Listymore core community meets somebody who he decides is English, or an official, or educated, or snooty, he is likely to slip into a childlike role, expecting the other to adopt that of the parent. The "child" here may, of course, be either compliant (becoming shy, reticent, or even embarrassed) or rebellious (exhibiting rudeness, a pointedly brusque manner, and an excessive determination to stand up for his rights).

As an educated Englishman, I have had much direct experience of both responses, but have also had much independent corroboration from both educated and English people familiar with the district. Here I concentrate upon one man's private rebellion, which took the form of wrong-footing.

James Wallace is a widower and a prosperous farmer. His forebears have lived on the present site of his farm for more than two centuries, and he recently placed some of the farm's buildings in the care of a semiofficial body so that they might be on show to the public. He invited me to the official opening.

On the morning of the opening, I happened to call at his farmyard. I found him and his employees cleaning out slurry from the tanks that lie beneath the cattle sheds near the old buildings. Presumably the job needed to be done, but the emptying of slurry tanks is not an everyday task, and it was interesting that he should choose to do it on that particular morning.

When, a few hours later, an assembly of civil servants, clergy, officials, local worthies, and press arrived, the aroma of cattle slurry hung over them like a cloud, providing a major topic of conversation. Perhaps, I thought for a while, it was just a coincidence.

I joined James Wallace and was introduced to his sister and another relative, a local historian of some note. It soon became clear that all around us were people of importance. The dominant dialect was conspicuously English. For a time we exchanged pleasantries and enjoyed the summer day. The only slightly untoward event occurred when a Catholic priest arrived. James made a private but ostentatiously offensive remark to his sister concerning the priest.

Soon, however, his relative discovered some factual errors in the newly printed brochure about the farm. This man, being interested in local history, was clearly concerned to set the record straight. Wallace too showed his concern, and they all went off to find an official to complain to. As they departed it was noticeable that Wallace was hoping to add another dimension to the situation. He wanted to have some fun.

They provisionally settled the matter, allowing the ceremony to take place. We stood politely listening to a succession of speeches. Wallace, however, did not merely stand politely. Instead, throughout the speeches, he whispered what were presumably witty remarks into the ears of his companions, eliciting from them barely suppressed guffaws.

The speeches over, the throng moved off to look at the now open building, while Wallace and his relatives once more laid siege to the officials. I was not privy to their conversation. However, I noted the glee with which Wallace approached them and the officials' glazed politeness as they settled down to sort the matter out for a second time.

As tea drew to a close a group gathered to be photographed by the local press. Wallace and his party were by now out in the sunshine. I watched as people gestured toward Wallace to join in the photograph. I too looked at Wallace and saw him observe the beckoning group out of the corner of his eye. He soon became aware of what they wanted. Immediately he fixed his gaze on some distant object and began to stride resolutely toward it, away from the photographer.

His sister, however, was too quick for him. She grasped his arm and, with a sweetly unconvincing smile, began, in the best of humors, to drag her brother toward the group. For a moment they were in friendly combat, though both pretended they were not. He pulled one way, she pulled the other. Wallace seemed to be muttering that he was not going to be in any photograph.

The sister, however, now put resolution into her step, and Wallace began to be hauled off. For a moment he resisted the inevitable. Then, with the cheerfulness he had displayed throughout, he meekly accepted defeat and went off to be photographed.

The Morphology of Wrong-footing

Wrong-footing characteristically consists of bad behavior directed against one or more individuals. There is, so to speak, an aggressor and a victim. It is constructed in such a way that the victim knows, or thinks he knows, that the act is taking place, but for some reason cannot retaliate. The performance characteristically takes place in front of a legitimating audience. Typically this audience is a parent figure, who redefines the action as play. Such bad behavior ceases to be playful only when the likelihood of punishment becomes real.

In the case we are looking at, the wrong-footing depends upon a manipulation of metamessages in such a way that the victim has difficulty in framing his experience. Specifically, the metamessages in question are those indicating that aspects of the wrong-footer's behavior are playful. The wrong-footer shares the playful frame with his audience, but he subtly excludes the victim from the play.

Let me concentrate first upon a small part of James Wallace's quite complex behavior. Immediately upon discovering that there was a fault in the brochure, James went off to find an official. The message (call it the primary message) that he went to convey was fairly straightforward. Roughly speaking, it was, "There are mistakes in the brochure and it must be rewritten." Such a message was judgmental. It carried authority. It was, indeed, that of a parent figure. Since it was an accurate representation of the situation, the appropriate response of the officials would have to be to apologize and offer to make amends.

Qualifying this message, however, was a metamessage of the type that Goffman (1975, 40ff.) calls a "keying." This transformed the message into the frame of play. It was perfectly clear both to Wallace's relatives and to myself that he regarded his forays to harass the officials as play. By noticing his sideways glances and secret smiles, but also by observing the general pattern of his behavior, it was easy for us to see that he was playfully hoping to discomfit the officials by issuing his complaint. There was, for us, no paradox involved in his behavior. The reason is simple: he made it clear to us that he was playing.

The situation for the officials was quite different. They were confronted with the primary message, delivered, as far as they could confidently be sure, in a parentlike frame. It pointed to an error for which they were responsible. This they had to act upon. Wallace was not apparently trying to make things awkward, and he was entitled to satisfaction in the matter of the brochure.

Only gradually, and in occasional glimpses, could they become aware of the keying that defined the situation as play. Had they been sure that Wallace was being playful, the officials might have done something about it. Specifically, they might have been able to describe the situation as one in which Wallace was merely trying to be difficult.

Unfortunately, because they could not be sure that Wallace was playing, they were unable to send him away with a deserved flea in his ear. To have tried to do this would, in any case, have been hazardous in the midst of the reception. Wallace could quickly have stopped being playful and become angry (acting as a parent) and have described more forthrightly their ineptitude. This would have been, at the least, embarrassing.

Conversely, however, there was a strong suspicion that the primary message was, indeed, delivered in a playful frame. This placed the officials in the invidious position of having to behave courteously and correctly (like a compliant child) with a complaint that they first suspected and later knew to have been in part concocted with the devious purpose of inconveniencing them.

Thus were the officials deftly placed in that celebrated version of Epimenides's paradox which Bateson and his colleagues call a double bind (Bateson et al. 1956). The other instances here exhibit a similar pattern.

The effusion of a spectacular smell over a respectable gathering has considerable potential as a message. Ordinarily there is an implied qualification upon such agricultural messages to indicate that they are not intended to be a nuisance. Here, however, Wallace's overall behavior cast the truth of this apologetic metamessage into serious doubt, though not to the extent that anyone could retaliate by complaining.

The rude remark that Wallace made on the arrival of the Catholic priest may be seen in the same light. In part it was a direct snub to the priest, of course, and to the religion he represents. Wallace shares in the locally common opposition to Catholicism. However, the "English" who invited the priest and who were there in profusion are notoriously ecumenical in spirit. They also have a lax attitude toward the central issues of contemporary Ulster politics.

Wallace's gesture should therefore be seen in part as defiance, not merely against the priest, but also against those who had invited him. The fact that this remark, though obviously offensive, was private in nature again prevented any complaint.

The finale of the occasion came when Wallace saw that he was required to take part in the photographs. His initial reaction was to pretend that he had not seen the people gesturing at him, to fix his eyes on the horizon and walk toward it.

His was not an open defiance of the photographer and officials, for he was pretending merely to walk across the lawn. However, it was not difficult for me, or indeed anyone else who was looking, to see that it was a pretense. Was he even pretending to pretend?

His sister also knew what he was up to, so she grabbed his arm. Really, she was trying to drag Wallace toward the photographer: she pretended, however, merely to be walking arm in arm with her brother. Perhaps she too was pretending to pretend.

As they stood there tugging in different directions, each wearing an unconvincing smile, the pretenses began to slip away. Lurching into view came the unambiguous fact that Wallace was, indeed, trying to be disruptive. At the instant that this became clear, however, his demeanor changed. In mock submission, he walked cheerfully over to be photographed.

In all of this, nobody could claim with any degree of certainty that anything had been going on. If anyone had been foolish enough to complain about Wallace's behavior, brother and sister would have stuck to the theory that they were merely strolling across the lawn.

A distinction is made here between honest play and paradoxical play, which is one form of wrong-footing. In honest play, there is a straightforward definition of the situation such that certain actions — punching, insults, being untidy, being drunk — take place in a context in which everyone knows that the actions do not denote what they would denote in a serious frame. The witnessing parent figure is thus invited to relax the rules of acceptable behavior. In so doing, however, the parent is still able to exercise legitimate control. The reason is that there is no profound confusion created by the playful frame. The parent is still able to describe, if necessary, what is going on, and description is the characteristic stratagem of social control exercised by someone in a parent frame.

In paradoxical play, the situation is quite different. Here there may be a parent figure acting as an audience who is privy to the entire drama. However, the victim is also a parent and this person is unable to describe what is going on.

Robbed of the parental mode of social control, he must fall back upon characteristically childlike behavior. If, like the English officials, he is also robbed of the ability even to be rebellious, he must be meekly compliant, a helpless, impotent child.

Thus is the victim laid low by playful dexterity. And thus, in the case given here, is made a complex rhetorical and metaphorical statement about more general social relationships and identities not only in Listymore, but in Ulster generally.

Having distinguished honest from paradoxical genres of play, I should point out that one may not always be certain which is which. In the pub, for example, were the rowdy bachelors trying to wrong-foot the owner into overreacting with a parental imposition of authority that would be inappropriate and thus foolish? Or when I noticed the ash scattered on the farmhouse floor, were my features being scanned for signs of typically English disapproval, which could be laughed at later? It is difficult to be sure, because, except for those who are most decisively in on the joke, paradoxical play evades description.

This chapter began by suggesting that playful genres of social interaction could dramatize relationships and identities, rather pointedly differentiating between those who were in on the joke and those who were not. As in the last chapter, play need not always be an aggressive form of action, but in given instances it can be. The next chapter will examine an even more aggressive form of activity, the riot. What it will show is that rioting can be fun: a form of play that dramatizes identities and allegiances.

10

FIELDWORK BY M. C. KENNEY

WITH A. D. BUCKLEY

Fighting and Fun

Stone-
Throwers
and
Spectators
in
Ulster
Riots

Riots in Northern Ireland are often carnivalesque. They usually arise out of parades and other public celebrations, and they develop through the interaction of the divergent aims of the participants, marchers, police, bands, stone-throwers, and spectators.

Through this interplay, actions that would ordinarily defy norms are reframed and redefined. A riot, like a theatrical event or a pageant, is therefore a "keyed" frame (Goffman 1975), bracketed off from ordinary life. Rioting is a playful, dramatic form of social interaction, but within it, participants enforce the norms peculiar to that frame.

Riots often arise out of serious social conflict over both macro- and micro-territorial claims. A riot, by its nature, is brutal. There are injuries and sometimes deaths. Nevertheless, in rioting there is also a strong element of macabre fun. As with the most active participants in a real carnival, the stone-throwers in a riot express the disorder perceived to be inherent in daily life. They also reverse roles and become "king for a day."

This discussion of rioting returns to a subject raised in chapter 5. It also continues the theme of playful rebellion explored in the last chapter. In a riot, there is the same relation between the actor, who misbehaves, and his audience, who gives him active or tacit support.

In a riot there is also the same dramatization of social relationships. Only seldom is there a serious attempt by the rioters to win a battle or to defeat an enemy. Rarely, for example, is territory gained or authority defeated. Instead, through dramatic means, the riot makes a statement about the identities of the participants. This statement is set in the broader frame of social and political relations. This framed statement is, of course, heavy with rhetoric.

Like Pentecostal ritual, but in a very different way, the most surprising but most obvious feature of the riot is that it is fun. Despite the brutality, the real violence, and the injuries, the rioting is quite visibly a form of play for both stone-throwers and spectators. Not only does the riot often arise from a "carnivalesque" (Burke 1978, 190) event, but rioting itself is an extension and enhancement of a carnival atmosphere.

This fun element of riots has been observed in public disorders elsewhere in the world, even where these involved serious injury. During the American urban race riots in the 1960s, for example, the public authorities denounced the "carnival spirit" that marked some of these disturbances. There was a mood of exhilaration, so intense as to border on jubilation (Fogelson 1970). Marsh (1978) has described the similar phenomenon of "aggro," the ritualized and recreational aggression found in the football matches of the British Isles.

Studies of carnival show that pugnacious and libidinous activity is also a feature of carnival and carnivalesque festivals throughout the world (Burke 1978, 190). Abrahams and Bauman (1978) say, however, that in such situations, norms are broken only by specific segments of a community, often by a small minority. Both these observations help an understanding of the riots, both Catholic and Protestant, that occur in Northern Irish community festivals.

Not all parades in Northern Ireland are riotous. Nevertheless, rioting is predictably — one may say traditionally — associated with community festivals and parades. The most famous of these undoubtedly belong to the Protestants, but Catholics have a comparable, if less elaborate, cycle of parades and public rituals.

Nearly all these take place in what the press calls "the marching season," between March and the end of August. In addition to regular demonstrations, there are also occasional ones organized by the political parties, or by such bodies as the Orange Order and the Apprentice Boys clubs. Increasingly, too, in recent years, there has been a tendency for bands of musicians to hold their own parades independently of the ones organized by the different associations. The so-called band parades often have a stridently ethnic or political flavor.

The two authors attended, sometimes together, sometimes separately, riotous assemblies in Belfast, Cookstown, Holywood, and Portadown in 1985 and 1986. Here we focus on examples that we regard as typical: riots by nationalists in the Falls Road on 17 March and in Ardoyne on 8–9 August 1985, and loyalist riots in Woodhouse Street and Obins Street in Portadown on the Twelfth of July in 1985. In all these cases, several individuals threw missiles —

usually stones and bottles, but occasionally firebombs — at soldiers and policemen while other people stood and watched.

The Rhetoric of the Demonstration and the Riot

Parades, bonfires, and the riots that sometimes arise from these events usually
mingle with questions of territory. These issues exist at both a macro and a
micro level. At the macro level, as we have seen, loyalists typically feel under
siege in their province, subject to the imperialistic ambitions of the Republic.
Nationalists believe their country to have been invaded. Each side, therefore,
informs the rhetoric of its political aims with images of siege and invasion.

As chapter 5 outlined, in some parts of Ulster these macroterritorial images translate into much more local concerns. There are many neighborhoods
and districts in Northern Ireland that people describe as "mixed" or "neutral."
There are also many that "belong" either to Catholics or to Protestants (see
especially Boal 1982; Boal and Livingstone 1984).

The definition of such areas is, in large part, decided by the ethnic affinity
of the majority living there. Sometimes a minority from the other side can be
tolerated. In other cases, where the ethnic identity of an area is in dispute, there
can be consternation when somebody of the other side comes to live locally.
There have been in recent years numerous instances in which people have
been so strongly intimidated that they have had to leave their homes. Commonly, such aggression is intended to reduce an ambiguity in the composition
of a particular street. There is often a further definition of the area as belonging
to one's own group by means of graffiti, painted curbstones, or more elaborate
and often quite artistic wall paintings (Loftus 1990).

Processions and bonfires have a similar territorial implication. One of the
things that a procession or bonfire asserts is the right of the ethnic group to
march or build a bonfire in a particular area. It is this aspect of such public
demonstrations that makes them likely to become violent.

Microterritoriality is what links rioting in Northern Ireland with non-
political violence in other societies. The rioting itself is mostly an activity of
working-class teenagers, ostensibly in defense of often exceedingly local
boundaries. It therefore invites comparison with teenage gang violence in
American and British cities.

Suttles, who has studied ethnic neighborhoods and street-corner gangs in
Chicago (1968), shows that this type of territorial action is a nonpathological
phenomenon found in street-corner society. Patrick (1973) describes violent

gang rivalries and maintenance of gang territories in working-class Glasgow. Some of these teenage rivalries have Ulster-related sectarian aspects. Marsh et al. (1978) show that in English soccer violence, territoriality has a significant place. In this case, the territory in question may be only a small piece of soccer field. Gill (1977) reports rioting of youths against police in Merseyside that closely resembles rioting observed in Belfast. White (1971) discusses similarly territorial street-corner gangs, locally called "mobs," in Birmingham. In all these studies of youthful working-class violence, neighborhood territoriality is a major theme.

In the particular riots described here, there was no attempt to drive anybody from their homes, though such activities were going on throughout the period under discussion. Here the dispute was over more symbolic issues, namely the diacritical markers that defined whether a territory was Protestant or Catholic.

The Falls Road incident arose out of an annual St. Patrick's Day parade, when a group of people began to throw stones and bottles near what was seen as an intrusive police station in the nationalist area of Andersonstown. The Ardoyne incident took place at a communal bonfire on the eve of the parade commemorating the anniversary of Internment. The nationalist riots described here, therefore, had almost a routine nature. Not only are the processions from which the riots arose built into the calendar, but also this kind of riotous activity has become almost woven into the fabric of life in these particular districts.

In contrast, the loyalist riots arose out of more specific political circumstances, though these too were associated with periodic festivities. In Portadown, it had long been the practice on the Twelfth of July, and similar occasions, for Orangemen to "walk" (that is, process) through Obins Street and Woodhouse Street toward the Portadown town center. This practice had not ended despite the building of a housing estate occupied by Roman Catholics.

In 1985, loyalist processions were prohibited from using this traditional route. The prohibition allegedly came from an agreement between Dublin and London in the context of the Anglo-Irish Agreement of the previous year. Police built barricades both at Obins Street itself, on the outskirts of the town, and at Woodhouse Street, in the town center. Orangemen who set out on the Twelfth of July, therefore, found their route impeded.

The local Orange lodges, together with musicians, families, friends, and onlookers, encamped themselves close to the Obins Street barricades in the early morning. Other local lodges paraded through the town center. At both places, rioting developed. The Woodhouse Street riot lasted for only two hours; that at Obins Street continued on and off until nightfall.

As the nationalist riot dramatized the iniquity of the British invasion of their country and locality, so the drama of the Orangemen's situation echoed their sense of being besieged. The ostensibly peaceful parade by Protestants was through a territory that traditionally had been theirs. Now it belonged to the opposition. One public figure claimed that an Ulsterman "had the right to walk down his own thoroughfare." He also said there should not *be* any nationalist areas.

Both the prohibition on parades and the Anglo-Irish Agreement from which it allegedly came had the same implication. This was that the Lundy-like authorities were giving nationalists, and more especially Dublin, too much influence over Ulster's internal affairs.

For the loyalists here, the police were not really intruders: such an idea was inappropriate. Nevertheless, the siege image persisted. The police were at best Lundys who, since they were perceived to be Protestants themselves, were traitors to their own people.

The Peaceful Event and Its Transformation

In most of the cases we saw, and all those described here, the rioting arose out of an apparently peaceful demonstration. Individuals or small groups acted to change the situation, giving a new set of actions and interactions a new defining frame.

This new riotous pattern was frequently unstable. The riot tended to lapse back into a peaceful demonstration. Individuals could sometimes keep the riot going, but at other times it simply petered out. Sometimes it was transformed further as respectable participants left the scene. Then, with little difficulty, policemen could arrest the handful of stone-throwing youths and bring the riot to an end.

The parade is the most common form of political demonstration among both nationalists and loyalists in Ulster. Its structure is inherently quite simple. There are marchers (who are often, but not always, members of specific organizations) and there are bands, sometimes hired for the occasion. Usually a crowd gathers to watch and give explicit or implied support. Such a crowd usually comprises a good cross-section of the relevant ethnic group, and it will often include marchers' relatives.

Figure 13. A flute band. (Courtesy of the Ulster Folk and Transport Museum)

Bands of musicians have a special importance. These are a major vehicle for youth and female participation in what is, particularly on the Protestant side, often a formally adult and male event. Among the various types of bands are Scottish-style pipe bands and accordion bands. Protestant marchers are also likely to be accompanied by "silver" (brass) bands and "part flute bands" (involving several sizes of flute). Bands such as these are often hired for the occasion. As is the case with bands in the rest of the British Isles, their members are mainly people who enjoy playing music.

There are also to be found unison (or melody) flute-and-drum bands. As the name suggests, these bands play only the tune upon their flutes, accompanied by exuberant drumming. These, usually made up wholly of youths and young men, have a more direct political orientation. On the loyalist side, the members of such bands, sometimes called kick-the-Pope bands or blood-and-thunder bands, formerly dressed in distinctive sweaters and plumed berets. They now increasingly wear more elaborate uniforms, some carrying their own expensively painted small banners.[1] On the Catholic side, the favored costume is quasi-military battle dress.

Unlike other groups of musicians, these melody flute bands have a distinctively aggressive style. They frequently attract roving groups of teenaged supporters, who mingle with the watching crowds. Such young people (and especially poor young people) are frequently among those who translate the symbolic challenge of the bands' stirring music into more direct action by starting stone-throwing episodes. The formal and aggressive role of these exuberant teenage flute bands in the parade is a major factor in attracting youthful thrillseekers who begin riots (cf. Bell 1985).

The Riot in Woodhouse Street, Portadown

The loyalist riot in Woodhouse Street in Portadown began as an essentially peaceful procession. It moved down the main street, where it passed the police barricade that blocked the opening to Woodhouse Street. Across this street the police had tightly wedged a row of their Land Rovers. Behind this they stood, wearing helmets and other riot gear and carrying batons.

At first the procession captured the attention of the crowd lining the main road. Early on, however, a knot of people gathered around the opening to Woodhouse Street. Gradually, almost imperceptibly at first, empty bottles were thrown high in the air. They landed on or behind the barricade of Land Rovers.

The crowd took more interest in these developments. More people gathered round. They began to cheer whenever a bottle shattered in an especially spectacular way. Despite this activity, it became apparent that the police would not retaliate.

One policeman, in ordinary uniform, ambled over from elsewhere. He fell into casual chit-chat with an acquaintance in the crowd who was watching the bottle-throwing. The bottle-throwing began to die away.

During this lull, three somewhat intoxicated young men traversed the open space immediately in front of the barricade to talk to the policemen. One of the officers (senior in both rank and age) engaged them in what seemed like amicable negotiations.

A fourth young man joined the others. He could be described as a comedian. As he sauntered across the empty space his hips waggled, his eyes rolled, and he grinned at the crowd. His hands waved in imitation of a black-faced minstrel. The comedian remained with the negotiators for a minute or two, and then he returned, making similar gestures. His antics raised considerable cheers from the crowd.

Despite the comic intrusion, mock discussions with the senior policeman continued to go well. Then, however, one of the young men placed an inebriated but affectionate arm around the policeman's shoulders. The policeman suddenly became irritated and shrugged the arm off. The young man repeated his affectionate gesture three or four times. Each time the policeman repelled it with a show of annoyance. The conversation continued for a while. It seemed as relaxed as before.

Suddenly, however, tempers flared. The affectionate young man grasped the policeman's head with his arm. Then, with his other hand, he punched the policeman several times, very hard, full in the face.

This overt show of anger changed the atmosphere in a moment. There was a joyous shout from the crowd. Everyone surged forward and occupied the empty space that, until that moment, had existed in front of the police barricade.

There followed a rather uneasy pause. Nobody seemed to know quite what to do. The barricade was impenetrable, but the closeness of the police inhibited the throwing of bottles.

Once again the situation changed. Somebody hurled a bottle high against a nearby wall, showering the crowd with broken glass (and incidentally causing some injury). With another shout, the crowd returned to its original position some distance away from the police.

From this point the situation continued much as before. The number of bottles and, more occasionally, stones being thrown gradually increased. Then it settled down.

A number of people went off to buy hamburgers and soft drinks. Gradually the bottle-throwing became rather boring to watch. From the two or three hundred people who had been watching from near Woodhouse Street, the number dwindled to no more than fifty. Only about a dozen youths remained, still throwing the occasional bottle or stone.

Suddenly, out of a side street, four Land Rovers drove dramatically toward Woodhouse Street. Several policemen, clad in riot gear, climbed out and took up rehearsed, formal positions. Two policemen ran toward a young man who was confused by the new events. One tapped him firmly on the head with a baton and he was put into a Land Rover. This little flying squad then drove away. Soon two Land Rovers began to drive up and down the main street, their noisy engines blaring defiance.

Neither the arrest nor the sight of policemen driving up and down the street noisily in low gear exactly served to disperse the crowd. But somehow the spirit of excitement and fun had gone. Everyone looked rather depressed and bored and began to wander off.

The Riot in Obins Street, Portadown

In Obins Street in Portadown occurred a pattern that seems to be mainly (but not exclusively) the preserve of Protestant demonstrators. This is the use of music as a symbolic form of aggression. Here musical instruments — classically Lambeg drums, but also other kinds of instrument — are played *at* the policemen (see Glassie 1982, 272–73).

As at the riot in Woodhouse Street, the rioters faced the problem of preventing the riot from becoming boring or sliding back into a merely peaceful demonstration. Buckley arrived from Woodhouse Street in the early afternoon. There had already been much stone-throwing. Policemen had already rescued some journalists from violent attacks and established them safely behind the large police barricades. Now, however, the events had settled down. Lunches had been eaten, and Orangemen were conversing with the policemen in riot gear. They were trying (or pretending to try) to persuade them of the error of their ways. There seemed no question of the police taking retaliatory action. Only an occasional stone was being thrown.

A religious service then began a little way off from the barricade. Its sermon was based on Ephesians 6 ("Take unto you the helmet of salvation; and the sword of the spirit"). Despite the military imagery, it had a depressing effect on the general excitement, and this depression continued after the service had ended.

It was in such circumstances that Buckley watched as a man persuaded a young female drum major to form up her accordion band of young teenage girls. Following the man's suggestion, the band marched off. It turned around a rough traffic island until it came face to face with the police cordon. The girls played some delicate little tunes for about five minutes, and then moved off.

It was perhaps a little odd to choose an accordion band for such a task. Accordion bands are hardly the most aggressive of Ulster's bands. This band was made up of small girls in drum majorette–type uniforms. Nevertheless, the impact on the crowd was considerable. As soon as the band had marched out of the way, stones and bottles began once more to fly.

Inspired by the accordion band, a melody flute band marched to the edge of the crowd. There it reassembled and returned with a swagger toward the police barricades. With a clatter of drums, it played for some minutes at the police until it too turned and marched away, allowing people to throw stones.

Another flute band followed this example. On and off, for over an hour, the two flute bands took turns playing at the policemen. On one occasion, the two bands formed up into one massive procession.

As these activities developed, the stone- and bottle-throwing continued, intensifying with each symbolic assault by the bands. Soon the bands were leading a largely female crowd of cheerfully capering teenagers. Missiles showered over the heads of the bands onto the helpless policemen beyond. The excitement came in waves, coordinated with the movement of the bands. Between each pass there continued to be a great deal of missile-throwing.

In the midst of this new-found enthusiasm, somebody spotted a group of people in a very distant housing estate. They seemed to be holding up an Irish tricolor. This drew the attention of several people to the rear, where they spied groups of policemen, no doubt strategically placed to stop sorties in that general direction.

One small group of policemen was especially vulnerable. Soon it was attacked by a group of small boys (about six to eight years old). At first the policemen crouched in a group, covering themselves skillfully with their shields. Then they released themselves from this ingenious but undignified posture and rushed at the small boys, who scampered off. These were soon replaced by older teenagers, who continued this minor battle well into the evening. In this vicinity, policemen fired an occasional plastic bullet.

The main event continued as before, until the approach of five o'clock. It then became clear that many members of the crowd were going home. Mothers began to collect their children and to clear up the picnics. This general stirring was accelerated by a sudden and fierce shower of rain that stimulated large numbers to move off toward where buses and cars were waiting.

At this point, Buckley also joined the movement homeward. The fighting had by no means stopped. He judged, however, that once most of the spectators had disappeared, the police would gird themselves for attack. Sure enough, about an hour later, the radio said there had been baton charges. He also heard a leading unionist politician, employing a familiar rhetoric, complain of the brutality of the police.

The Riot on the Falls Road

The St. Patrick's Day parade on the Falls Road, Belfast, began as an inherently peaceful demonstration. There had, however, already been some exuberance among the younger members of the crowd, who threw snowballs at each other and at the procession from its beginning.

Kenney attached herself to a small group of working-class teenage boys (about fourteen to eighteen years old) roaming along in the wake of the parade.

Many of these were dressed skinhead-style, with shaved or close-cropped heads, paratrooper boots, old jeans, and short nylon bomber jackets. Some of them were carrying stout sticks made from sawn-off broom handles painted with an Irish tricolor motif. Several also carried bottles of cider or cans of beer that they tipped with a flourish into their mouths. They were all excited and cheerfully boisterous.

At the top of the Falls Road there stands a massive fortification, the Andersonstown police barracks. As they passed this edifice one of the young men suddenly smashed a full cider bottle on the window of the jutting observation post. He celebrated this deed by laughing, jumping, and dancing. He clenched his fists and turned his face up to the sky with an expression of pleasure and excitement.

Then, with the aid of his friends, he climbed up on top of the observation post, where, with two other boys, he jumped up and down on its corrugated metal roof. Presumably there were police inside to receive this noisy challenge.

Someone then passed the boy an Irish tricolor flag. With it, he climbed up a further fifteen precarious feet. There he tried to stuff the tricolor into the wire mesh stretched around the top of the fort. Meanwhile, a crowd was peeling off from the parade and gathering in front of the fort to watch the boy make his ascent and to cheer him on.

After he had climbed down, a few bottles sailed through the air and smashed on the front of the fort. This initial volley suddenly erupted into an extremely dense bombardment of stones and bottles fired by a crowd of about a hundred boys and young men. This lasted for five or ten minutes.

Then the big double doors of the fort opened and a convoy of gray police Land Rovers rolled slowly out to confront the crowd. Battle was then joined and the stones and bottles flew. The considerable crowd that had gathered to watch began rapidly to disperse, leaving the stone-throwers to fight it out. Kenney too retreated at this point. News broadcasts later reported that the crowd had thrown firebombs at the police.

The Riot in Ardoyne

If a riot is to begin and continue, in general there is a need for someone to seize the initiative and create activity (though not all riots start in this way). On Internment Eve in Ardoyne one year (8 August 1985), this role fell to a convoy of police vehicles.

Here there was a huge bonfire bedecked by union flags and flags of Ulster. (Orange Order bonfires on the eve of the Twelfth of July similarly have a branch of greenery, an effigy of the Pope, or an Irish tricolor). There were some four hundred people nearby, waiting for the lighting of the fire, which was scheduled for midnight. This gathering was peaceful except for the sporadic appearance of three police Land Rovers. They drove repeatedly around the bonfire site in close formation and at great speed, buzzing the gathering in precisely the same manner as they had done at Woodhouse Street in Portadown. In the context, they could only have hoped to provoke a reaction. Increasingly, as they zoomed around the corner, boys and young men chased after them on foot, hurling bricks, bottles, sticks, and insults.

Between passes, the youths waited until the Land Rovers came to receive another volley. As they drove past, a roar would arise from the crowd. Members of the crowd were heard to say, "Here they come," or "They'll be back," as the Land Rovers sped to and fro.

Someone told Kenney of a "little Molotov cocktail factory" behind a nearby row of houses. Sure enough, later, in the darkness, when the Land Rovers sped past, about five young men in their late teens bombarded the policemen with homemade firebombs. When eventually the bonfire was lit, its damp state required that it be ignited by some half-dozen Molotov cocktails.

Thus it was that policemen had a major part in this particular game of territorial assertiveness. There were policemen staked out at night on the edge of the Ardoyne area, it being presumably too dangerous to undertake normal patrols. The mobile convoy perhaps had to enter the area for the rhetorical purpose of asserting the territorial claims of the state. Perhaps they hoped too to localize the likely conflict, diverting attention away from more vulnerable groups of policemen. Whatever the reason for the police's assertive actions, these were integral to the development of the event. The tantalizing movements of the mobile convoy undoubtedly stimulated the onslaught of stones and firebombs.

In all four incidents described above, the initiative of individuals produced a riotous framework out of an otherwise peaceful gathering. These riots tended to settle into a rather dull shower of stones or bottles onto an unresponding line of policemen. When this happened, it became obligatory for someone to take the initiative and restore the excitement. In one case, the initiative was taken by the police. In the others, venturesome youths fulfilled this function. And among Protestants, bands have a special responsibility for starting and maintaining a riotous situation. In nearly all cases, however, the spirit in which the riots began and continued was one of ribaldry and fun, not anger.

Rioters and Their Audience

In the earlier discussions of play, considerable emphasis was placed upon the role of an audience. At a riot, the actors can be differentiated from the spectators. Apart from the police, a major distinction can be drawn between those people whom we call stone-throwers and the rest, who watch them.

The number of stone-throwers tends to vary somewhat with the ebb and flow of excitement. Some individuals who begin in the role of spectator get caught up by the drama of the situation and engage in aggressive and destructive acts. Such people, when the attack recedes, will fall back into the more passive role of spectator. Some individuals thus switch from one category to another. Others remain consistently willing to throw missiles. Still more, however, remain spectators throughout.

At no time — at least while we were actually present at the different riots — did the number of stone-throwers exceed that of the spectators. The overwhelming majority of people present never threw a stone, bottle, or firebomb. They only watched. The stone-throwers themselves were all young, in their teens and early twenties. Most were male. Often it was clear they had been drinking. One reason for this is the need to drain a bottle before one can throw it. Young rioters were often seen urgently passing round liter bottles of cider so that they could then throw the empty bottle.

The young men engaged in this sort of activity were usually of an easily identifiable type. They were young men from the lower working class, the kind known generally in Ulster as "rough." They also included those especially aggressive individuals called "hard men." Their attitude to the police in all the observable riots was only sometimes overtly aggressive. Rather, in hurling their missiles, they were engaging in a display of braggadocio.

In this type of situation the police are not really unwelcome enemies to the stone-throwers. This was most clearly displayed at the Ardoyne bonfire. Rather, they play a more ambiguous role as adversaries. Without them there would be no thrill-seeking, and no opportunity to act out the aggressive, half-comic drama.

Many of the police themselves come from urban working-class backgrounds. For them, no doubt, the game is already quite familiar. In part, rioting among both loyalists and nationalists is part of the ritualized animosity toward the police that goes on in poorer working-class neighborhoods throughout the British Isles. It is a dramatization of their honor or self-esteem against authority, but it is simultaneously a dramatization of their ethnic honor (Wallis 1986 et al.).

This formalized hostility is intertwined in the wider context of the United Kingdom with the bravado surrounding soccer matches. Particularly at loyalist demonstrations, one can see youthful spectators wearing the scarves and insignia of soccer teams. It was comic, but not wholly unexpected, to hear a loyalist crowd confronting policemen at an inherently similar riot in Cookstown. They sang the soccer chant "Liverpool, Liverpool, Liverpool."

Again, many of the activities associated with the riot are done for dramatic rather than quasi-military effect. We have described how a youth climbed with an Irish tricolor onto that symbol of British power, the police station in Andersonstown; and that another engaged in drunken "negotiations" with a senior policeman in Woodhouse Street. The aim in these cases was less to injure the policemen than to discomfit them, to make them laughingstocks. Even in the nationalist riots, the police appeared not so much as enemies but as targets.

One must wonder, too, whether many actual murders by paramilitary forces are not also symbolic or dramaturgical in their intent, an idea that makes them seem even more bleak and horrific.

There is in the riot a strong element of what the last chapter described as wrong-footing. The police are compelled to withstand taunts and showers of stones, broken glass, and burning gasoline. They are trapped by the need to maintain decorum and to avoid injuring those whom the press might define as innocent, such as women, children, and old people.

The spectators, being by far the largest body of people present, were also the most highly differentiated. Here too there were young men from the lower working class, but other types of people were also present. Many old ladies, for example, some very elderly indeed, were to be found in all the locations. There were young couples with toddlers or with babies in strollers. It was astonishing to see at a Cookstown riot not only a disabled child in a wheelchair but even a middle-aged blind woman carrying a white stick.

The polarity between active stone-thrower and usually passive spectator corresponded in part to their proximity to the police. This was true at the Falls Road and Ardoyne riots, but it was most obvious at the Woodhouse Street riot, where the flow of occasional traffic forced spectators to organize themselves into distinct layers. Those on the farthest sidewalk were that type of quite ordinary lower-class citizen who spends much time standing on street corners. These people were interested in this new form of excitement, but only casually, and they did not disperse even when the riot had completely ended.

Those standing on the traffic island in the middle of the main road were more agitated. Though they generally supported the stone-throwers, they also made disinterested comments about those more actively involved. One young man in this group said that a firebomb would be needed to shift the police. He believed that oil mixed with gasoline was particularly effective. His neighbor replied, with equal detachment, that she could not see why the police did not come out and arrest the stone-throwers.

Even among the people standing on the nearest sidewalk, clustered around the intersection, by no means all of them were throwing missiles. Most were simply standing there. These, however, expressed a more direct excitement, and they gave a more obvious encouragement to the throwers, cheering their more accurate shots in the manner of a tennis crowd.

The atmosphere at Obins Street was very similar, but here the crowd was even more highly differentiated. Here it was possible to look away from the front line and quite literally believe oneself to be at a church garden party.

The atmosphere was very much that of a "field" at the end of a normal Twelfth of July procession. Ordinarily, when the main Twelfth of July procession has walked along a route, usually through a small town, the marchers and bands gather together in a large field, near where their leaders give speeches, and have refreshments. This occasion (itself called a "field") is usually a pleasant one. When they have rested from their march, men saunter about, renewing acquaintanceships with brethren from other lodges, whom they may not have seen since the last Twelfth. Women and children, who are only seldom part of the actual procession, arrive before their menfolk and provide tea and sandwiches. Occasionally beer is drunk, though not in the quantities that the Orangemen's opponents like to claim. The atmosphere is lighthearted and the occasion is a family picnic.

So too at Obins Street. Because it was a Twelfth of July demonstration, many participants were well dressed in Sunday suits or summer dresses. Scattered around were family parties picnicking or buying food or soft drinks from impromptu roadside stalls. The women sat and chatted to each other, gave out food, and looked after children. Men ambled about, greeting old friends and discussing the day's news.

In one direction, there was a relaxed, family atmosphere — including, for a time, a religious service. In the other, there were riot police defending themselves with shields against stones and shattering bottles. It was all a bit surreal.

Play and Permission

The form of activity and atmosphere described here is remarkably similar to that found in carnival. In carnival, staid and respectable individuals do not throw off their respectability to do outrageous and extravagant things. Rather, people who ordinarily behave outrageously, but behind closed doors or in secluded streets and bars, are allowed in carnival to exhibit themselves and take center stage (Abrahams and Bauman 1978).

Those who riot are like those who take part in carnival. They are curators of a kind of culture. This culture may comprise only an ability and willingness to be foolhardy and aggressive. It can, however, be occasionally useful to a wider community.

The ordinary peaceful parades from which riots commonly develop are, of course, not merely *like* carnival. They actually *are* a type of carnival, if a politically motivated kind. Around these parades there are ordinarily clusters of teenagers indulging in exuberant if mild misbehavior. There are also adults behaving and dressing in an unusual and mildly flamboyant way. The teenage melody flute bands, in particular, have in these parades a setting where they may display, in a controlled if taunting way, an aggression normally kept hidden away. When the parade develops into a riot, however, the social control exercised over the younger, wilder people erodes even more.

In the riots described here, the individuals who throw stones and bottles are not the people pushing baby strollers, the old ladies, or the married couples. They are the young men who are to be seen fighting and drinking and being rowdy on Saturday nights when the public houses close down. What distinguishes their behavior in the riot from that of their more ordinary existence is the social framework. In the riot, the people who would ordinarily object to them throwing bottles at policemen instead give them sometimes explicit, sometimes implicit permission to do so. Social control over the young men has been relaxed.

This relaxation of social control takes several forms. First, the people around the stone-throwers give implicit permission. Most obviously, there are people nearby who cheer whenever a bottle smashes sensationally, or when a stone makes a particularly good hit. The atmosphere in this context is like a sports tournament, where spectators applaud good play. This kind of direct encouragement usually comes from the peers of the stone-throwers, that is, from young people, and teenage girls in particular.

Less obvious but, we feel, more important is the more tacit approval given by older or more respectable people. This approval takes the rather passive form of not voicing disapproval, or of otherwise not interfering. Minimally, it consists of not walking away from the situation.

In the riots we attended, the refusal of the majority to discourage riotous behavior was highlighted by the exceptions. Occasionally there were protests.

In such circumstances, we feel that women are particularly well placed to intervene. Kenney has seen women intervene to stop destructive activity in Belfast. They succeeded because criticism of rough behavior is an accepted part of the female role. Partly, too, women are effectively shielded from retaliatory violence by the general prohibition against hitting women.

A woman tried to control events at the Falls Road disturbance. She urgently pushed away a baby carriage as the police loomed from their barracks to confront the ranks of stone-throwing teenagers. She shouted in disapproval at the rioters, "Oh, see what you've done. Haven't youse done enough?"

There was a similar case at Obins Street in Portadown, where a middle-aged woman, obviously distressed at the ferocity of the attack upon the police, rushed away from where she had been standing with her small child. Looking for a sympathetic ear into which to pour her anger, she shouted out, "There was a policeman over there. He had blood pouring down his face." The group of women to whom these remarks were directed were dispensing soft drinks to their children. They undoubtedly heard what she had said, as did many other people, but they pretended not to.

In these particular instances, the pleas of the women for peace were ignored. The respectable people present quietly watched what was going on and did not take steps to prevent the action or to walk away. And this allowed the riot to continue.

At a disturbance at Holywood, outside Belfast, on 4 January 1986, politicians intervened to end a riot. Here, unlike the riots we have focused on, there seems to have been more direct paramilitary involvement. The politicians had initially given speeches from a nearby platform. When the rioting began, they first urged the rioters to cease their more extravagant exploits. They then asked respectable onlookers to withdraw their effective support by going home. Here, as elsewhere, once the crowd had gone, the remaining, comparatively few stone- and bottle- and firebomb-throwers could be dealt with efficiently by the police.

Even within a continuing riot, there are sometimes successful attempts to exercise control and to moderate behavior. At one riot, a man threatened Buckley with violence if he did not immediately leave the scene. Another man, overhearing the exchange, interceded. He took the heat out of the situation by politely advising Buckley to leave.

Of course, the major constraint upon rioters is the police. Part of the thrill and enjoyment for both stone-throwers and spectators is to escalate the riot in order to inconvenience or embarrass the police. There is, however, a risk of pushing the police too far. They may then give up a tolerant posture and react with more dangerous force. The police can show directly that while they will provisionally accept some types of bad behavior, other forms are to them less tolerable.

We came to believe that there was an unspoken rule that one does not throw missiles directly *at* policemen. The tacit agreement, only sometimes broken, is that rioters will only throw stones and bottles high in the air. In this way, the policemen can clearly see the missiles and deflect them with their shields.

In Obins Street, when excitement was at its height, one stone-thrower threw a stone at a policeman's shin, instead of aiming the usual high lob. The policeman quickly lowered his shield. A second man, seizing his opportunity, threw another stone directly at the policeman's briefly exposed throat. Fortuitously, the policeman's visor saved him from injury.

His fellow policemen clearly disapproved of this type of stone-throwing. From casually and good-naturedly fending off missiles, the policemen excitedly and fiercely began to point. Wagging their forefingers in rhythmical unison, they indicated to each other the culprit.

The man who had thrown the stone became very agitated. He was, as it happened, extraordinarily noticeable, since he was wearing a bright, almost incandescent, new Orange collarette. Immediately, an older man who appeared to have some authority with the crowd began to intercede. He urged both the man to behave himself and the policemen to stop pointing at him.

The meaning of the policemen's gestures had been clear. If there was to be a baton charge — as seemed plausible at that moment — the man would have been a target. He floundered. His pride would not let him retreat, yet his fear would not let him stay. His situation transmitted a clear message about the inadvisability of overly aggressive stone-throwing. By such means as this, within the difficult bounds set by their situation, the police could impose restrictions and rules on the crowd that was pelting them with stones and bottles.

At all events, the police stood, without retaliating, sometimes for hours at a time, while a crowd hurled bottles and stones at them. Only when the spectators had drifted away and a few comparatively isolated individuals were still throwing bottles would the police move in. Then, often with great suddenness, they would bang them on the head and bundle them into a vehicle for later prosecution.

One reason for this iron discipline is clear. This is the presence of the press, for, it is alleged, the police are less scrupulous when the press are absent. On the Catholic more than the Protestant side, a prime aim of the rioters is to discredit the police. This they hope to do by tempting them to behave badly.

The press are usually welcome at republican demonstrations and riots.

First, in a general way, they draw attention to the republican cause. Second, the demonstrations and riots dramatize the supposed conflict between oppressor and oppressed (Briton and Gael) that republicans wish to claim is the dominant frame. If the police can be persuaded to misbehave in front of the press, then this is an added bonus.

In the Protestant riots described here, the situation was a little more confused. The police were, for them, representatives of the law and order that loyalists usually claim to uphold. It was only in an immediate and local sense that the police had become their opponents, because they had impeded the loyalists' right to go into their traditional areas. The loyalists' aims in demonstrating were to illustrate their opposition to an immediate injustice, not to present themselves as rebellious in any general way to a legally constituted authority. Many rioters, therefore, resented the press for portraying them in precisely the same light as comparable Catholic rioters. In consequence, there were direct and violent attacks upon journalists during the riots in 1985. Loyalists did not especially want to have their conflict with authority depicted on a world stage. For them, this was a private quarrel. It was intended to instruct not the world press, but the government and the police themselves.

Concluding Remarks

As in the last two chapters, these various incidents illustrate a symbiotic relationship between actors and spectators. In this case, we have discussed the relation between those who attack the police and those who condone the attacks.

Each group of people in a riot has its own distinctive goals. Both stone-throwers and spectators no doubt like to see the dramatization of the territorial rights of their own side. But the young rioters are also engaged in the pursuit of thrills, danger, and the joys of embarrassing and attacking their more general opponents, the police. The spectators, however, take a more vicarious pleasure in the sight. They are pleased to see a forceful expression of their viewpoint acted out before their eyes.

This scenario, of course, contains a constant danger that the stone-throwers, especially when directly influenced by paramilitary organizations, might act wholly beyond the expectation of the more passive onlookers. This, however, never seemed to happen in the riots that we witnessed in 1985.

Rioting, we have argued, is often a playful form of activity, comparable to certain kinds of carnival. Indeed, it is out of carnival-like occasions of loyalist and republican festivals that many riots actually develop. We suggest that the framework of a playful carnival is partly responsible for the frequency and pattern of rioting in Northern Ireland. Here, as elsewhere, norm-violating behavior by working-class youths receives a tacit permission and social value. At these times, socially inferior and insignificant individuals become "king for a day," achieving a brief leading role in the eyes of their social superiors. Here, as in the theater, they act out for their approving audience scenes that reflect a broader rhetorical truth about social and political realities.

11

FIELDWORK BY A. D. BUCKLEY   The
Chosen
Few

Biblical
Texts
in a
Society
with
Secrets

Like the Protestant churches, the Orange Order and its sister institutions, the Royal Arch Purple Chapter and the Royal Black Institution, can claim to represent and in some ways typify Ulster Protestantism. Their aims, in each case, are to uphold Protestantism as a religion and to uphold the interests of Northern Ireland's Protestants.

Compared with other groups in Northern Irish society, the Orange, Arch Purple, and Black institutions are fairly moderate. They describe themselves as religious, and they are anxious to rid themselves of any rowdy elements. In the previous chapter we have just described riotous activity in which Orangemen were involved. Also, we have shown that rioting has long been associated with festivals organized by the Orange Order. Despite this, these organizations themselves are made up of law-abiding citizens, and their activities are usually nothing but peaceful.

The three orders are in many respects like their Catholic equivalent, the Ancient Order of Hibernians, whose demonstrations have also sometimes been accompanied by riot. Each of them certainly represents a segment of society eager to uphold the interests of their ethnic group. But none of them is, in Northern Irish terms, extreme.

As with the churches, the more active members of each of these three different organizations occupy a special world that has its own preoccupations. These interests seem somewhat esoteric to outsiders. Enthusiasts in these bodies are curators of a highly elaborate tradition that includes rituals and other genres of symbolism. Because of the continued interest and activity of the experts and enthusiasts within the institutions, less enthusiastic members and sometimes complete outsiders can participate more occasionally.

All these organizations employ an elaborate array of metaphors that originate in biblical texts. This chapter will concentrate on the symbolism of one of these organizations, the Royal Black Institution, suggesting that the continuing popularity of this association is due in part to the perceived relevance of these metaphors and texts to social, political, and religious issues in modern Ulster.

This chapter will continue to argue that a person's identity is partially structured by being translated into other, more prototypical images. The biblical texts used in the social dramas of the Royal Black Institution provide a set of metaphors that allow Blackmen to see themselves as similar, in certain respects, to the Israelites, Jews, and Christians in the Bible. As members of an institution devoted to the defense of the Protestant faith, Blackmen can see themselves as "God's chosen few."

The symbols and rituals that connect the Blackmen with the Bible are not, however, only rhetorical in their purpose. Although rhetoric can enhance a person's self-respect, it is more properly directed at others. The significance of Orange and Black imagery is actually kept secret from nonmembers. The symbolism is, therefore, to use Goffman's expression (1959), part of the "backstage" life of the Royal Black Institution. It may be considered as part of the means whereby Blackmen work out the operational implications of their shared Protestant identity.

In two most useful studies, Santino (1983; 1989, 68ff.) has described the backstage conversations of people who work on Pullman trains in the United States. These men exchange free-ranging anecdotes exploring the infinity of subtle variations upon the fixed relationship that they have with their customers. Using his approach, this chapter will show how the members of the Black Institution use biblical metaphors to confront the variety of situations that arise out of their common identity as Ulster Protestants.

The biblical images do not contradict the standard forms of Protestant rhetoric. In some ways, they reinforce them. The more central function of the images, however, is to act as operational models. The Bible-based symbols of the Blackmen provide not so much rhetoric as food for practical thought.

The Brotherhood Tradition

The Imperial Grand Black Chapter of the British Commonwealth is more commonly called the Royal Black Institution, or simply the Black. Like its sister organizations, the Orange Order and the Arch Purple Chapter, it has its origins in the melange of secret societies that proliferated in the late eighteenth century both in Ireland and elsewhere. In the last century, it was one of a very large number of brotherhoods.

The brotherhood tradition reached its peak in the fifty years before World War I, though its origins are much older (see Buckley and Anderson 1988). Historically, the most important of these brotherhoods has been the Order of Freemasons, whose Grand Lodge in Dublin was set up in the early eighteenth century. The Freemasons, in turn, modeled themselves primarily upon the guilds that controlled the local governments of the major cities of Britain and Ireland well into the nineteenth century. Many Masonic higher degrees were modeled upon orders of chivalry, and not least upon the crusading orders, the Knights Templar and the Knights of Malta (see, for example, Forster 1982–84; Given 1959).

The eighteenth and nineteenth centuries produced a plethora of agrarian societies as well as the Masons. These agrarian societies were devoted in part to squabbling with each other and in part to engaging, sometimes through violence, in a variety of economic, religious, or political causes (Bartlett 1985; Biggar 1910; Donnelly 1978, 1981; Moody 1968; Robinson 1986; Williams 1973). No doubt in imitation of the Masons, but also copying directly the official guilds and chivalric orders, these bodies used secret oaths, passwords, signs, handshakes, and elaborate catechisms, legends, and rituals as an intrinsic part of their activity.

From the mid-nineteenth century on, there also grew up a number of large friendly societies, dedicated to the provision of health insurance (Buckley 1987). Many of these had headquarters in Britain. Sometimes these bodies too gave themselves the names of crafts, such as Foresters, Shepherds, or Gardeners. Thus they modeled themselves either directly upon the craft guilds or indirectly upon the Freemasons or each other. By the end of the nineteenth century, it had become almost obligatory, in Ireland as elsewhere, for any voluntary association formed for whatever purpose to have the form of a brotherhood (Buckley and Anderson 1988). They would typically have regalia and jewels, secret handshakes and signs, and a range of degrees and rituals.

Brotherhoods in Ireland included temperance societies such as the Good Templars, the Sons of Temperance, the Pioneers, and the Rechabites; drinking clubs such as the Buffaloes; religious groups such as the Roman Catholic sodalities and the Knights of St. Columbanus; and boys' clubs such as the Boy Scouts. All these were recognizably within the same brotherhood tradition, though they had differing purposes. All belonged to different "worlds," in Finnegan's sense of the term (1989), and they had separate identities that were often jealously guarded.

This brotherhood tradition still persists in Ireland, though it has declined. Individual bodies usually recruit their members from a fairly narrow segment of society. Nevertheless, the broader tradition transcends differences of social class, ethnic affiliation, and even gender. It provides a striking example of how one set of social relationships can be copied as an operational model for another set of quite different relationships.

Orange, Arch Purple, and Black

The Orange, Arch Purple, and Black institutions are three interrelated loyalist brotherhoods, of which the most famous is the Orange Order.[1] The Orange Order was founded in 1795 after the Battle of the Diamond, a skirmish in County Armagh between Protestant and Catholic agrarian secret societies called, respectively, the Peep o' Day Boys and the Defenders. Nowadays the Order is organized locally into lodges, each with its own Worshipful Master, secretary, treasurer, and other officers. Each local lodge is represented in a district lodge and a county lodge, with the Grand Lodge at the apex. Its administrative headquarters are in Belfast.

The second institution of this trio is the Royal Arch Purple Chapter (see Cargo et al. 1943). Each of the local chapters of this organization is drawn from a specific Orange lodge. Nevertheless, even locally, the officers of an Orange lodge are different from those of its corresponding Royal Arch Purple chapter. The hierarchical organization at district, county, and Grand Chapter levels is wholly distinct from that of the Orange Order. It has no fixed headquarters and is the least well known of the three bodies.

The third body, the Royal Black Institution, is organized in preceptories, each drawn from several Arch Purple chapters. It too has its own distinct hierarchical form of organization. Its headquarters are in Lurgan in County Armagh.

Of the three organizations, the Black Institution has the most extensive symbolism. Like the others, the Black Institution is a society with secrets, the secrets consisting of rituals, handshakes, signs, and passwords. Despite the secrecy, the Black Institution, like the Orange Order, regularly holds public demonstrations and parades at which much of its symbolism is openly displayed.

As well as having officers and hierarchical structures of administration,

Figure 14. Member of the Orange Order, wearing collarette and carrying banner. (Courtesy of the Ulster Folk and Transport Museum)

the three institutions also have degrees. The Orange Order has two degrees, Orange and Purple, each with its own ceremonial and ritual of initiation. When an Orangeman has passed through the Purple degree, he may join the Royal Arch Purple chapter associated with his lodge. Of all the degrees through which an Orangeman may pass, this is the most elaborate and the most terrifying. Emblems of the Royal Arch Purple, derived from its ritual, are worn on Orange collarettes at demonstrations organized by the Orange Order. They include the Arch itself, which has a prominent keystone; a three-stepped ladder, the steps signifying faith, hope, and charity; and a five-pointed star, signifying the five points of fellowship. Other images belong to the Royal Arch Purple but are also found in Black symbolism. These are the Ark of the Covenant, pots of manna, Aaron's rod, and other images related to the Israelites' sojourn in the desert.

The Royal Arch Purple degree seems in some ways similar to the Royal Arch degree in Irish Freemasonry. It is the first of the higher degrees in both systems, and the two degrees share much symbolism. But the degrees are signif-

Figure 15. Orange Order collarette emblems. (Courtesy of the Ulster Folk and Transport Museum)

icantly different. The Masonic Royal Arch in Ireland recounts the repair of Solomon's temple by Josiah, while the Royal Arch Purple tells the story of the Exodus. Moreover, many Orangemen feel that the Royal Arch Purple has a similar status in Orangeism to the third degree in Craft Masonry, being a consummation of the earlier Orange and Purple degrees. However, not everyone in the Orange Order chooses to be initiated into the Royal Arch Purple. For them, and indeed for many who actually become Arch Purplemen, this third degree is but a stepping stone into the degrees of the Black.

There are eleven degrees in the Royal Black Institution.[2] A member will ordinarily be initiated through each of them at successive monthly meetings.

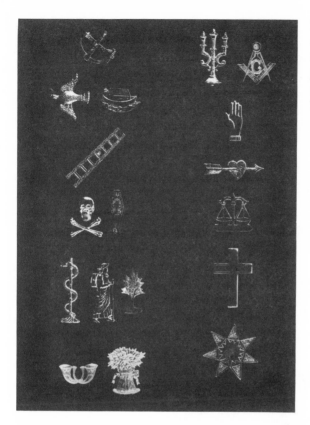

Figure 16. Collarette emblems of a Royal Black Institution preceptory. (Courtesy of the Ulster Folk and Transport Museum)

For most of its members, the Black Institution is the highest form of Orangeism. Other Orangemen are sometimes skeptical of this opinion. Orangemen who are also Freemasons sometimes describe the Black rites as an inferior form of Masonry.

As the Royal Arch Purple degree is similar to the Royal Arch degree of Freemasonry, so the Black Institution resembles the Masonic Order of the Temple. Both institutions regard themselves as orders of chivalry. Both are referred to as "the Black" and both have black emblems. Their members address each other as "Sir Knight." The name *preceptory* is common both to the Black Institution and to the Masonic degrees of Knight Templar and Knight of Malta. There is, moreover, a similarity between the Masonic Knight Templar ritual and that of the first Royal Black degree in their use of the skull and crossbones. And both organizations have Constantine's motto, "*In hoc signo vinces*" (In this sign [the Cross] you conquer). Both organizations perceive themselves as defenders of Christianity, although the Black Institution understands "Christianity" to mean Protestantism.

Biblical texts occur in four major contexts in the Black Institution: in rituals, in emblems, in banner pictures, and in the sermons given each year when the Orange lodges and Black preceptories hold a parade and a church service. Initiation rituals in the Black Institution, as in the Royal Arch Purple Chapter and, to a lesser extent, in the Orange Order itself, are founded in specific biblical texts. Two lecturers who supervise these ceremonies give a lecture as part of the proceedings. This is actually more like a catechism during which Bible stories are read out and explained. The initiate, as part of these rites, sometimes takes the role of one or even successively several of the characters in the plot. Once initiated into a specific degree, the candidate may be told the chapters and verses of the texts upon which the rite has been based. He may then, at his leisure, read the texts for himself.

It is common for an individual, once initiated into a Black degree, to wear a metal emblem of that degree on the black-colored collarette that he wears during ceremonial parades. These emblems are not always related to their texts in a way that outsiders will readily recognize. Typically they depict gardeners' tools, a dove with an olive branch, Noah's Ark, a seven-stepped ladder, a skull and crossbones, a bush, a man, a stick with a snake wrapped around it, two crossed trumpets, a square and compasses in which is inscribed the letter G, a hand, an arrow piercing a heart, a balance, a red cross, and a seven-pointed star. Since few outsiders are even certain that the different emblems correspond to biblical texts, their meaning is fairly obscure. They may have been deliberately contrived at the outset to disguise from outsiders the ritual content of the different degrees. Not everybody collects all the emblems to which he is entitled. Many Blackmen who have been through the eleven degrees wear only the emblem of the highest degree, the Red Cross.

These same emblems are also to be found on the wall charts, printed for purposes of instruction, that adorn the walls of Orange halls where Black preceptory meetings take place. On such charts are not only Black but also Orange and Arch Purple symbols, and other images — the all-seeing eye, a beehive, an hourglass, and expressions such as "Cemented with Love" — that are found among brotherhoods generally. Similar emblems decorate certificates, warrants, and other official documents of the Institution.

These same biblical texts appear on the banners displayed at Black demonstrations. Some Black banners have designs made up entirely of emblems. Some of these are embroidered. Most, however, are painted on silk in the manner established by George Tutill of London (Gorman 1973, 49ff.). These typ-

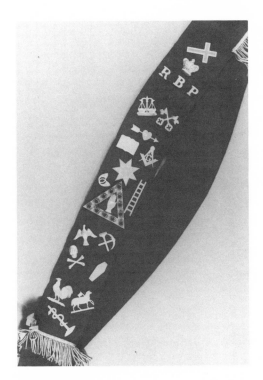

Figure 17. Royal Black Institution preceptory sash. (Courtesy of the Ulster Folk and Transport Museum)

ically give the name and number of the preceptory (for example, Mount Horeb RBP 270), and sometimes say that this Royal Black Preceptory is "encamped at" the particular place where it meets. On the painted banners is sometimes to be found the coat of arms of the Black Institution, on which these same emblems are an important feature. But much more important here are the pictures that are the main feature of most Black banners. Nearly all of these illustrate a biblical text.

It is important to note that not all the paintings on Black banners that portray biblical scenes relate to Black initiation rites. Whereas collarette emblems do have a direct reference to Black degrees, a minority of the banner pictures were chosen because the preceptory members happened to like the particular story.

This chapter will not describe the rituals of the Black Institution or connect the rites of specific degrees to specific biblical texts. The rites are in any case secret, known to this writer only in outline. The lecturers who organize them learn the texts by heart. No recordings are made, and nobody may write them down. The only real way to learn the rituals is not only to become a mem-

Figure 18. Member of a Royal Black Institution preceptory, wearing collarette and apron. (Courtesy of the Ulster Folk and Transport Museum)

ber of a preceptory, but also to become a lecturer. Unfortunately, one can do this only after making a solemn undertaking to keep the ritual secret.

Apart from this, some of the rites are clearly great fun. Part of the fun lies in the ignorance of the initiate about what will happen next. People say, for example, that an Arch Purple initiate must "ride a goat." This is not strictly true, but it is not far from the spirit of what happens. It is not for a researcher to publicize what little he knows of these amusing mysteries and spoil the fun.

Toward an Interpretation of the Texts

Discussion here will be confined to the texts referred to in pictures and emblems seen at the Black Institution's public ceremonies. There will be reference too to wall charts and to other readily available documents. The aim is to show what meaning these texts might have for an Ulster Protestant who participates in a Black preceptory.

Figure 19. Wall chart of the Orange Order and Royal Black Institution, showing emblems. (Courtesy of the Ulster Folk and Transport Museum)

Figure 20. Royal Black Institution preceptory banner. (Courtesy of the Ulster Folk and Transport Museum)

*Figure 21. Demonstration by
members of a Royal Black
Institution preceptory. (Courtesy
of the Ulster Folk and Transport
Museum)*

*Figure 22. Banner of a Royal Black Institution preceptory.
(Courtesy of the Ulster Folk and Transport Museum)*

The difficulties in doing this are twofold. First, Orangemen and Black-men are often unwilling to discuss these matters with outsiders. Second, my strong impression is that the contents of the rites and the related texts are sel-dom a topic for conversation even among these organizations' members. There is nothing very peculiar about this second point. It certainly does not imply that participants find no meaning in the rites and related texts. To take part in a rite, to read a text, to follow a banner, even to wear an emblem, is rather like con-versing with a person. One does not need to discuss the conversation with a third party for it to have an impact.

Clearly it would have been useful if more Blackmen had been forthcom-ing about the significance of their pictures and emblems. Since what Turner (1962) calls "native exegesis" was sadly lacking, however, I must fall back upon studying the symbols in their social context and in their relation to other sym-bols. This is to explore their "positional meaning" (Turner 1962). My feeling is that the meaning of the texts is not inordinately obscure. The lack of obscurity, indeed, may be a good reason why Blackmen do not trouble to discuss their rites: there is, quite simply, nothing much to discuss.

It may be useful to try to separate out some layers of meaning that exist in the emblems and banner pictures. First, there is the emblem or banner picture itself. This is a very specific sign that refers to a particular element in the larger biblical text. A bystander who is not a Blackman may merely glimpse the ban-ner or collarette emblem as it flashes past him in a procession. Such a person may not be able quickly to do the act of translation that relates the emblem or picture to its text. This is particularly true of the collarette emblems, whose relevance to the text is usually far from clear. Even from a banner painting, the casual observer who sees, say, Elijah receiving food from an angel, or Daniel in the lions' den, may have only the dimmest recollections of what these stories are about. For him, the emblems and paintings form part of the public display. They can, therefore, be understood only within this important, and indeed complex, but restricted frame.

For the Blackman too, the emblems and paintings are part of the public display, but for him they may have an additional significance. First, a Blackman will have learned during his initiation which emblem belongs to which degree and to which text. He will, therefore, have enacted in a serious or half-comic drama the relevant Bible story. Second, even if he did not quite catch all he was told at his own initiation, he is likely to have witnessed frequently the initiation of other candidates. For him, therefore, the emblems and pictures are part of a frame provided by a biblical text.

It is possible to explore the levels of meaning to be found in the texts themselves. There is first the immediate sense of the words of the text, which refer to the adventures of Noah, Moses, Daniel, and others. At this level, there is not much room for interpretation. The words mean simply what convention and the dictionary say that they mean.

Turner (1965) and Charsley (1987) have written about the multivocality of symbols. Using their approach, one might hope to be able to distill many more allegorical meanings from the narrative. But it is doubtful that the texts referred to in Black emblems and banner paintings are multivocal. On the contrary, they have a quite restricted range of possible allegorical meanings. From the perspective of a unionist Ulsterman in an organization that upholds Protestantism against Catholicism, the allegorical meanings seem few and inescapable.

The Black rites and their related texts do not provide Blackmen with complete allegorical solutions to the social and political problems of being loyalist Protestants. Nevertheless, by identifying himself with the various Israelite and Jewish heroes in the texts, a Blackman may at least find food for thought. He can use them as metaphors to construct operational frameworks for dealing with new and immediate situations. With only a few exceptions, the problems that the texts confront are the difficulties faced by God's chosen people when dealing with heathens, foreigners, and other villains.

One should not, however, think that the different texts represented in banners and emblems all have the same structure or convey the same message. Most of the texts do have similar frameworks, telling of an individual or a people living in a foreign land or among sinners or heathens. But within this pattern, the texts explore many possibilities. The texts provide a means for Blackmen to explore a central feature of their fixed situation. This is the relation — social, political, and theological — between Catholicism and Protestantism.

The strictly limited sample of banner pictures to be discussed here were photographed by personnel from the Ulster Folk and Transport Museum at the annual Black demonstrations held in the towns of Antrim, Dromore, and Lisburn on the last Saturday of August 1982. This collection forms part of the much larger slide collection concerned with the Orange, Arch Purple, and Black institutions in the museum's photographic archive.3 Consideration will also be given to emblems on Black collarettes, sashes, wall charts, and certificates. These also exist in the Ulster Folk and Transport Museum's material culture and photographic collections.

The Texts

The following is a brief summary of the texts referred to in banner paintings, wall charts, and collarette emblems. Informants kindly told me the precise biblical references. Also given here are the related emblems found on sashes, collarettes, and wall charts. There is also a mention of the number of occasions on which a scene from the particular texts appeared in the restricted sample of banner paintings under consideration.

It would be easy to gain an impression that the texts referred to in the pictures and emblems give a simple résumé of the Bible from beginning to end. While the texts do include both the Garden of Eden and the City of God, this selection strongly emphasizes certain biblical themes while systematically avoiding others. To draw out the peculiarity of the texts, it will be useful, therefore, to list fourteen of the most characteristic texts or groups of texts. When this has been done, the few remaining texts can be shown to provide a contextual frame for the majority.

1. Noah escapes from the flood (Genesis 2–3). Emblems: dove, Noah's ark. 18 banners.

   Noah is among wicked men. When God destroys the world with a flood, Noah escapes with his family. God condemns Noah's grandson Canaan and his heirs to serve the descendants of Noah's other sons.

2. Abraham, Isaac, and the sacrifice (Genesis 22). Emblems: none. 2 banners.

   God commands Abraham to sacrifice Isaac, his son. In consequence of Abraham's loyalty, God finds him a substitute sacrifice. Isaac escapes.

3. Jacob's dream: the promise of Canaanite land (Genesis 25–28). Emblem: seven-stepped ladder. 5 banners.

   God promises the land of Canaan to Jacob in a dream. Jacob, unlike his hairy brother, Esau, refuses to marry Canaanite women.

4. Joseph rules in Egypt (Genesis 37–50). Emblems: skull and crossbones, coffin, *in memoria mortua*. 8 banners.

   Jacob's favorite son, Joseph, is sold into slavery by his brothers. Because he has favor with God, Joseph escapes death, becomes servant to the king, and rules over Egypt.

5. Moses escapes from the Egyptians (Exodus). Emblems: Aaron's rod, Moses, the burning bush, tablets of stone. 22 banners.

   The Hebrews are enslaved by the Egyptians and their male offspring are thrown into the Nile. The child Moses escapes, and finally leads his people out of Egypt. God gives him the law on tablets of stone.

6. Joshua conquers Jericho (Joshua 2–6). Emblems: trumpets, corn, twelve stones. 1 banner.

   With the help of a Canaanite harlot, Rahab, the Israelites conquer Jericho. Rahab and her family escape the slaughter.

7. The two and a half tribes (Joshua 22). Emblem: Three triangles marked R, G, and M. No banners.

   When the Israelites conquer the land of Canaan, the tribes of Reuben and Gad and half the tribe of Manasseh are given land from the other tribes. When they build an altar, the main body of tribes construes this as rebellion. Nevertheless, they stay faithful. Eventually the altar is interpreted as a sign of the bond between the separated groups.

8. Gideon's chosen few (Judges 6–7). Emblems: none. 1 banner.

   Gideon selects a small band to defeat the numerically superior Midianites.

9. Ruth and Naomi (Ruth). Emblems: none. 1 banner.

   In time of famine, an Israelite woman, Naomi, goes to live among the Moabites. Her sons marry local women. When the famine recedes and Naomi returns home, one of her daughters-in-law, Ruth, insists on returning with her. Ruth remarries in Israel and her son becomes grandfather to King David.

10. David defeats Goliath (1 Samuel 17–18). Emblems: five stones, a sling. 45 banners.

    David the shepherd boy defeats the giant Philistine Goliath with a sling.

11. Elijah defeats the prophets of Baal (1 Kings 16–19). Emblem: a hand. 19 banners.

    When King Ahab marries a foreign woman and worships Baal, Elijah proclaims a drought. Elijah challenges the prophets of Baal to a contest. When they lose, they are slaughtered, and the drought ends. God rescues Elijah from his enemies. He later ascends to heaven in a chariot of fire.

12. Jehu's purge (2 Kings 10–12). Emblem: an arrow (sometimes piercing a heart). No banners.

    Jehu kills the apostate Ahab's son with an arrow, defeats the prophets of Baal, and restores the temple.

13. Daniel (Daniel 2, 3, 5, and 6). Emblem: a balance. 12 banners.

    When some Jews refuse to worship a golden image, they are put in a furnace, from which they escape unscathed. Daniel, because of his prophetic abilities, becomes ruler over Babylon. When, however, he prays to God, he is fed to the lions. He emerges unhurt.

14. New Testament references (Matthew 3, John 19–21). Emblem: a red cross. 6 banners.

    Matthew 3 tells of the escape by Jesus from the slaughter of the innocents. John 19–21 is an account of Christ's victory over death at the resurrection.

It is clear enough that these fourteen texts do not deal with identical or even precisely similar situations, but there are strong resemblances among them. The dominant pattern is of an individual or group of people, who have found favor in the eyes of God, confronting alien peoples. These aliens are not all of the same kind. Some are wicked people, as in the story of Noah; some are upholders of a rival religion; others are merely foreigners.

Another major theme is faithfulness. When God chooses someone who in return is loyal to God, then that person will prosper. Perhaps he will be rescued from God's wrath; perhaps the rescue will be from the wrath of his enemies. He may gain a victory, sometimes against the overwhelming strength of his opponent. When a heathen or foreigner changes allegiance and becomes loyal to God (as with Rahab or Ruth), that person may be saved and may prosper. Where, as with Ahab, one of God's chosen people turns to a foreign religion, he must expect ruin. The different texts therefore all explore variations upon the same theme: the encounter between God's chosen people and heathens or foreigners or the wicked.

The remaining four groups of texts do not significantly alter the picture. Rather, they provide a frame for the main body of texts. They are as follows:

15. Adam and Eve (Genesis 2–3). Emblem: gardener's tools, Adam and Eve, angel with flaming sword. 4 banners.

    The text tells of Adam and Eve, the forbidden fruit, and the expulsion from the Garden of Eden.

16. The building of Solomon's temple (1 Kings 5–8, 2 Chronicles 2–8). Emblems: a royal-blue apron, square and compasses, builder's tools. 7 banners.

    The texts elaborate at great length the building of the temple.

17. The City of God (Revelation 21). This text is found with the other New Testament references (number 14 above). Emblem: red cross. 1 banner.

    John the Divine has a vision of the City of God.

18. Star and Garter (Exodus 28, Hebrews 7, Genesis 14, 18ff., Revelation 5:7–10). Emblem: seven-pointed star, (formerly) a garter. No banners.

These texts are unusual here in that they are not really stories. Exodus 28 gives a detailed account of the Levitical priesthood, describing the garments worn by Aaron the Levite and his descendants, the priests of Israel. Hebrews 7 recalls how Melchizedek, king of Salem and priest of God, blessed Abraham and was given tithes in return (Genesis 14, 18ff.). The Epistle to the Hebrews explains that, like Melchisedek, one need not be a descendant of Aaron to be a priest, but merely a believer. And in Revelation 5:7–10, a song is sung to the Lamb: "Or thou was slain, and hast redeemed us to God by thy blood . . . and hast made unto our God kings and priests and we shall reign on the earth."

The first story, that of Adam and Eve, provides a setting and explanation for the frankly depressing scenario of conflict, destruction, and alienation to which even the chosen people are subject in this world. The building of Solomon's temple rounds off the story of the sojourners in the desert. And the final glimpse of the City of God concludes the journey of those who struggle in the world today.

The references labeled "Star and Garter" (the name of a degree), based in the Epistle to the Hebrews and rather tenuously reinforced by the text from Revelation 5, make an allegedly anti-Catholic point. This is that the priesthood since Christ consists not of the descendants of Aaron, but of those who are faithful to Christ. For this reason, Hebrews is sometimes called the Protestant Epistle.

It is worth pointing out that although these texts are indeed biblical, they concern themselves only with certain themes, avoiding others. Consider some the themes that are omitted. Most glaring of all is the lack of references to the great Pauline emphasis upon sin and redemption that is so important to the fundamentalists (see chapter 7). There are certainly sinners in the above narratives, but these sinners are not redeemed of their sins. Rather, their most common role in the various narratives is as villains. They are there to be defeated, not saved. There is little reference here to loving one's neighbor or turning the other cheek. The "wisdom" literature (Proverbs, Ecclesiastes) is excluded. Where there are prophecies and prophets (Joseph, Elijah, Elisha, Daniel, Revelation), the prophecies provide mere incidents in the more important superordinate narratives. Nowhere are there speculations or insights into the timing or nature of Christ's second coming. Missing are the sufferings of Job, the sexuality of Solomon's Song, and Hosea's marital problems. There is no reference to those who grind the faces of the poor (Isaiah 3:15) nor to camels who cannot climb through the eyes of needles (Matthew 19:24). In short, the Black Institution's banner pictures and emblems point to an unrepresentative or biased sample of the Bible as a whole.

This does not mean that the Black Institution is non-Christian. Christian critics of Freemasonry often point to the Old Testament bias of that organization. They say it is theologically Jewish rather than Christian (Hanna 1963; McCormick 1984). I do not argue this kind of case here. At least in principle, but often in practice, Blackmen are also churchgoers. They do not see Black rites as a substitute for church services. Whatever Christianity they fail to pick up in the preceptory, they no doubt hope to learn in church. Moreover, whatever teachings are absent from Black ritual and symbolism, what remains is still genuinely biblical. The themes evoked by the Black rites and the public symbols are major and legitimate biblical themes.

The Black Institution nevertheless has a very distinctive emphasis in its selection of texts. The texts' most prevailing theme is of God's chosen people confronting those who are apostate, alien, heathen, or merely wicked. Since the texts are encountered in an institution whose primary declared purpose is to reinforce Protestantism against Catholicism, their significance is unambiguous. One could hardly fail to recognize the similarity between the situation of the Ulster Protestant and that of the heroes of the various stories.

Like the Israelites in Canaan, Ulster Protestants have been given, and now occupy, an alien land. The foreigners whose land they occupy are — like the Canaanites, the Midianites, the Philistines, and others — adherents of an alien religion. Like Jacob, Ulster Protestants steadfastly avoid marrying the daughters of their enemies. Like the heroes of the stories, they lay great stress on loyalty, both to their religion and to the crown.

Concluding Remarks

Black symbolism invites the Blackman to see himself and his fellow Ulster Protestants as similar to God's chosen people in the Bible. But one should not draw conclusions that are too radical. If one were to ask a Blackman directly whether he believes himself to be one of God's chosen people, he would probably respond with appropriate embarrassment. The idea of having been chosen by God, however, is one that has some significance in Protestant thought in Ulster, and it takes a variety of forms.

At its mildest, individuals will maintain that when they do God's work, they do so by the grace of God. This implies that they have been chosen by God to do His work. Sometimes such an image is meant only lightly. In other cases, however, as chapter 6 showed, this idea is powerfully and literally intended.

One version of this opinion occurs among conservative Presbyterians. Such people adopt a view, which they attribute to Calvin, that they are of the elect. This is but another way of saying that they have been chosen by God.

A group of people in Northern Ireland, small but influential, are called British Israelites. They hold that the peoples of the United Kingdom (and hence those of the United States and the white Commonwealth) are descendants of the ancient Israelites. The British Israelite version of history begins with the division of Solomon's kingdom into two parts. The southern kingdom of Judah, they say, was conquered by the Babylonians, and the history of this people, the Jews, appears in the later books of the Bible. The remaining ten tribes of Israel, who made up the northern kingdom, were lost. British Israelites say they were dispersed throughout northern Europe. There, as Angles, Saxons, Jutes, Vikings, and Normans, they reassembled in Britain and Ireland to form the British people.

According to the British Israelites, at the time of the Babylonian exile the prophet Jeremiah set off northward. He carried with him the Ark of the Covenant, and also the stone that had served as a pillow for Jacob when he had his dream at Bethel. Jeremiah traveled with the daughters of Zedekiah, the last preexilic king of Judah. They landed in Carrickfergus in County Antrim. One of these daughters, Temar-Tephi, married the Israelitish High King of Ireland, Eochaidu. British Israelites have traced the descent of the present queen, Elizabeth II, through James I of Scotland and the Irish king Fergus the Great to Eochaidu and Temar-Tephi and thence to King David. For the British Israelites, the people of Britain (and especially those who are loyal both to the Queen and to the Protestant faith) are, in an Old Testament sense, God's chosen people.

The stone used by Jacob at Bethel is said to have been taken to Tara in County Meath, where it was used at the coronations of the ancient kings of Ireland. It is said to have been moved later to Scone in Scotland, where it was used in Scottish coronations. The stone beneath the Coronation Chair in Westminster Abbey is said to be the same stone. Just as the stone was used to promise land to Israel, and just as it was used to crown the ancient Israelitish kings of Ireland and of Scotland, so it is used today to crown the monarchs of the United Kingdom, who are descended from King David.

The symbolism of the Black Institution reflects a more general tendency in Ulster Protestantism that conceives of Ulster Protestants, or perhaps a select group of such Protestants, as having an especially close relationship to God. The relationship is defined in two ways. The first says that they are beneath God's protection. The second says that they are the instrument of God's will (see chapters 7 and 8 above).

The symbols and rituals of the Royal Black Institution are not, however, narrowly dogmatic. They do not just provide a set of beliefs that rigidly define the place of Protestants in Ulster or in the world. Rather, their emblems and images relate to a fairly big set of quite different stories. These, in turn, can serve as metaphors, generating more immediate operational frames to define practical circumstances. As such, the stories have a direct bearing on the practical construction of Ulster Protestant identity.

The Black banners, emblems, and rites do not refer merely to an arbitrary collection of Bible stories. Rather, they tell of a people who inherited a promised land that had once belonged to someone else. By confining their Bible study to this narrow range of texts, Blackmen can perceive Ulster Protestants as, in some sense, God's chosen people. In this framework, the Black Knights may feel themselves to be, like the followers of Gideon, God's chosen few.

12

Ethnic and Other Identities

FIELDWORK BY A. D. BUCKLEY

Are There Really Two Traditions?

We have argued that, despite their obvious differences, distinct kinds of identity, such as those based on gender or social class or ethnicity, are interrelated. One reason is that the frames that define identity are structured by similar metaphors. Thus, different institutions or groups — even individuals — are said to be besieged or invaded (or besieging or invading), or superior or inferior to another, and so forth. Often, too, one frame is a direct metaphor for another.

The discussion will now end by returning to issues raised in chapter 1. The first section of this chapter considers again ethnic stereotypes. Because identities of many different kinds are so similar, we can show how the ethnic groups in Ulster have often borrowed their supposedly distinctive cultural traits from other forms of identity. Cultural traits that allegedly belong to one or the other of the two ethnic groups are often better described as belonging to a geographical region or a social class.

The second section considers the social construction of a unified identity. We have said that as a person enters and leaves any of countless frames, so his or her identity will also change. A question therefore arises: How, despite presenting so many different partial identities, can someone nevertheless be always the selfsame person? We shall claim that these different identities can fit together sequentially into a narrative. Also, an individual can present several different partial identities simultaneously, constructing an image of himself as a multifaceted human being. One effect of this, however, is that any given feature of the individual's identity — say, his ethnicity — will be very specific to that one person. It will reflect his other statuses and roles. It will even reflect his immediate situation.

In chapter 4, we looked at individuals who were members of the Long Stone Mission or the Long Stone Orange lodge, organizations that are directly concerned with ethnic identity. Later, we looked at the symbolic and ritual activities of Pentecostalists and Blackmen in more detail. It was clear that these people differed quite radically from one another and from nonmembers in the way they defined their ethnicity.

In the same way, members of a particular social class or gender will define their ethnicity differently than someone of a different class or gender. A person's ethnic identity is affected by his or her other partial identities because it is expressed in relation to these other identities. What ethnic identity means to one person, then, will be very different from what it means to another, and makes it difficult to define in abstraction what a Catholic or Protestant identity might be.

Given this, is it proper to speak of two distinct traditions or cultures in Ulster? This question will lead us to restate our earlier argument that identity is primarily a matter of social interaction. Ethnic identity arises through interactions that maintain social boundaries, and through consequent competition over resources. It is not primarily a consequence of cultural differences.

The conclusion will be that the two ethnic groups in Ulster have remarkably similar cultures. They differ from each other only in detail. More than this, even where there are differences, these differences are often elements in the same system. The two ethnic identities are, in effect, constructed in similar ways from the same cultural materials. As with the two sides in a soccer match, the two ethnic groups attack and defend different goals and they wear different colors. Nevertheless, they play the same game. Who a person is cannot be reduced to a set of emblems, however important these emblems may sometimes seem to be.

Geography, Class, and the Social Divide

We have suggested that a person's identity is often represented in a particular frame structured by metaphors. The person and his context are represented as though they were in a sense some other type of person or some other type of context. Thus upper-class Irish gentlewomen are described as though they were English. Thus God (a divine being) is described as though He were a nondivine being: a parent or an advocate, a son or a judge (see Feuerbach 1841). And thus people in everyday situations are treated as though they were subject to siege or invasion.

We shall now argue that many allegedly distinctive aspects of ethnic identity in Ulster are similarly borrowed from other forms of identity. In particular, many supposed cultural characteristics of the ethnic groups do not, in reality, belong to the ethnic groups at all. Some have been borrowed from real or supposed cultural traits belonging to geographical regions. Others are attributes of social classes.

Take geography first. According to Gregg (1972), there are four readily differentiable groups of English dialect spoken in the different regions of Ireland. These seem to correspond broadly to distributions of other cultural patterns.

The Republic of Ireland has a remarkably uniform dialect of its own. The major exception to this is in the *Gaelteacht* (Irish language–speaking) areas of the west of Ireland. There, not only do people speak the Irish language, but also there are dialects of English heavily influenced by Irish.

North of an area that corresponds roughly to the Northern Irish border, people speak the dialect known to linguists as Ulster Anglo-Irish. In addition, Ulster is divided geographically by the River Bann. Roughly (but not precisely) east of this river, but excluding the Glens of Antrim and including the northeast of Donegal, is another dialect. This is the Ulster Scots dialect, called by North Americans the Scots-Irish or Scotch-Irish dialect. There is also a differentiable Ulster Scots urban dialect in the larger towns (Gregg 1972).

There are other cultural peculiarities in these regions of distinctive dialect. Gailey has shown, for example, that some folk customs of a distinctively Scottish type occur only in those parts of Ulster where the Scots-Irish dialect is spoken. This is true of New Year "first-footing" and Christmas rhyming traditions (Gailey 1975). Ó Danachair has shown that with at least some folk customs (but not all), there exists a similar division along that other cultural divide, the Northern Irish border (Ó Danachair 1957, 1965, 1977).

It is sometimes argued that these regional variations are the results of invasions, population movements, and cultural contact. This contact has been primarily with Great Britain, though also with the Continent (Ó Danachair 1979).

On the basis of linguistic evidence, Barry (1972) suggests that a linguistic division existed long before the sixteenth century. The Irish spoken in the south of Ireland at that time was significantly different from that of the north, which was closer to Scots Gaelic. Onto this preexisting linguistic division, he argues, came later settlement from Britain. Those areas that now speak the Ulster Scots dialect (roughly east of the Bann) were settled by Scottish people. The division between northeast Ulster and mid-Ulster thus reflects the division between Scots and English settlement in the seventeenth century and earlier (see Gailey 1975; Robinson 1984, chap. 5).

The other linguistic divide, between Northern Ireland and the present Republic of Ireland, reflects the more prevailing contact with Britain. Ulster has been affected by continual contact with Scotland. The south of Ireland has been affected by contact with England. The dialects of the far west are due to the comparative isolation of these areas from both Scotland and England.

This kind of work can tempt the unwary. Cultural differences between the Irish regions can, for example, be seen as analogous to the differences between the nations and regions of the wider British Isles. These cultural-geographical areas can then be seen respectively as Scottish, English, and Irish in essence, with the west of Ireland claiming an especially undiluted form of Irishness. A further translation leads to Presbyterian, Episcopalian, and Catholic denominational identities.

Such a leap, however, should be made with the greatest of care. There is little doubt that the origin of this cultural diversity lies partly in the different forms of British cultural influence in these different regions. However, as the historian of the Ulster Plantation, P. S. Robinson, has written, "Cultural fusion, the mutual adoption of traits, interdependent development and subsequent evolution have given rise to patterns of cultural development that are neither 'Irish' and 'Catholic' nor 'British' and 'Protestant' in type" (Robinson 1984, 193–94). Within each region is a culture in which all of the people participate, whatever their politics, religion, or ethnicity.

Many writers have drawn attention to the fact that Catholics and Protestants allegedly have different traits of both personality and ethos. Donnan and McFarlane summarize these stereotypes neatly: "Protestants contrast their industriousness, cleanliness, loyalty to the State and freedom of religious expression with Catholic laziness, scruffiness, treachery, clannishness and priest domination. Catholics contrast Protestant bigotry, narrow-mindedness, discrimination and money-centredness with their own tolerance, openness and interest in 'culture'" (Donnan and McFarlane 1986, 386; see also Buckley 1982, chaps. 2 and 3; Harris 1972, chap. 8). Many of these differences, though here expressed in pejorative forms, are real enough, but are more accurately attributable not to ethnic so much as to regional and class differences.

Consider, for example, this joke: "What is the difference between a Ballymena man and a coconut? You can get a drink out of a coconut." Thus a man from Ballymena has allegedly "Scottish" characteristics, for the town of Ballymena is thought in some respects to typify the Ulster-Scots region east of the

Bann. In the popular imagination, however, as well as in statistical fact, the Ballymena man is not merely "Scottish"; he is also typically a Protestant. No great leap of imagination is needed to conflate both supposed and real regional differences into ethnic stereotypes. This readily occurs even though the culture of a Catholic in, for example, Ballymena is much the same as that of his Protestant neighbor. As Heslinga has shown, stereotypes of northerner and southerner derived from real cultural differences are often translated into stereotypes of Protestant and Catholic (Heslinga 1962). But in practice, the cultural differences between northerner and southerner are much more substantial and transcend both religious and ethnic boundaries.

Another dimension to the presumed cultural divergences between ethnic groups in Ulster is social class. In the present, and more so in the recent past, it has been a fact that Protestants have typically been wealthier than Catholics. This idea is still strongly present in popular stereotypes. Predominantly Catholic areas have tended to be poorer than areas where there are more Protestants.

In Ulster, those areas east of the Bann, where Protestants predominate, have historically been wealthier than those west of the Bann, where there are more Catholics. West Belfast, where Catholics predominate, has been poorer than east Belfast for a variety of reasons, including discrimination. And in Ireland as a whole, areas with the strongest Protestant influence, notably the south, east, and north coastal counties, have been wealthier than the Catholic midlands and west.

The classic statement of the intertwining of ethnic identity with social class at a more local level is made by Harris (1972, chap. 8). In the town that she calls Ballybeg, she says, those who live in the valley are better off than those who live in the hills. The valley contains more Protestants than Catholics, while on the hillside the proportions are reversed. Hence, the lifestyles of comparatively wealthy and comparatively poor people are perceived to be Protestant and Catholic lifestyles, respectively. On closer examination, however, Harris finds that the many Protestants who live in the hills participate wholeheartedly in the supposedly Catholic way of life. Conversely, many valley-living Catholics have a style of life barely distinguishable from that of their allegedly more respectable Protestant neighbors.

What we have in ethnic stereotypes of this kind is that special form of metaphor known as *synecdoche*. It is the case that for generations, Catholics have generally held lower-paying occupations than Protestants and have also had a higher rate of unemployment. From this came the well-known jibe that Catholics were "loyal to the half-crown [of social security] but not to the

Crown." It is also true that statistically speaking, Catholics have long been more numerous in the south and the west of Ireland than in the north and the east. In a similar way, Protestants are sometimes supposed typically to be clean-living fundamentalists, or at least evangelicals devoted to a strict morality (see Buckley 1982).

But not all Catholics are poor and unemployed and from the south or the west. Not all Protestants are wealthy and powerful and from the north or the east. And while fundamentalists and evangelicals have an important place among Protestants in Ulster, it is not the case that these people are in any sense typical. The idea that a segment of each ethnic group is prototypical of the whole group is ultimately very misleading.

What is true of rural Ballybeg is true of most of the different areas of Ulster. Catholic and Protestant university lecturers are likely to hold very similar social and political attitudes, colored only a little by their respective social origins. There are many Catholics whose attitudes toward tobacco, alcohol, and gambling are scarcely different from those of Protestant fundamentalists. Nowadays there are even born-again, Bible-believing Catholics. And a Catholic working men's club is likely to have a very similar ethos to that of a club frequented by Protestants of the same social class.

It is important not to overstate the case, for there are significant cultural differences between Protestants and Catholics. Most of these are to be found in particular subcultures or worlds. These include associations of different kinds that, under the curatorship of professionals and enthusiasts, are devoted to the preservation of "our culture." The distinctiveness of these cultural forms is often quite small, however. The Orange Order, for example, is often thought to epitomize important aspects of distinctively Protestant culture. But the Orange Order arose out of a much broader context of activity in Ireland that embraced agrarian secret societies such as the Ribbonmen, the Molly Maguires, the Rockites, and the Defenders, many of which were predominantly Catholic.

In the expression of political and religious differences, there has long been much borrowing. Indeed, to try to project present-day symbolism into the past and call it a "distinctive tradition" will often come to grief. The Lambeg drum is a case in point. This large, loud, and ferocious drum is now a distinctively Protestant instrument. Yet I have interviewed old men belonging to divisions of the Catholic Ancient Order of Hibernians who recall storing Lambeg drums in their halls. They say Lambeg drums were played by Hibernians in much the same way as they are still played by Orangemen.

Such comparisons are endless, and can descend into triviality. A common loyalist graffito consists of the initials *F.T.P.* It is now imitated by nationalists, who scrawl *F.T.Q.* (The initials refer to the Pope and the Queen, respectively.) Curbstones painted in red, white, and blue echo curbstones painted green, white, and orange. The rise among Protestant youths of distinctively aggressive flute bands soon afterward had its counterpart on the Catholic side; each side, however, has distinctive uniforms and plays separate tunes.

Thus it is not only in the nonsectarian aspects of life that the two sides are culturally similar. They are often similar in the way they assert their separate ethnic identities. The broad sweep of these so-called traditions is very much the same. All that differs are the narrowly specific details, which are what they use to assert their difference.

Though these symbols of differentiation have immense significance in the culture, they scarcely add up to two discrete traditions. To a considerable extent, the significance of these diacritical elements is much the same for one side as it is for the other. People in Ulster take elements from a shared culture or heritage (which has, however, regional and class differences) and make use of them to differentiate and identify social groups. They use them also to assert rhetorically the importance of these groups.

These diacritical elements in the culture provide a clear and visible gauge of which side is winning in the perennial battle for power, prestige, and influence. Thus if there are more Irish tricolors in the streets, more Irish-language street names, or a greater Irish dimension to government, or if Protestant street parades are curtailed, then this is a sign that nationalists have increased their influence. When these various indicators recede, then nationalist influence is perceived to have receded.

There are, of course, intricacies involved in some of this distinctive culture. This is why so much of it is looked after by small groups of specialists. Gaelic football, hurley, Irish dance, Lambeg drumming, and the symbolism of the Royal Black Institution are each quite difficult to learn. Some individuals become deeply immersed in the learning of these specialized skills, while most do not. Nevertheless, most of these skills are expressed in an idiom that is understandable to both sides. And, indeed, much of it is socially useful just because it *can* be understood by people on both sides.

Those activities that differentiate the traditions or the culture of Catholics and Protestants are, in practice, only a small proportion of what most Catholics and Protestants actually do. Except for enthusiasts, most people use the available culture and tradition for more mundane purposes. These have to do with earning a living, making a family, enjoying entertainment, eating, drinking, and so forth. Only a small amount of energy is typically used for the narrow purpose of identifying oneself as a member of an ethnic group, or to assert the group's political claims.

As Akenson (1991) discovered, the whole point about a culture is that it enables those who participate in it to move and thrive in many different worlds. Northern Ireland's people, like other people, take their culture where they can find it — from the south of Ireland, Britain, the United States, continental Europe, Asia, Africa, and elsewhere. Most of what Catholics and Protestants do is not distinctively either "Catholic" or "Protestant." Still less is it distinctively "Irish" or "British." While there *are* distinctive practices of this kind, most of what people do does not derive from any distinctive canon of ethnic tradition.

With only very limited and specific exceptions, the cultural heritage of a Catholic is likely to be much the same as that of a Protestant of the same social class living in the same geographical area. There are no distinctively Protestant or Catholic dialects, nor agricultural practices, nor house types, nor pottery techniques, nor styles of cooking. Family life is much the same on both sides, as indeed is the broader social morality.

In much of day-to-day existence, then, we may say not that there exist distinct Catholic and Protestant cultures in Ireland, but rather that there are cultural differences that coincide with both regional and class distinctions. These divergences have often been used to give weight to the respective identities and claims of the two conflicting endogamous groups in society. But the definition of these does not arise from the facticity of cultural variation. Instead it arises out of the use to which these variations are put.

Once more, therefore, one should be wary of placing too much emphasis on cultural diversity as a determinant of identity. Nor should shared culture be looked to as a means of determining an identity that transcends ethnic division. A minority of Protestants sometimes hopes that ethnic identities can be submerged in the common culture and identity of Ulster. There are Catholics who similarly look to the Irish culture and identity that the two sides have in common. Both approaches, we believe, hold out false hopes. There are indeed cultural differences and similarities between the Irish regions. It does not, however, follow that one can circumnavigate ethnicity just by emphasizing an Ulster or Irish identity. Ethnic and other forms of identity are not rooted in the ephemera of cultural difference. They are rooted in patterns of social interaction whose consequences can last for generations. The identification of Catholics with the whole island of Ireland and of Protestants with Ulster and the United Kingdom has little to do with cultural similarities and differences. It has a lot to do with power relationships between the endogamous social groups.

Unity in Diverse Identities

We wish now to consider how a person can have so many quite different partial identities and yet always seem to be the selfsame person.

Cohen (1994) suggests that an individual will strive to synthesize his different personae into a unified identity or self through a reflexive self-consciousness. Fortunately one does not need to penetrate the privacy of this introspective self in order to examine this process, for an individual will frequently dramatize or otherwise represent to others synthetic definitions of himself. These representations define several partial identities simultaneously. They do so, however, in particular circumstances and for particular purposes. If they do not convey the whole truth about the person, then at least they point to the idea that the separate partial identities of that person have a measure of integrity or unity.

Part of the solution to the "unity of diversity" question is fairly simple. Most people can, at will, construct a simple narrative that unites their particular worlds into a single, overarching, syntagmatic framework: "I go to work most weekdays; in the evenings I come home and we watch television; most Saturdays I go fishing; we take the kids to church on Sundays; and then we go to see the wife's mother for Sunday lunch," and so on. Similar autobiographical narratives can be constructed for the day, the year, the lifetime: "I was born in Belfast; soon I went to live in Ballymena, and there I started school. . . ." Such narratives, which draw together composite versions of the self, are likely to differ according to the purpose of the narrator and the situation in which they are told.

We have shown that a directly metaphoric relation as well as a wholly metonymic one can exist between worlds. We shall now show that in specific interactions a person will sometimes dramatize several different identities simultaneously. This enables that person to dramatize the notion that his different identities are compatible. He is, therefore, not several people, but only one.

For example, a dramatization of an ethnic identity can also dramatize an identity grounded in social class or gender. A person may present to others a framed definition of himself as a particular kind of *man*. He may do this by simultaneously dramatizing a framed definition of himself as a particular kind of *loyalist*. In the process he will dramatize himself as a unified being. He will show that in this case his masculinity and his loyalism are both compatible and intertwined.

Specific social dramas can draw together several of an individual's multifarious partial identities into a single unified identity. Our main discussion, therefore, will end by considering social interactions that dramatize or describe several separate identities simultaneously.

The early part of this chapter showed that cultural differences of class and region can be used metaphorically to define an ethnic cultural identity. Similarly, the more specific emblems of ethnicity can be used to depict rhetorical versions of other, nonethnic identities. For example, in concrete social interactions, the depiction of ethnicity is often clearly intertwined with ideas of authority, gender, or social class.

Two points are of interest here. The first is that when an ethnic identity is presented in a given framework of other events, the presentation usually incorporates elements drawn from a common culture. A presentation of self is never just of a Protestant or a Catholic person. It is of someone who is multifaceted and complex. The second is that, in such presentations, a person can dramatize to others that his different partial identities are indeed mutually compatible. He may imply that they combine into a single, unified, and integrated identity.

It is useful here to think of actions as being organized at different levels (Goldman 1970). If someone, for example, is playing chess, he gains a victory over his opponent *by* checkmating him; he does this *by* moving his pawn to king's knight seven; he does this *by* lifting the pawn and putting it down on the correct square; he does this *by* making a series of complex movements with his hand. Each of these actions is simultaneous with the others, yet each has a different level of organization.

In order for someone to organize his actions at any one of several discrete levels, that person must first have learned a skill. Most of these skills, including perhaps even the ability to manipulate objects, have been learned while watching and imitating other people; that is, they come from operational models (Caws 1978) transmitted from a previous generation.

I shall now examine certain specifically sectarian aspects of Northern Irish culture as they were actually used in specific social interactions. When such actions are treated as highly complex permutations of skills, the idea that there exist discrete cultures or traditions melts away.

In given situations, the Irishness or Britishness of what somebody does, its distinctively Catholic or Protestant character, is never the only thing that is relevant. Much more important is the fact that the person's ethnic identity is inseparable from other, nonethnic kinds of identity. Together these emerge into a composite and unified identity. In such an identity, ethnicity is only one component.

An Eleventh Night Procession

The large and loud Lambeg drum (see Scullion 1981) has a special place in the events of the annual Twelfth of July festival. Lambeg drums are taken out and beaten on 1 July, when the arches are built across the streets and the flags are put out. They are also used in the Twelfth of July procession itself. The drum, however, has a particular place on the evening of 11 July. During fieldwork in Listymore, I watched as Lambeg drums were beaten on the Eleventh Night.

I have said that inhabitants of Long Stone sometimes complain that the people who live in Killycarnon are "snooty," and that Long Stone is sometimes stigmatized as "rough." Most people in the area are Protestant. Insofar as there is a distinctively Catholic area in Listymore, it is in a comparatively isolated part of the countryside, near a Catholic chapel.

At midnight on 11 July one year, I watched some two dozen men take out the Lambeg drums from Long Stone Orange Hall. As they marched off, rattling the drums, a cheerful crowd of some one hundred other people — mostly, but not all, teenagers — followed them.

It is widely supposed that the purpose of beating the Lambeg drums on the

Figure 23. *Protestants beating Lambeg drums outside Belfast City Hall. Belfast, March 1985. (Courtesy of Mary C. Kenney)*

Figure 24. Lambeg drumming. (Courtesy of the Ulster Folk and Transport Museum)

Eleventh Night is to assert a territorial claim. The drums assert that a given area belongs specifically to Protestants. They are also said to intimidate any Catholics who might happen to hear the noise. The sound of Lambeg drums is indeed intimidating, particularly when the drummers bring with them an inebriated crowd. That day, however, the intimidation of Catholics did not appear to be the prime purpose of the exercise.

It is clear that in marching around at midnight playing two extremely loud drums in celebration of the Twelfth of July, the body of people was indeed asserting a distinctively Protestant identity. Moreover, the imprecise message of their drumming was also that, as Protestants, they had a right to dominate their immediate surroundings. What I want to suggest, however, is that this is not the whole of what these people were doing. When they marched off from the Long Stone Orange Hall, they did not go anywhere near the local Catholics. Instead, they went, by the quickest possible route, straight to the village of Killycarnon. There, until at least two-thirty in the morning, when I went to bed, they regaled the no-longer-sleeping inhabitants with an unbelievably loud musical offering. The Lambeg drum did here affirm a Protestant identity; but it did something else, too. It also asserted values of plainness, straightforwardness, bluntness, and good fellowship. These, in Listymore, are identified with the village of Long Stone, with the working classes, and with the masculine camaraderie of "the boys."

Although there were teenage girls present, and indeed some Killycarnon residents, this was emphatically a Long Stone occasion, a youthful occasion, and one that belonged to the men. These men were dramatizing a rhetoric that stated the importance of masculinity, the working classes, and youth. It was a ritual of rebellion (Gluckman 1954) against the allegedly snooty, educated, female, and elderly population of Killycarnon. Using Goldman's idiom, these people were affirming this rather complex plain man's identity *by* affirming a Protestant, anti-Catholic identity. And they were doing this, in turn, *by* playing the Lambeg drum long after midnight through the streets of Killycarnon.

To limit this description to the undoubted fact that Eleventh Night processions with Lambeg drums are specifically Protestant occasions would be to miss most of the point of what was going on. The dislike of the comparatively poor for the comparatively rich, of the teenage young for the figures who represent authority, and, more specifically, of inebriated young males for the more upright and respectable citizenry, is quite as traditional a feature of Irish (indeed British) life as the more celebrated traditional hostility between Catholics and Protestants. It is this that the Eleventh Night procession in Listymore dramatized. And, incidentally, it is one that wholly transcends the so-called sectarian divide.

A Use for a Tricolor

What is true for Protestant emblems is also true for those of the other side. In a precisely similar (but opposite) way to the Union flag, the Irish national flag is an object commonly used in Ulster to affirm an Irish nationalist identity. The Irish tricolor is typically raised on housing estates, sports grounds, and even public buildings. It then makes at least a claim that such spaces are specifically nationalist territory. Sometimes the claim may be that the British (government, police, or people) have no jurisdiction in such an area. As such, it has much the same significance as the Lambeg drum. It is a way of identifying or claiming a territory as the special preserve of one segment of the population. The pattern here is clear and well known. However, when used in an actual situation, there can be much subtlety.

I attended an Orange procession on the Twelfth of July in Downpatrick. When the march was in full swing, a small group of women unfurled a large tricolor outside the police station, some fifty yards from the march. Not only was the tricolor held by women, but they also organized a half-dozen young children, six to eight years old, to stand in front of it.

This was a most elaborate situation. In particular, it was a great quandary for the police. Fifty yards away were several thousand Protestants — Orangemen, bands, and onlookers — liable to become incensed at the sight of the flag. Also nearby were the press, including a television crew. The police were fully entitled, under the law, to remove the tricolor, as it was likely to cause a breach of the peace. If they had done this, however, they would have gained massively adverse publicity. Policemen would have been photographed attacking a peaceful demonstration of women and small children. If, on the other hand, the police did not remove the tricolor, they ran a real risk of precipitating an unpleasant riot. Tension had already been high in Downpatrick that year, which was why the press were there in force. Also, once the scene appeared on television, the local police would be criticized by loyalist politicians for not doing their duty. So while in abstraction the showing of a tricolor can be seen as the affirmation of a Catholic, nationalist identity, in this particular situation much more was going on.

The activity of the women and children in this context was an especially deft example of what chapter 9 described as "wrong-footing." This consists of maneuvering someone, usually a figure of authority, into a situation where he is ridiculously incapable of defining what is going on, or of making a sensible decision. This form of skillful manipulation is as much part of Protestant culture as it is of Catholic.

In this instance the senior policeman on the spot was quite as deft and agile as those who held the flag. He quickly shooed away all the press, and deployed his forces to seal them out of the street. He then stood near the small demonstration. With the pose of a Nelson refusing to see a signal, he turned his head and looked studiously in the opposite direction. After a while, the demonstrators, themselves outmaneuvered (but perhaps having won a victory worth recounting to their grandchildren), packed up their flag and departed.

In this instance, as in the last, emblems and activities widely recognized as specifically factional were used for purposes that are found on both sides in Northern Ireland: irritating the snooty, or wrong-footing policemen. Indeed, such purposes belong to a more general popular culture found in the British Isles and beyond.

Uses of a Stereotype

As the focus for two final examples, I return to the oral history that I collected in the area of Ulster that I call the Upper Tullagh (Buckley 1982). This area was predominantly, but not exclusively, Catholic.

There, people spoke of two main categories of people existing in the past: one rich and the other poor. According to this history, the poor lived an old-fashioned sort of life. They ate homemade bread, butter, and other simple fare. Their lives were ones of easygoing tolerance. Gambling, drinking, the playing of games, and the telling of stories about fairies and ghosts all had a part in a rich community life. Above all, there was neighborliness. Each gave to each when there was need.

In contrast to the poor, the rich lived lives of steely rationality. They did not just reject superstition and drink; they also ignored the genuine morality of neighborly give-and-take, replacing it with a harsher morality of rules and regulations.

This dichotomy broadly amounts to a conflation of Weber's opposition of *traditional* and *bureaucratic-rational* with that of *Gemeinschaft* and *Gesellschaft*. It is a very potent image. In Ulster it is one version of the stereotype of the Catholic and the Protestant.

In the Upper Tullagh, the good, kindly, neighborly, fairytale-telling people of the past were poor farmers and laborers who were usually Catholic; and the nasty, oppressive, rational people were wealthy farmers, who were usually Presbyterian.

In a largely Catholic area, one might expect such a mythology to be used to explain modern interdenominational relationships. It could justify an assertion of Catholic dominance over local Protestants, or generally advocate the cause of Irish nationalism. And no doubt this history is sometimes used in this way. When I heard the story told, however, it made a rather different point.

In an area where there were remarkably good relations between Catholics and Protestants, individuals on both sides tended to tell the same oral history. The stories were told to uphold the virtues of being a good neighbor, to denigrate excessive devotion to making money, and in particular to emphasize the importance of maintaining good, friendly relationships across the sectarian divide. Thus, a version of the past that articulates stereotypes of Protestants and Catholics and which has every possibility of being used as nationalist propaganda is, in the cases I heard, used as an operational model, a cautionary tale, for developing harmony between the two sides (Buckley 1982, chap. 2).

The use of Catholic and Protestant stereotypes, however, can be even more flexible than this. In the following example, Catholicism and Protestantism were identified with quasi-Weberian traditional and rational values, respectively. But this identification was used to articulate quite different ideals among people who had an interest in the creative arts.

Alan lives in the countryside, teaching art in a nearby college. His house is old and traditional. He has made an effort to furnish it in a manner compatible with its age. Alan disapproves of being too rational. He says it is important to be open to nature. By conceptualizing objects, he says, one limits one's experience of them. Evidence of this can be seen in County Donegal (the epitome, for many Ulster people, of traditional, rural, Catholic Ireland). Here, an object that has outlived its usefulness can be redefined for another purpose. For example, a bedstead can be used as a fence.

Alan and his wife bake their own bread. Where possible, they use natural herbal medicines, believing them to be gentler than those provided by modern doctors. Although they are of Protestant descent, they send one of their children to a Catholic school, and their children have names whose origins lie in ancient Irish legends.

For them, as for the people of the Upper Tullagh, there is an ostensible rejection of modernity and bureaucratic rationality. They identify their views with an essentially Catholic past still found, they believe, in the west of Ireland.

They are not, however, nationalists. I would guess that when they have the chance, they vote for the nonsectarian Alliance Party. Also unlike most people in the Upper Tullagh, they do not stress the community aspects of the life of the poor Catholic laborer or farmer in the past.

In somewhat marked contrast to views that are found in the Upper Tullagh, their opinion is that the Catholic farmer of the past had a somewhat independent and creative style of life. The virtues that they prize most of all are creativity and thinking for oneself. These they see in the Catholic peasant of the past, who is, for them, someone rather like themselves: in touch with nature, open to the supernatural, and with an artist's creativity and independence of spirit.

Each of these two versions of the past takes stereotyped versions of Protestant and Catholic identities and transforms them. Each asserts a nonsectarian — even antisectarian — rhetorical identity. In the one case, the stereotypes assert community values; in the other, the values are individualistic and creative. For both, however, the identities asserted are ones that transcend sectarianism and reject conflict.

Concluding Remarks

Ethnicity in Ulster is but one example of a type of identity that is structured by metaphors. It is not only sieges and invasions and their related body- or self-based images that provide metaphors for ethnicity; so do images of people from different social classes and different geographical regions. Sometimes the metaphors are reflexive. Thus social class can be expressed through ethnicity, and ethnicity expressed through social class. Sometimes the metaphors are a form of synecdoche, as when lower-class Catholics from the west of Ireland are thought typical of Catholics as a whole.

Despite this interpenetration, and despite the undoubted and obvious importance of ethnicity in Northern Ireland, one should be careful not to exaggerate this importance. Just as, for example, gender is only one important feature of life in Ulster, so too there is a limit to the importance of ethnicity.

Catholics and Protestants do not spend all or even most of their time and energy affirming the distinctiveness of their ethnic identities. There is even much evidence that they frequently decide such affirmation is undesirable. Ulster people, for example, often avoid controversial subjects in mixed company to avoid giving offense (see Harris 1972, 146–47). In other ways, too, they try to get on well with people from the other side (Buckley 1982; Donnan and McFarlane 1986). Ulster people do indeed present themselves to others as Catholics or Protestants, but only when it is useful for them to do so.

Ben-Amos (1984) makes the point that when folklorists themselves identify certain elements of folklore as a canon or tradition, they usually consider this tradition to be in danger of being overwhelmed by outside forces. Thus they may regard folklore as a little tradition under threat from the great traditions of education, science, literature, and so on. Or they may see a traditional culture threatened by mass popular culture.

Not only professional folklorists think like this. Ordinary people who identify with an "Irish tradition" or a "Protestant tradition" or an "Anglican tradition," or whatever, tend to conceive their tradition as being subject to attack. Thus the national traditions of Ireland — its dance, language, music, games — are supposed to be in danger of being swamped by the culture of the United States and especially that of Britain. And Ulster Protestantism is similarly thought to be in danger from the culture of Gaelic nationalism.

When people speak of culture or tradition in the narrow canonical sense — when they say, "This is our tradition," or even "This is what we believe" — they usually want to define the identity of their social group in order to assert its importance or to defend it against somebody else. Culture or tradition in this sense, therefore, is a rhetorical rather than an analytical device, and as such it can be beguiling.

This book has argued that individuals are defined — that is, their identities are constructed — against a background of framed circumstances. These frames are given a conceptual structure by means of metaphors. Identities are constructed when people act and interact with each other, for it is in action and interaction that a person's definition in a particular world ceases to be a mere representation and becomes concrete. Identity is not just a matter of arbitrary labels, nor merely of cultural diversity. Still less is it a simple fabrication. Identity is rooted in what people do.

In social interactions, however, rhetoric plays an important part. Rhetoric may persuade others that a particular structured situation or social world exists. Then, if other people act as though that situation or world exists, they will help create it by their actions. And since rhetoric defines people as having (or not having) value, it is connected to the allocation of resources. Praise and condemnation, riches and poverty, power and impotence, reward and punishment all depend in part on the success or failure of competing rhetorics.

Rhetoric also provides the occasion for social interaction. Statements about the nature of the world occur in interactions that define the identity of participants. Social dramas provide some of the most important ways in which rhetorical statements can be made. In social drama, individuals usually dramatize who they and other people are, or who they hope others will take them to be. And rhetoric and its symbolic expression, especially in the form of social drama but also in the form of gossip, history, and other narratives, provide a focus for allegiance.

Certain socially constructed identities, we have shown, would not exist without rhetoric. A persuasive speech or a quasi-dramatic act can therefore be the start of a socially constructed real identity. Identity can be constructed during conversation, in processions, in religious and other kinds of ritual, in rioting, in comic exchanges, in different kinds of misbehavior — indeed, in the countless different genres of interaction in which rhetorical presentations of defined frameworks of reality have a part.

Arising from this analysis is the idea that individuals do not have merely a single identity, but rather identities that are negotiated in particular circumstances. Individuals create particular worlds and situations by their interactions, and it is against the background of these that identities have their shape. The unity of an individual identity, the "essence" of a person, the idea that someone seems always to be the selfsame individual: these are themselves social constructions, dramatized or otherwise presented to others in particular circumstances for particular purposes.

This work has focused upon ethnic identity in the north of Ireland. We have argued that ethnicity arises out of patterns of social interaction. Of these patterns, the most intractable are those founded in kinship. The reluctance to marry across the sectarian divide establishes patterns of practical interaction that span the generations. Upon these are built other patterns of interaction based on school, church, voluntary society, and geography, among other factors. And these in turn provide the basis for economic and political rivalry.

We have shown that rhetoric plays a major part in the definition of ethnicity, as it does in the construction of all kinds of identity. There are rhetorical statements made about the past and the present of the different ethnic groups. Rhetorical social dramas of all kinds — rituals, ceremonies, processions, riots, and others — give often-conflicting definitions of both the ethnic groups themselves and the different groupings that claim to represent them.

It follows that in Northern Ireland, where the social boundaries between the two ethnic groups are firmly built, there is not much room for negotiating ethnic identity. Nevertheless, ethnicity, even in Northern Ireland, is not a simple matter. It is deeply intertwined with other forms of identity — especially class, gender, and geography, but also identities that are tied to wholly local or immediate circumstances — that in themselves are unconnected to ethnicity. Different individuals define their ethnic identities, as they define the rest of their identities, in highly individual ways according to their particular situations and circumstances.

Since identity is forged in practice rather than in ideas, it is appropriate to end on a pragmatic note rather than a theoretical one. We shall therefore conclude this book with a postscript discussing the work of Northern Irish schools and museums. In the next and final chapter, we shall try to show that the approach used in this book is relevant to practical attempts to find solutions to the social conflict in Ulster.

13

Postscript

Identity
in
Schools
and
Museums

We shall now consider how our findings are relevant to the work of educational establishments in Northern Ireland, looking at schools and museums. We argued in chapter 2 that any theory that describes humanity should be applicable to the theorists themselves. Since one of the present authors is a museum curator, we shall especially consider how this approach to identity has had practical application in the institution where he works, the Ulster Folk and Transport Museum.

Three of the points made in this volume are especially relevant. First is the idea that identity is defined in the frameworks provided by specific relationships, situations, and "worlds." Second, ethnic identities arise because of the way individuals typically interact. They do not come out of cultural difference. Third, individuals do define themselves during the presentation of rhetorical definitions of reality. Identity is defined during conversation, commemorations of history, music, dance, ritual, ceremonial, and social drama of all sorts. Some of these forms of discourse and social drama are cared for by individuals and organizations who act as curators.

Our argument is that each of these three points has a direct practical implication for schools and museums. Each defines a stratagem in relation to the problem of providing greater social harmony and peace in Northern Ireland.

The three stratagems in question are not new. They have been available for some time and have been much used by educational bodies. In recommending them, we do not therefore advocate any revolutionary changes. On the contrary, we believe that our findings provide a theoretical underpinning for policies already in place.

The stratagems even have labels already well established in the Northern Irish educational vocabulary. They are: (a) that schools and museums should be "oases of calm"; (b) that schools and museums should encourage intermingling between the two groups to inspire "mutual understanding"; and (c) that schools and museums should enable members of the two groups to explore their own and each other's "cultural heritage."

Oases of Calm: Living in Different Worlds

The idea that educational institutions ought to be oases of calm has long permeated the world of education in Northern Ireland. Its unstated theoretical premise is that each person lives in several distinct and separable worlds.

There is a myth of origin for the phrase "oases of calm." People say it originated in the early 1970s, when it referred specifically to "maintained" (that is, Catholic) schools in what then were the intensely battle-torn inner-city nationalist areas of Belfast. At that time, soldiers nightly raided homes for weapons; rioting was an everyday occurrence; explosions and gunfire regularly rattled the windows.

Despite this, one could walk into a school and find peace. In the schools were orderliness, cleanliness, civilization, and spirituality. The calm was only heightened by the devastation immediately outside the school railings. Children who spent their evenings "bricking peelers" (or worse) would next morning come into the school, where, surrounded by vases of flowers and statues of saints, they would sit at their desks, working in the quiet discipline of a classroom.

Whatever the origin of the expression, the practical goal of creating oases of calm came to permeate the world of education. It extended into the state (Protestant) schools and into the world of museums. Schools and museums were neutral territory into which the troubles should not intrude.

The desire for an oasis of calm is, of course, a version of the siege metaphor, closely related to ideas of the temple and to what Feldman (1991) has called "sanctuary." Schools and museums may be, in their way, neutral territory, but they are territory nevertheless. The ambition of the teachers and others who sustained this policy, often individuals of great personal courage, was to maintain the boundaries of their spiritual havens against the forces of barbarism without.

There was more to this policy of boundary maintenance than the physical exclusion of "the men of violence." Centrally, there was also a wish to keep out of the classroom and museum gallery the contentious forms of debate that might politicize these places.

Maintaining oases of calm might have been much more difficult if the cultural differences of sectarianism had been more central to Northern Irish culture. In reality, however, as we, following Akenson (1991), have argued, the cultural differences between Catholics and Protestants are remarkably few. Most of the cultural differences that do exist are confined to comparatively discrete worlds overseen by enthusiasts, professionals, or other curatorial figures.

There are many other worlds in Northern Ireland broadly untouched by the distinctive marks of sectarianism. Indeed, the school curriculum exemplifies the division of the cultural universe into worlds. It exemplifies, too, just how marginal the culture of ethnicity is in these different worlds.

In a school there are some subjects, notably history, religious education, the Irish language, and certain kinds of physical education, that might raise sectarian issues. Greer, for example, noted in 1972 that the study of social problems, or of Hinduism, Buddhism, and humanism, often found its way into religious-education courses. The subject of the Catholic/Protestant division, however, was carefully omitted (Greer 1972, 83). However, particularly where education is ethnically segregated, it is possible to deal with even these issues without raising contentious hackles. Also, for the most part, students could study physics, chemistry, biology, art, woodworking, metalworking, geography, or literature without reference to sectarianism or social conflict. Catholic physics is no different from Protestant physics, and the same is true of most school subjects.

In the 1970s and even later, teachers could therefore take refuge in the pluralism of the curriculum. They could also work toward a classical educational ideal of producing well-rounded individuals. A well-rounded individual, in the terms of this book, is one whose identity is defined broadly in relation to the worlds of literature, science, and the rest. A well-rounded person is not someone defined in relation only to those wholly local worlds where ethnicity is relevant.

The situation in schools found a parallel in the two so-called national museums in Northern Ireland, the Ulster Museum in Belfast and the Ulster Folk and Transport Museum at Cultra in County Down. Of these two institutions, the Ulster Museum has a breadth of concern precisely similar to that of a school. Inside its walls are departments concerned with antiquities, art, botany, geology, textiles, and zoology. These topics do not rouse sectarian hackles.

The Ulster Museum, however, also has a department of local history. In this, though with a different emphasis, it shares concerns with its sister institution, the Ulster Folk and Transport Museum. This latter body is charged, by act of Parliament, to study and represent the "traditions and way of life of the people of Northern Ireland past and present." It is, therefore, centrally concerned with those matters that might undermine that institution's aspiration to be an oasis of calm.

In fact, neither the local-history department of the Ulster Museum nor the Ulster Folk and Transport Museum has been highly controversial. The reason for this is that the cultural universe is divided into diverse worlds, few of which are differentiated by marks of distinctive ethnic culture.

Since its establishment in the 1950s, the Ulster Folk and Transport Museum has consisted principally of an open-air museum. This depicts a dispersed rural community and a small town in Ulster in about the year 1900. Apart from a few replica buildings, the exhibits in the open-air museum have been dismantled and brought to the museum brick by brick from different parts of Ulster. There are also galleries suitable for both folk and transport exhibitions. The museum stages entertainments, demonstrations of skill, and other events as well.

The themes considered over the years by the Ulster Folk and Transport Museum have been many and various. An important one has been the depiction of the buildings themselves. The buildings exemplify older forms of vernacular architecture. The exhibits also illustrate how different kinds of people used the buildings. Presentations of aspects of domestic life, in the form of furnishings and matters relating to cookery and so on, give life to the display of buildings. Another theme has been the variety of agricultural practices; these practices are reconstructed in the landscape of the open-air museum. In addition, the museum's agriculture department has encouraged the preservation of rare breeds of farm animals. There is a lively textile department, which collects and displays textiles and materials related to their manufacture. It does this not only for their own intrinsic interest but also for the light that textiles throw upon the social lives of the people who made and made use of them. Crafts such as blacksmithing, printing, spade making, and woodworking are regularly illustrated and displayed. Music is performed in the open-air museum and is a major feature of the museum's work. The transport department is concerned with the display of all kinds of transport, including shipping — a major aspect of Ulster life — and road and rail transport. Recently a large gallery devoted entirely to railways was opened.

In all this activity, the topic of ethnicity scarcely arises at all. One could, of course, if one chose, allow ethnicity to intrude into the storyline of any and every exhibition. This, however, would be inappropriate, for, as in any other society, there are many other stories to be told.

Thus a popular exhibition in the late 1980s told the story of the *Titanic*, the famous doomed ship that was built in a Belfast shipyard. This exhibition, quite correctly, had nothing at all to do with ethnicity. Despite its local relevance, it has also been successfully displayed in museums in England and the United States.

There have also been gallery exhibitions on marriage, domestic furniture, agriculture, the harp, the life of a local motorcycling hero, and so forth. In these exhibitions, ethnicity very occasionally peeped into the picture, but not to any great extent. This is because in most of the worlds that exist in the north of Ireland, the culture of one side is not very different from that of the other.

The attempt to create oases of calm in the schools and museums in Northern Ireland was therefore largely successful, due in large part to the good sense of both teachers and curators. It was also because, in a pragmatic way, everyone knew that the cultural universe of Northern Ireland was not in fact divided into sectarian dichotomies.

The idea of an oasis of calm, however, was a response by teachers and curators to the very extreme conditions of the 1970s, when physical intimidation threatened the very foundation of education itself. As a policy, it tended to evade (with ample good reason) some of the central issues of Northern Irish life. From the mid-1980s on, however, a new atmosphere became apparent. Although there were hiccups, government began to take renewed steps to encourage reconciliation between the two ethnic groups. Also, and again with some hesitancy, local politicians responded with cautious goodwill. At the same time, educators also felt able to take on a more positive role.

Social Interaction: Education for Mutual Understanding

We have argued that ethnic identity, and also other forms of identity, are formed during social interaction. Broadly speaking, ethnic identity consists of social interaction of a discriminatory nature. It persists through the construction and continuing existence of worlds in which ethnicity is relevant to interaction. The most important interactions that maintain the boundaries between ethnic groups are those involved in the socialization of children. And not least of these is segregated education.

Since at least the early 1970s, there have been those who have sought to provide opportunities for children of different ethnic backgrounds to intermingle. One aspect to this has been the establishment of several integrated schools. The most famous of these schools is Lagan College in Belfast (see Irwin 1991). Here, as in the others, the ethnic composition of the students is carefully monitored. Selection procedures ensure that no one ethnic group predominates.

Government has, from time to time, declared itself to be in favor of these schools. And, indeed, integrated schools are funded by the state in much the same way as are the Catholic schools. Despite this, government has left the impetus for the creation of integrated schools to the initiative of parents. Although there is an undoubted demand for integrated schools, few parents are so enthusiastic that they will go to the trouble of building their own school. Thus, the development of integrated education has been slow.

The reason for the muted nature of government support for integrated education undoubtedly lies in the political opposition that such schools could generate. Existing schools not unnaturally fear that resources might be diverted away from them toward the new integrated schools. And despite growing pockets of support, especially in the professional classes, popular opinion is also at best ambiguous toward attempts to enforce integration.

There is also a widespread suspicion, well articulated in a pamphlet by Frank Wright, that the commonly stated support for integration can disguise a desire to "put something across on the others." "Do you know either of the following?" he writes. "Someone with a fantasy of Catholics and Protestants standing reverently before a Union Jack fluttering from the school flagpole; or someone with the fantasy of Protestant and Catholic children dutifully absorbing a history syllabus which puts Protestants 'right about their Irishness'" (Wright n.d., 3). Separate education, he suggests, may be a means of managing mistrust. Too rapid an erosion of segregation may destroy the quiet that is currently in most schools.

The main thrust of educational endeavors toward intermingling in the classroom comes, therefore, not in schemes for integrated education but through Education for Mutual Understanding (EMU). EMU was undoubtedly set up in face of a widespread recognition that to force the pace of integration in schools would be unwise.

EMU is now one of six cross-curricular themes built into the Northern Ireland curriculum. Those who support it take care to insist that it is neither "a threat to particular cultures or traditions" nor "an attack on the concept of segregated education in Northern Ireland" (NICC 1990). Indeed, there are critics who suggest that, as such, it is insufficient, and therefore ineffectual (e.g., Dunlop 1987).

Central to the stratagem of EMU has been the systematic cultivation of regular and practical links between maintained (Catholic) and controlled (Protestant) schools. Typically, classes from different schools come together regularly for lessons in common, or they will undertake occasional projects, often involving field trips or other outings together.

In this work, the education departments of the different museums have taken an active part. During school terms, an average of three EMU groups visit the Ulster Folk and Transport Museum for EMU workshops every week. The children are usually divided into small ethnically mixed groups of six to eight children to do practical work involving farming, cooking, candlemaking, embroidery, laundry, and so on. They may then form into larger groups to take part in another activity. This could be a visit to a building in the museum's open-air collection to complete a workbook, or a lesson given by one of their teachers in the museum's village school.

The schools that participate in these activities are almost always a pair of schools, one Catholic, the other Protestant, that have closely cooperated for months or even years. Classes from these schools usually visit the museum on four separate days. On each occasion, the children will work together in the same small groups. Often their visits to the museum culminate in a longer visit to the residential unit in the urban area of the museum's open-air collection. This gives the children a chance to live together for a few days, working and making friends with one another.

In cultivating such contacts, staff ensure that the effect will be positive and not negative. Following research in this field (e.g., McWhirter 1983), the aim of the work is to encourage practical interdependence among the participants. It is part of a long-term relationship between groups of Catholics and Protestants, not a transitory relationship between individuals.

Cultural Heritage: Curatorship

The final policy to be considered here is one that arose most clearly in Northern Ireland in the late 1980s. This is the policy of encouraging schools and museums, and also private individuals and groups, to explore their cultural heritage.

This policy has operated mainly through two government agencies. One is the Cultural Traditions Group of the Community Relations Council; the other is the Department of Education (Northern Ireland). The first of these bodies, through a judicious use of funding, helps individuals and associations in the exploration and portrayal of the cultural heritage of Northern Ireland. The other is more concerned with specifically educational matters.

Like EMU, cultural heritage is now a cross-curricular theme that permeates every subject in the Northern Ireland schools' curriculum. Some aspect of specifically Northern Irish life must now enter into every course of study. This will often include materials from the distinctive traditions of one side of the community or the other.

At first sight, the idea of encouraging cultural heritage in schools and museums seems to contradict the practice of the early 1970s, when educational bodies generally avoided such topics in order to sustain oases of calm. They feared that such subjects might stir up dissent among students within the institutions, and invite the attention of politicians and others from outside.

We have said that, in the 1970s, the Ulster Folk and Transport Museum had created an oasis by representing only the less controversial Northern Irish worlds. The museum, however, never had the wholly negative purpose of not stirring up trouble. On the contrary, under its director at the time, George Thompson, the museum's vision was very positive. Thompson's frequently restated purpose was to present a vision of the Northern Irish heritage around which all inhabitants could unite. The aim was to present what Ulster people had in common.

Seen in this light, the policy represented by the work of George Thompson at the Ulster Folk and Transport Museum is not very different from the new one of emphasizing cultural heritage. The old policy presented a vision of society in which the people living in Northern Ireland had much in common. The new vision also concentrates on what people have in common. It only adds to this the extra feature that the ethnic differences that do exist should also be explicitly recognized and given respect.

And, indeed, the new policy is not a shift of principle but of circumstances. It would have been irresponsible to have explored distinctive ethnic cultures in the 1970s, when tensions were acute. Now that the problems are perceived as chronic, one can hope to be more adventurous.

The idea that individuals can come together around rhetorical dramatizations and other presentations, including versions of the historical past, is one that has been central to this volume. We have claimed that social groups, and especially ethnic groups, can cohere around such representations of the past.

In this context, we have used the term *curatorship*. Organizations such as the Hibernians, the Orange Order, Cómhaltas Ceoltóiri Éireann, the Gaelic Athletic Association, the Ulster Society, the churches, and others have a quasi-curatorial function. They conserve different kinds of intellectual property on behalf of a wider ethnic group, enabling this property to be commemorated or reproduced and transmitted to a wider public and to subsequent generations.

In using the idea of curatorship in this way, we suggest that museums are in many ways similar to these other bodies. These bodies, however, differ from the official museums in that the former are more concerned with the preservation and presentation of specifically *ethnic* knowledge. The museums and other educational bodies are concerned, in principle, with *all* forms of intellectual property. Their task is to care for all this property (both the distinctively ethnic and the nonethnic) so that members of the whole society can make use of it.

Chapter 4 suggested that individuals in Northern Ireland sometimes organize their understanding of their social institutions (including those with curatorial functions) using the metaphor of the temple. Museum people are very familiar with the idea that a museum is a "treasure house, educational instrument, or secular temple" (Baxandall 1991, 33). The idea of museum as temple has been well elaborated by Duncan (1991), but it permeates current debate about the nature of curatorship. Alpers, for example, uses a religious imagery when she emphasizes that objects are selected for display in museums because of their visual interest. She notes that the ancient Egyptians and the Renaissance Italians used tombs and chapels as places to look at beautiful pictures (Alpers 1991, 26). Horne also speaks of "temples," though he raises an eyebrow to mock his own usage. He describes museum-visiting tourists as "pilgrims" traveling from holy place to holy place. He calls this pilgrimage "the way of the tourist" (Horne 1984, part 1).

Cameron, however, has argued that the modern museum need not always be a temple. Instead, he says, museums should move toward another classical form, the "forum" (Cameron 1972). In a forum, there is no mere reverence for the treasures and symbols of the dominant groups in society; there is, rather, a coming-together of diverse opinions for disagreement or debate (see Karp and Lavine 1991). Unfortunately, the idea of museum as forum is not very useful when ethnic tension is acute. A forum can too easily cease to be a place for civilized debate and become disputed territory.

The Ulster Folk and Transport Museum has always tried to show the considerable variety of the worlds within which people of different kinds live and move. It has tried to provide versions of the past, and sometimes of the present, that all members of the public could enjoy. Complementing those other curatorial bodies that strive to care for the culture only of their own ethnic group, the museum has performed the same function, but consciously on behalf of people from all Northern Irish groupings. By so doing, the museum hopes to present culture that symbolizes ethnic groupings, but within a more general framework to which members of the entire society can give assent.

This is not to say that the museum has (or indeed should) set itself only the evangelistic purpose of reconciling the two sides of society. On the contrary, the museum has seen itself as representing Northern Irish life (within reason) in *all* its complexity. It has not tried to represent merely *two* aspects of that complexity.

As we have suggested, individuals in Northern Ireland, as elsewhere, live in multitudinous different worlds. A museum's task is to explore a large number of these worlds. It is also to present to a general public what the participants in these worlds see as vital and valuable. By so doing, it recognizes and celebrates their identities in *all* of these diverse worlds. The idea must be to represent a vision of life in Ulster or in Ireland in which all major groups have a valued and respected place. Ethnic culture is one means by which the importance of ethnic groups can be given recognition. In a public museum, the presentation of ethnicity can be done within a framework that is noncompetitive but that gives each group its due.

If, then, the museum is to be a temple, then it has to be one built for the whole of society. Such a museum may give recognition to the reality of ethnic cleavages. It can also hope to provide a vision of society in which everyone can take some pride, and around which everyone can, in due course, cohere.

Two Exhibitions

We shall now consider two exhibitions at the Ulster Folk and Transport Museum that tried to address distinctively ethnic culture directly: Brotherhoods in Ireland, and Remembering 1690: The Folklore of a War.

Both exhibitions arose out of a piece of library and field research undertaken by A. D. Buckley but supported by his colleagues, especially T. K. Anderson, C. McCullough, and P. S. Robinson, and also by M. C. Kenney. The research began as a study of the Orange Order, but it extended, little by little, to include other bodies. Among these were the Hibernians, the Knights of St. Columbanus, the Freemasons, the friendly-society movement, the temperance movement, the trade unions, the Roman Catholic sodalities, and the guilds.

They were selected because of their manifest similarity to one another. Because of this similarity, an all-inclusive name was sought, and eventually P. S. Robinson hit on the name Brotherhoods in Ireland. This became the title of the first exhibition.

The Brotherhoods in Ireland Exhibition

The Brotherhoods in Ireland exhibition was a temporary display presented in 1988. Its main storyline was based on the somewhat abstract ideas of Goldman (1970), namely, that actions are complex, and stratified at different levels. Its central theme was that of unity in diversity. In some respects (i.e., at some levels of organization), the ritual and other actions performed by these brotherhoods were different. In other respects (i.e., at other levels), what they did was very similar. In apparent diversity, the exhibition implied, one could find the unity of a common culture.

The exhibition was organized into sections, each devoted to materials from a different brotherhood or type of brotherhood:

Introductory section
The urban guilds
The Sovereign, Military, and Hospitaller Order of St. John of Jerusalem, of Rhodes, and of Malta (once a crusading order, now a charitable body devoted to medical care)
The Order of Ancient, Free, and Accepted Masons of Ireland
The Orange and Royal Black Institutions (bodies devoted to upholding Protestantism; see chapter 11)
The Ancient Order of Hibernians (a body similar to the Orange Order, but devoted to upholding Catholicism)
The Archconfraternity of the Holy Family (a Roman Catholic sodality)
The Knights of St. Columbanus (an order devoted to upholding Roman Catholic values)
The Ancient Order of Foresters (a friendly society)
The Irish National Foresters (a friendly society, now mainly a social club)
The Independent Order of Odd Fellows (Manchester Unity) (a friendly society)
The Independent Order of Rechabites (Salford Unity) (a temperance friendly society)
The British Order of Ancient Free Gardeners (a friendly society)

The Loyal Order of Ancient Shepherds (Ashton Unity) (a friendly society)
The Royal Antediluvian Order of Buffaloes ("the poor man's Freemasonry" —
a social club)
The trade unions

In this array of different organizations there was, first of all, much diversity. Part of the display's purpose was to emphasize ethnic diversity, and this feature of the exhibition was evident to anyone with even slight local knowledge. Several bodies — the Orange Order, the Black Institution, the Hibernians, the Order of Malta, the Knights of St. Columbanus, and the Confraternity of the Holy Family — had purposes explicitly related to a religious tradition. The other organizations, with the trade unions in general being a notable exception, had an informal tendency to confine their recruitment to one or the other ethnic group.

The diversity, however, went beyond religion and ethnicity. Some of these bodies had a policy of strict temperance. Others were primarily drinking clubs. Some were organizations to encourage piety. Others had quasi-political goals. Many had the narrowly practical aim of organizing health insurance.

The political ethos of the different groups varied considerably. Some were straightforwardly nationalist or unionist, but others, notably the friendly societies and the trade unions, had ideological roots in forms of socialism.

They also varied considerably in the social classes from which they recruited. The Order of Malta, in its more exclusive reaches, restricts membership to Catholics with a claim to aristocracy. The friendly societies (now largely defunct in Ireland) drew their support from among the skilled or white-collar workers. So do the Freemasons, who also appeal to the well-to-do.

The aim of the exhibition, however, was to show the unity underlying the diversity. The diversity of purpose, ethnicity, and ethos, portrayed through the segregation of the exhibition into sections, was challenged by the similarity among the sections. As far as was practical, each section displayed a similar set of artifacts. Most sections contained

Regalia in the form of collars, aprons, sashes, or uniforms
Lists of officers, often with high-sounding titles such as Worshipful Master,
Chief Ranger, or Worthy Primo
Lists of degrees, again with elaborate titles, such as the Sublime Degree of
Master Gardeners, or the Excellent and Perfect Prince Rose Croix of
Heredom and Knight of the Eagle and Pelican Degree, and officers'
certificates
Jewels to signify degrees and honors obtained

Wall charts and similar teaching materials for instruction in the significance
of the organization's symbolism
Banners for use in processions

The point behind all of this was that the diversity in the different organizations was expressed through inherently similar cultural forms.

It is not the goal of museum exhibitions to provide an opportunity for commingling between different groups of people. Nevertheless, it seemed appropriate that the guests invited to the exhibition's opening should include members of significantly opposed organizations. Hibernians, Orangemen, National Foresters, Freemasons, clergy of different denominations, and others were present. Many of these could be considered curators of their group's cultural heritage. All of them had contributed — by giving advice, and by lending items — to the production of a single exhibition. This exhibition celebrated a tradition that was common to each of the two ethnic groups, a tradition so multipurpose that it could express and provide a focus for division.

Remembering 1690: The Folklore of a War

The second exhibition was constructed in 1990 to commemorate the three hundredth anniversary of the Battle of the Boyne. This battle, as everybody in Ulster knows, is annually commemorated by the Orange Order as the moment that established a Protestant ascendancy in Ireland (see chapter 3). Its title, Remembering 1690, evoked the slogan "Remember 1690," which, as "REM 1690," is often written on Northern Irish walls.

This exhibition was only one of several exhibitions and events put on over several years to commemorate the events of the Williamite-Jacobite Wars. Apart from the 1690 celebrations, there were also commemorations of the siege of Derry. These were organized, with a remarkable show of goodwill on all sides, not only by the unionist Apprentice Boys of Derry but also by the mainly nationalist Derry City Council. There were official celebrations in the city of Dublin, and the city of Limerick also joined in with a commemoration of its own two sieges.

In the world of Northern Ireland's museums, the exhibition at the Ulster Folk and Transport Museum was not the most important of the 1690 exhibitions. The Ulster Museum in Belfast put on a magnificent, specifically historical display entitled Kings in Conflict. This other exhibition recounted the Williamite-Jacobite conflict in Ireland within the broader framework of European history. It was a war between *three* kings: not only William III and James

Figure 25. Wall inscription, "REM 1690." (Courtesy of the Ulster Folk and Transport Museum)

II, but also Louis XIV of France. This context relegated the Irish campaign to a small place in the wars. The focus on the conflict in Europe obscured much of what Irish folk history considers important. Ireland did, however, feature in the exhibition's most splendid part, a tableau showing the signing of the Treaty of Limerick. In the tableau, the faces of actors delivering speeches were projected onto the faces of life-size models to give the effect of talking heads.

In the Ulster Museum's exhibition, therefore, the emphasis shifted from Ireland to Europe, and from the Battle of the Boyne (sacred to Orangemen) to the Treaty of Limerick. This treaty was no doubt historically more important, for it concluded the war and settled Ireland's fate for the next century. By shifting the framework for the war to include Europe, the Ulster Museum's exhibition also implied another message. This was that the popular histories had created a false impression of the events of 1688–92. The *real* events of the war (known to professional historians) had little to do with modern-day identities.

The Ulster Folk and Transport Museum's exhibition was more modest. In contrast to that of the Ulster Museum, it dealt with the "folklore of the war," that is, with the popular history as depicted in banners, bonfires, trinkets, songs, and narratives. Its central materials for display consisted of rhetorically divergent representations of the traditional histories of Ireland (see chapter 3).

While researching this topic, it was noted that certain organizations had effectively appropriated certain events of the war. To use the terminology of the present volume, they had unofficially become curators of these specific traditions.

We have already mentioned that the Apprentice Boys of Derry twice annually commemorate the siege of Londonderry, and that on the Twelfth of July the Orange Order commemorates the Battle of the Boyne. In addition, certain historical events that took place in the southwest of Ireland have become the intellectual property of nationalist traditions. These are, more specifically, the Battle of Aughrim, the two sieges of Athlone, and the two sieges of Limerick — in short, the Fight for the Shannon — as well as the aftermath of the war. These events were most readily accessible through pictures on banners preserved by the mainly Catholic National Forester and Hibernian movements, and also through Jacobite and nationalist songs and Irish dances that refer to these events.

To tell the story of the Williamite-Jacobite wars through its folklore, it was simplest to divide the exhibition into four sections. These dealt with the Siege of Derry, the Route to the Boyne, the Fight for the Shannon, and the Aftermath.

The first two sections concentrated mainly upon narratives and practices derived from Apprentice Boys and Orange tradition. As well as paintings on banners and drums, the museum also borrowed precious commemorative glassware in the Williamite tradition. The exhibition was fortunate in obtaining paintings of the siege by Robert Jackson, a well-known painter of murals from Londonderry. Robert Jackson's family has long been involved in building the effigy of the traitor Lundy that is ceremonially burned each year in Londonderry. He lent the museum models that illustrated the former practice of burning this effigy as it hung from the massive Walker monument (which has since been destroyed by an explosion). One of his models was a full-size half model of the Lundy effigy. It stood some fifteen feet high, and was magnificently clad in a full dress uniform made of cardboard. Lundy also had a handsome face with rouged cheeks and a mustache of which Salvador Dali would have been proud.

The other two sections dealt with the Fight for the Shannon and with the aftermath of the Treaty of Limerick. These stories were told mainly through banner paintings of the National Foresters and the Hibernians. The sections also included glassware, trinkets, photographs of statues, and other objects relating both to the battles and sieges and to the Treaty of Limerick.

There was also a videotape presentation. This was in two parts, one drawn

Figure 26. The Jackson family, builders of the Lundy effigy. (Courtesy of the Ulster Folk and Transport Museum)

roughly from Williamite and loyalist culture, the other from Jacobite and nationalist. The first half dealt with processions, bonfires, drumming, and other practices relating to the siege of Derry and King William's journey to the Boyne. The second commemorated the later stages of the war in the southwest. Inevitably, it too had processions, but it also focused upon the narrative, poetry, music, and dance in the Jacobite and later the nationalist traditions.

As this exhibition was being prepared, many who ventured an opinion or who were consulted, not least those involved in the teaching of history, thought that the purpose of the exhibition should be to correct the mistakes of folk history. This temptation to debunk was resisted. Instead, the exhibition adopted the rhetorical conceit that the specific popular histories of the Williamite-Jacobite wars were not incorrect but incomplete. In chapter 3 we argued that what Smith (1984) calls "ethnic histories" often have rhetorical purposes. We also claimed, however, that they are usually founded in verifiable fact. The exhibition suggested that the incompleteness of the two popular historical traditions could be overcome by putting the two of them together. By putting the unionist and nationalist traditions side by side, a complete and indeed broadly true picture of the war could be presented.

Livingstone and Beardsley (1991) have said that museums in divided societies have a problem of how to include the points of view of several different publics "without sacrificing . . . coherence and aesthetic will." Because of the nature of the ethnic division in the north of Ireland, the Ulster Folk and Transport Museum daily confronts this problem in an especially acute way. It was not the museum's place to declare baldly that the ethnic histories were wrong. Nor should it claim merely that the professionals know best. At the same time, it had to tell a limited and coherent story that was true.

The exhibition, therefore, sought to affirm the validity of the popular histories of both sides. By so doing, it hoped to uphold the worth not only of the popular curators who looked after these histories, but also of the more general public, who gave the histories more-distant support. The exhibition did not disparage the popular histories. Nor did it condemn the largely working-class and ethnically based groups that espoused them. It did not try to uphold the value of one section of society against another. Instead, it declared, by implication, that each section of Ulster society has as much right to have its importance confirmed as any other.

Concluding Remarks

This postscript has suggested that the approach to identity given in this book is compatible with current educational thinking in the province. The idea that identity is forged in social interaction and in the context of different frameworks is compatible with forward-looking policies aimed at reconciliation. These policies encourage, in a controlled environment, social interaction between schoolchildren of different ethnic backgrounds. They also strive to create oases of calm in which the common and distinctive cultural heritage of all groups can be explored, recognized, and valued.

When discussing Northern Ireland, however, it is always appropriate to add a note of pessimism. There is a limit to what policies of cultural heritage and mutual understanding in schools and museums can achieve, and the limitations ought to be pointed out.

Museums in Northern Ireland have tried to create images of a common heritage around which the population might unite. This is a laudable objective, and the discussion here suggests that such images are ultimately necessary for peace. However, we have also argued that ethnic division does not arise out of cultural differences and similarities. Rather, ethnic differentiation and ethnic conflict arise out of the uses to which culture is put in specific interactions.

There are, moreover, more substantial issues than distinctively ethnic culture that stand in the way of rapprochement. There are, for example, many people in Northern Ireland who feel intimidated. Sometimes this intimidation comes directly from paramilitary groups, or even from the security forces. Sometimes it comes, more indirectly, from the mere political ambitions of the other side. It even comes from displays of chauvinism by one's opponents. Wherever it comes from, it renders individuals and their spokespeople unwilling or unable to engage wholeheartedly in constructive interactions that might lead to peace. Confronted with intimidation, a person can too readily, and with justification, retreat into frameworks structured by ideas of invasion and siege.

Another issue is social inequality. An obvious question here is the long-standing social inequality between Catholics and Protestants, which is still a source of continuing resentment among nationalists. The impact of fair-employment legislation, for example, has been painfully slow. Also, in a period of endemic unemployment, fair-employment legislation can not only soothe but also arouse hostility, as when it is suspected of being a way of discriminating unfairly against Protestants.

Beyond this, the very existence of social inequality between the social classes is a source of hostility. We have shown that ethnic identity is defined by means of metaphors taken, *inter alia*, from the language of social class. More than this, violent dramatizations of ethnic identity are often challenges both to authority and to inequalities of wealth, education, and power. These inequalities are basic to the social organization of Western society.

We have said above that Wallis et al. (1986) correctly claim that the poor are especially jealous of the self-esteem or "honor" attached to their ethnicity. While the rich and the educated can find self-esteem through careers, erudition, and displays of consumption, the prestige due to ethnicity is also available to the poor. The self-esteem that comes from the ethnic group's rhetorical histories, its demonstrations, and its culture is not, therefore, easily abandoned. To woo poorer people from their ethnic loyalties, to stop them from feeling besieged or invaded, one may have to do more than just point to a common culture.

In such a framework, the answers provided by schools and museums can only be part of a more general solution. Schools and museums cannot, on their own, solve the major political conundrum of the Irish border; they cannot heal social inequality; they cannot by themselves make Catholics and Protestants want to give up their preferred social distance from each other.

The kinds of identities that will emerge in Northern Ireland will not, therefore, be built in schools and museums. In the last resort, Northern Irish people will negotiate and construct their own identities in the worlds that they themselves create in their day-to-day social interactions.

Schools and museums can, however, provide calm and neutral territory where members of the two sides can come and sometimes meet. In such neutral territory, people can learn about the things they have in common and the things that divide them. Here they can find building blocks with which they can themselves socially construct harmonious relationships. They can then hope to renegotiate their identities.

Notes

Chapter 1. Negotiating Identity in Ulster

1. This belief in physical difference is part of a half-serious folklore. It is jokingly alleged that the eyes of Catholics are closer together than those of Protestants. A Catholic friend therefore claimed, in mixed company, that she had a "Prodometer" that allowed her to measure this distance and thus identify Protestants (Prods).

2. As far as possible, Buckley has chosen fictitious names for people and places, in order to protect his informants. Because Kenney's work was bound up with a readily recognizable geography, she has hidden the identities only of people.

Chapter 2. Some Theoretical Remarks

1. St. Paul is famous for having misunderstood this particular paradox (Titus 1, 12).

Chapter 3. History as Rhetoric

1. Connell, whose 1968 book has the evocative title *Irish Peasant Society*, casts doubt upon the traditional nationalist romance of an impoverished, spiritual, Catholic, peasant Ireland. In a collection of witty historical essays, he attributes Ireland's odder kinship arrangements not to religion but to economics; he investigates the curious practice of drinking ether; and he suggests that the symbol of Irish poverty, the potato, was nutritious and indeed responsible for the robustness of the Irish when compared to the sickly English.

Chapter 4. The Siege Metaphor in Listymore

1. It is the custom, especially in country areas in Northern Ireland, to speak about and address both men and unmarried women by their first names, no matter how senior (in age or status) they are. In contrast, married women, no matter how young, are addressed as "Mrs. So and So," even, sometimes, by very close friends. There are exceptions to the rule, as for example when occasion demands that one be formal, or with elderly, respectable single ladies, especially of the gentry class. The practice was almost universal in rural areas twenty years ago, when I began my fieldwork, though now it is declining. Here I have followed native usage in referring to individuals.

Chapter 6. Interlocking Identities

1. Some of the best-organized criticisms of paramilitary groups have come from women, both Catholic and Protestant: the names of Mairaid Corrigan and Betty Williams, of the Peace People, and Sadie Patterson, of Women Together, are especially notable. In a similar vein, one of Alan Feldman's informants remembers the brawling common among the men from Belfast's largely Catholic Dockside area. He says, "The women would have stopped the fights. They would have clipped you in the ears and dragged you home for your tea!" (Feldman 1991, 52). The humorous tone of this remark seems to show that the role of women as controllers of male bad behavior is well recognized, and that in this role the women were relatively free from physical danger.

Chapter 9. Dramatizing Identity: Playful Rebellion

1. One can also contrast modern opinions with those of Schopenhauer, who writes,

> Women are suited to being the nurses and teachers of our earliest childhood precisely because they themselves are childish, silly and shortsighted, in a word, big children their whole lives long: a kind of intermediate stage between the child and the man, who is the actual human being, "man." One has only to watch a girl playing with a child, dancing and singing with it the whole day, and then ask oneself what with the best will in the world a man could do in her place. (Schopenhauer 1970, 81)

It is not just that this view is politically incorrect or offensive to women. Much more interesting is the fact that today we find this opinion *implausible*. The opposite view, often expressed by women in Northern Ireland, that the hobbies and enthusiasms of men make them "just like children" seems, in contrast, transparently apposite.

Chapter 10. Fighting and Fun

1. The fine distinctions between these grades of band are sometimes difficult to follow. A young man came to Buckley's door one day before Christmas in 1993, col-

lecting money for instruments. "Is it a melody flute band?" he was asked. "No," came the reply. "I *was* in a melody flute band, but now I've changed. Now I'm in a blood-and-thunder band."

Chapter 11. The Chosen Few

1. Freemasonry in Ireland is similarly divided among different but interrelated bodies. The essence of Freemasonry is Craft Masonry. Craft Masonry has three degrees: Entered Apprentice, Fellow Craft, and Master Mason. Craft lodges are controlled directly by the Grand Lodge of Free and Accepted Masons of Ireland. The Supreme Grand Royal Arch Chapter of Ireland controls the Mark Master and Royal Arch degrees. The Grand Council controls the Knight of the Sword, Knight of the East, and Knight of the East and West degrees. The Order of the Temple and Great Priory of Ireland governs the Knight Templar, Mediterranean Pass, and Knight of Malta degrees. The Grand Chapter of Prince Masons of Ireland is the ruling body of the degree of Knight of the Eagle and Pelican and Prince Grand Rose Croix of Heredom. This degree is the same as the eighteenth degree of the Ancient and Accepted Rite, as worked elsewhere. The Supreme Council of the 33rd Degree, Ancient and Accepted Rite for Ireland, controls the degree of Knight of the Sun (28th Degree), Philosophical Mason Knight Kadosh (30th Degree), Grand Inspector Inquisitor Commander (31st Degree), Prince of the Royal Secret (32nd Degree), and Sovereign Grand Inspector General (33rd Degree).

2. They are called, respectively, Royal Black, Royal Scarlet, Royal Mark, Apron and Royal Blue, Royal White, Royal Green, Royal Gold, Star and Garter, Crimson Arrow, Link and Chain, and Red Cross.

3. This collection (Ulster Folk and Transport Museum photographic slide archive BF149-240 BG1-176) is a complete record of the banners on display in these places. The flapping of banners, the necessity of changing film, and other contingencies of a fast-flowing public parade created only occasional omissions. Necessary choices between banner pictures were determined by the need to photograph a range of different designs.

Bibliography

Abrahams, R. D., and R. Bauman
    1978   Ranges of Festival Behavior. In *The Reversible World*, edited by B. Babcock. Ithaca: Cornell University Press.

Adamson, I.
    1974   *The Cruthin: The Ancient Kindred*. Belfast: Donard.
    1982   *The Identity of Ulster: The Land, the Language, and the People*. Belfast: Pretani.

Akenson, D. H.
    1991   *Small Differences: Irish Catholics and Irish Protestants, 1815–1922*. Dublin: Gill and Macmillan.

Alpers, S.
    1991   The Museum as a Way of Seeing. In *The Poetics and Politics of Museum Display*, edited by I. Karp and S. D. Lavine. Washington, D.C.: Smithsonian Institution Press.

Ardener, E.
    1970   Witchcraft, Economics, and the Continuity of Belief. In *Witchcraft, Confessions, and Accusations*, edited by M. M. Douglas. London: Tavistock.
    1975   Belief and the Problem of Women. In *Perceiving Women*, edited by S. Ardener. London: Malaby.

Ballard, L. M.
    1988   Three Rural Storytellers: A Perspective on the Question of Cultural Heritage. In *Monsters with Iron Teeth: Perspectives on Contemporary Legend*, edited by G. Bennet and P. Smith. Sheffield: Sheffield Academic Press.

Bardon, J.
  1982   *Belfast: An Illustrated History.* Belfast: Blackstaff.
Barnes, S. B.
  1969   Paradigms, Scientific and Social. *Man* (n.s.) 4:94–102.
Barry, M. U.
  1972   The Southern Boundaries of Northern Hiberno-English Speech. In *Patterns in the Folk Speech of the British Isles,* edited by M. F. Wakelin. London: Athlone.
Barth, F.
  1969   Introduction. In *Ethnic Groups and Boundaries: The Social Organisation of Cultural Difference,* edited by F. Barth. London: Allen and Unwin.
Bartlett, T.
  1985   Select Documents 38: Defenders and Defenderism in 1795. *Irish Historical Studies* 24:338–39.
Bateson, G.
  1955   A Theory of Play and Fantasies and Phantasy. APA *Psychiatric Research Reports* 2:39–51.
Bateson, G., J. Haley, D. D. Jackson, and J. H. Weakland
  1956   Towards a Theory of Schizophrenia. *Behavioural Science* 1, 4:251–64.
Baxandall, M.
  1991   Exhibiting Intention: Some Preconditions of the Visual Display of Culturally Purposeful Objects. In *The Poetics and Politics of Museum Display,* edited by I. Karp and S. D. Lavine. Washington, D.C.: Smithsonian Institution Press.
Beck, B. E. F.
  1978   The Metaphor as Mediator between Semantic and Analogic Modes of Thought. *Current Anthropology* 19:83–97.
Becker, H. S.
  1953   Becoming a Marijuana User. *American Journal of Sociology* 59:235–42.
Bell, D.
  1990   *Acts of Union: Youth Culture and Sectarianism in Northern Ireland.* Houndmills: Macmillan.
  1985   The Loyal Sons of Ulster March Anew. *New Society* 3, 177:79–81.
Bell, J.
  1978   Relations of Mutual Help between Ulster Farmers. *Ulster Folklife* 24:48–58.
Ben-Amos, D.
  1984   The Seven Strands of Tradition: Varieties in Its Meaning in American Folklore Studies. *Journal of American Folklore* 21:97–131.
Berger, P. L., and T. Luckmann
  1966   *The Social Construction of Reality.* Harmondsworth: Penguin.

Berlin, B.
    1978   Ethnobiological Classification. In *Cognition and Classification*, edited by B. B. Lloyd and E. Rosch. Hillsdale, N.J.: Lawrence Erlbaum.

Berlin, B., and P. Kay
    1969   *Basic Color Terms*. Berkeley and Los Angeles: University of California Press.

Berne, E.
    1975   *What Do You Say after You Say Hello?* London: Corgi.

BICO (British and Irish Communist Organization)
    1971   *On the Democratic Validity of the Northern Ireland State*. Belfast: BICO.
    1972   *The Two Irish Nations: A Reply to Michael Farrell*. Belfast: BICO.

Biggar, F. J.
    1910   *The Ulster Land War of 1770 (the Hearts of Steel)*. Dublin: Sealy, Bryers and Walker.

Billig, M.
    1985   Prejudice, Categorisation and Particularisation: From a Perceptual to a Rhetorical Approach. *European Journal of Social Psychology* 15:79–103.

Black, R., F. Pinter, and B. Overy
    1975   *Flight: A Report on Population Movement in Belfast, August 1971*. Belfast: Community Relations Commission.

Boal, F. W.
    1982   Segregating and Mixing: Space and Residence in Belfast. In *Integration and Division: Geographical Perspectives on the Northern Ireland Problem*, edited by F. W. Boal and J. N. H. Douglas. London: Academic Press.

Boal, F. W., and D. N. Livingstone
    1984   The Frontier in the City: Ethnonationalism in Belfast. *International Political Science Review* 5:161–79.

Bohannan, L.
    1952   A Genealogical Charter. *Africa* 22, 4:301–15.

Bowen, D.
    1970   *Souperism: Myth or Reality?* Cork: Mercier.

Boyce, D. G.
    1982   *Nationalism in Ireland*. London: Croom Helm.

Boyd, M.
    1979   Metaphor and Theory Change. In *Metaphor and Thought*, edited by A. Ortony. Cambridge: Cambridge University Press.

Brett, C. E. B.
    1986   *Housing a Divided Society*. Dublin: Institute of Public Administration.

Brody, H.
    1971   *Inishkillane: Change and Decline in the West of Ireland*. Harmondsworth: Penguin.

Brown, C. H.
    1977   Folk-Botanical Life-forms: Their Universality and Growth. *American Anthropologist* 79:317–42.

Buckley, A. D.
    1987   On the Club: Friendly Societies in Ireland. *Irish Economic and Social History* 14:39–58.
    1985   *Yoruba Medicine.* Oxford: Clarendon.
    1982   *A Gentle People: A Study of a Peaceful Community in Ulster.* Cultra: Ulster Folk and Transport Museum.
    1979–80   Fall of a Landlord. *Yearbook 1979–80.* Cultra: Ulster Folk and Transport Museum.

Buckley, A. D., and T. K. Anderson
    1988   *Brotherhoods in Ireland.* Cultra: Ulster Folk and Transport Museum.

Bufwack, M. S.
    1982   *Village Without Violence: An Examination of a Northern Irish Community.* Cambridge, Mass.: Schenkman.

Burke, K.
    1957   *The Philosophy of Literary Form: Studies in Symbolic Action.* New York: Vintage.

Burke, P.
    1978   *Popular Culture in Early Modern Europe.* London: Temple Smith.

Burkitt, I.
    1991   *Social Selves: Theories of the Social Formation of Personality.* London: Sage.

Burton, F.
    1978   *Politics of Legitimacy: Struggles in a Belfast Community.* London: Routledge and Kegan Paul.

Cameron, D.
    1972   The Museum: A Temple or a Forum. *Journal of World History* 14:197–201.

Cargo, D., C. Kilpatrick, and W. Murdie
    1943   *History of the Royal Arch Purple Order.* Belfast: Royal Arch Purple Order.

Carson, J. T.
    1959   *The Great Awakening in Ulster: A Centenary Brochure.* Belfast: Nicholson and Bass for the United Committee of Irish Churches.

Caws, P.
    1978   Operational, Representational, and Explanatory Models. *American Anthropologist* 76:1–10.

Charsley, S.
    1987   Interpretation and Custom: The Case of the Wedding Cake. *Man* (n.s.) 22:93–110.

Clements, W.

    1982   "I Once Was Lost": Oral Narratives of Born-Again Christians. *International Folklore Review* 2:105–11.

Cohen, A. P.

    1994   *Self Consciousness: An Alternative Anthropology of Identity.* London and New York: Routledge.

Collier, G. A., G. K. Dorflinger, T. A. Gulick, D. L. Johnson, C. McCorkle, M. A. Meyer, D. D. Wood, and L. Yip

    1976   Further Evidence for Universal Color Categories. *Language* 52:884–90.

Compton, P. A., in association with A. Smith, M. Trainor, and R. C. Murray

    1978   *Northern Ireland: A Census Atlas.* Dublin: Gill and MacMillan.

Connell, K. H.

    1968   *Irish Peasant Society.* Oxford: Oxford University Press.

Connelly, S. E.

    1982   *Priests and People in Pre-famine Ireland, 1780–1845.* Dublin: Gill and Macmillan.

Darby, J.

    1986   *Intimidation and the Control of Conflict in Northern Ireland.* Dublin: Gill and Macmillan.

    1988   Intimidation and Interaction in a Small Belfast Community: The Water and the Fish. In *Political Violence: Ireland in a Comparative Perspective,* edited by J. Darby, N. Dodge, and A. C. Hepburn. Belfast: Appletree.

Delargy, J. H.

    1945   The Gaelic Story-teller: With Some Notes on Gaelic Folk-tales. *Proceedings of the Irish Academy* 31. Reprint. Chicago: University of Chicago Press, 1969.

Dixon, K.

    1977   Is Cultural Relativism Self-refuting? *British Journal of Sociology* 28:75–87.

Donnan, H., and W. G. McFarlane

    1986   "You Get On Better with Your Own": Continuity and Change in Rural Northern Ireland. In *Ireland: A Sociological Profile,* edited by P. Clancy, S. Drury, K. Lynch, and L. O'Dowd. Dublin: Institute of Public Administration and Sociological Association of Ireland.

Donnelly, J. S.

    1978   The Rightboy Movement. *Studia Hibernica* 17–18:120–202.

    1981   Hearts of Oak, Hearts of Steel. *Studia Hibernica* 21:7–73.

Douglas, E.

    1975   A Sociolinguistic Study of Articlave, Co. Londonderry — A Preliminary Report. *Ulster Folklife* 21:55–67.

Douglas, M. M.

    1966   *Purity and Danger: An Analysis of Concepts of Pollution and Taboo.* London: Routledge and Kegan Paul.

Duncan, C.

1991   Art Museums and the Ritual of Curatorship. In *The Poetics and Politics of Museum Display*, edited by I. Karp and S. D. Lavine. Washington, D.C.: Smithsonian Institution Press.

Dunlop, D.

1987   Inter-school Links: A Limavady Experience. In *Education for Mutual Understanding: Roles and Responsibilities*, edited by A. Robinson. Coleraine: University of Ulster, Faculty of Education.

Durkheim, E.

1933   *The Division of Labour in Society.* Translated by G. Simpson. London: Collier, Macmillan.

1977   *The Elementary Forms of the Religious Life.* Translated by W. Swain. London: Allen and Unwin.

Ebel, H.

1986   The Strange History of Cultural Relativism. *Journal of Psychoanalytic Anthropology* 9:177–83.

Ehn, B.

1989   National Feeling in Sport. *Ethnologia Europaea* 19:57–66.

Engels, F., and K. Marx

1845–46   *The German Ideology.* London: Lawrence and Wishart.

Erikson, E. H.

1974   *Dimensions of a New Identity.* New York: Norton.

Evans-Pritchard, E. E.

1965   *Theories of Primitive Religion.* London: Oxford University Press.

Feldman, A.

1991   *Formations of Violence: The Narrative of the Body and Political Terror in Northern Ireland.* Chicago: University of Chicago Press.

Fennell, D.

1983   *The Changing Face of Catholic Ireland.* London: Chapman.

1985   *Beyond Nationalism: The Struggle against Provinciality in the Modern World.* Swords: Ward River.

1986   *Nice People and Rednecks: Ireland in the 1980s.* Dublin: Gill and Macmillan.

1989   *The Revision of Irish Nationalism.* Dublin: Open Air.

Fernandez, J. W.

1974   The Mission of the Metaphor in Expressive Culture. *Current Anthropology* 15:119–33.

1975   On the Concept of the Symbol. *Current Anthropology* 16:652–54.

Feuerbach, L.

1841   *The Essence of Christianity.* Translated by G. Eliot. Reprint. New York: Harper, 1953.

Feyerabend, P.
  1975   *Against Method: Outline of an Anarchistic Theory of Knowledge.* London: New Left Books.
Fingarette, H.
  1965   *The Self in Transformation: Psychoanalysis, Philosophy, and the Life of the Spirit.* New York: Harper and Row.
  1969   *Self-deception.* London: Routledge and Kegan Paul.
Finnegan, R.
  1989   *The Hidden Musicians: Music Making in an English Town.* Cambridge: Cambridge University Press.
Fogelson, J.
  1970   Violence and Grievances: Reflections on the 1960 Riots. *Journal of Social Issues* 26:141–64.
Forster, R. W.
  1982–84 The Early Grand Encampments of Ireland and Scotland and England. *Lodge of Research No. CC Ireland, Transactions* 18:134–200.
Foster, J. W.
  1982   Yeats and the Folklore of the Irish Revival. *Eire/Ireland* 17:6–18.
Fox, J. R.
  1963   The Structure of Personal Names on Tory Island. *Man* 192:153–56.
  1966   Kinship and Land Tenure on Tory Island. *Ulster Folklife* 12:1–17.
  1968   Multilingualism in Two Communities. *Man* (n.s.) 3:456–64.
  1978   *The Tory Islanders: A People of the Celtic Fringe.* Cambridge: Cambridge University Press.
Freud, S.
  1921   Group Psychology and the Analysis of the Ego. In *The Standard Edition of the Complete Psychological Works of Sigmund Freud.* Edited and translated by J. Strachey. Vol. 18:69–143.
  1930   Civilization and Its Discontents. In *The Standard Edition of the Complete Psychological Works of Sigmund Freud.* Edited and translated by J. Strachey. Vol. 21:57–145.
Frykman, J.
  1989   Social Mobility and National Character. *Ethnologia Europaea* 19:33–48.
Gailey, R. A.
  1975   The Scots Element in North Irish Popular Culture. *Ethnologia Europaea* 8:2–22.
  1982   Folk Culture, Context, and Cultural Change. In *Folklorismus,* edited by E. Horandner and H. Lunzer. Neusiedl am See: Offsetschnelldruck A. Riegelnik.
Gallagher, F.
  1957   *The Indivisible Island: The History of the Partition of Ireland.* London: Gollancz.

Gans, H. J.
    1962   *The Urban Villagers.* New York: Free Press.

Gibson, W.
    1860   *The Year of Grace: A History of the 1859 Ulster Revival.* Reprint. Belfast: Ambassador Productions, 1989.

Gill, O.
    1977   *Luke Street: Housing Policy, Conflict, and the Creation of the Delinquent Area.* London: Macmillan.

Giovannini, M. J.
    1981   Woman: A Dominant Symbol within the Cultural System of a Sicilian Town. *Man* (n.s.) 16:408–26.

Girard, R.
    1989   *Violence and the Sacred.* Translated by P. Gregory. Baltimore: Johns Hopkins University Press.

Given, R. J.
    1959   *Two Centuries of Profit and Pleasure in Union Band Masonic Lodge No. 336, Banbridge, 1759–1953.* Newry: Hodgett Reporter Works.

Glassie, H.
    1982   *Passing the Time in Ballymenone: Culture and History of an Ulster Community.* Philadelphia: University of Pennsylvania Press.

Gluckman, M.
    1954   *Rituals of Rebellion in South East Africa.* Manchester: Manchester University Press.

Goffman, E.
    1959   *The Presentation of Self in Everyday Life.* Garden City, N.Y.: Doubleday, Anchor.
    1968   *Stigma: Notes on the Management of Spoiled Identity.* Harmondsworth: Penguin.
    1975   *Frame Analysis.* Harmondsworth: Penguin.

Goldman, A. I.
    1970   *A Theory of Human Action.* Englewood Cliffs, N.J.: Prentice Hall.

Gordon, C. W.
    1949   *The '59 Revival: Lest We Forget: The Wonders of Ulster in 1859.* Belfast: Baird.

Gorman, J.
    1973   *Banner Bright: An Illustrated History of the Banners of the British Trade Union Movement.* London: Allen Lane.

Green, A. S.
    1908   *The Making of Ireland and Its Undoing.* London: Macmillan.

Greer, J. E.
    1972   *A Questioning Generation.* Belfast: Church of Ireland Board of Education.

Gregg, R. J.

    1972   The Scotch-Irish Dialect Boundary in Ulster. In *Patterns in the Folk Speech of the British Isles*, edited by M. F. Wakelin. London: Athlone.

Haight, M. R.

    1980   *A Study of Self-deception*. Hassocks: Harvester.

Haley, J.

    1959a   An Interactional Description of Schizophrenia. *Psychiatry* 22:321–22.

    1959b   The Family of the Schizophrenic: A Model System. *Journal of Nervous and Mental Diseases* 129:357–74.

Hall, M.

    1986   *Ulster: The Hidden History*. Belfast: Pretani.

Hanna, W.

    1963   *Darkness Visible: A Revelation and Interpretation of Freemasonry*. London: Britons.

Harris, L.

    1984   Class, Community, and Sexual Divisions in North Mayo. In *Culture and Ideology in Ireland*, edited by C. Curtin, M. Kelly, and L. O'Dowd. Galway: Galway University Press.

Harris, R.

    1972   *Prejudice and Tolerance in Ulster: A Study of Neighbours and "Strangers" in a Border Community*. Manchester: Manchester University Press.

Harrison, S.

    1992   Ritual as Intellectual Property. *Man* (n.s.) 27:225–44.

Heald, S.

    1990   Joking and Avoidance, Hostility and Incest: An Essay on Gisu Moral Categories. *Man* (n.s.) 25:377–92.

Heggassy, L., and J. Webster

    1990   News Warped by the Lust for a Sexy Story. *The Independent*, 14 November 1990, 15.

Heslinga, M.

    1962   *The Irish Border as a Cultural Divide*. Assen: Van Gorcum.

Hewitt, C.

    1981   Catholic Grievances, Catholic Nationalism and Violence in Northern Ireland during the Civil Rights Period: A Reconsideration. *British Journal of Sociology* 32:362–80.

    1983   Discrimination in Northern Ireland: A Rejoinder. *British Journal of Sociology* 34:446–51.

    1985   Catholic Grievances and Violence in Northern Ireland. *British Journal of Sociology* 36:102–5.

Hippsley, P.

    1988   *Derry's Walls*. Derry: Guildhall.

Hofstadter, D. R.
    1980   *Gödel, Escher, Bach: An Eternal Braid: A Metaphorical Fugue on Minds and Machines in the Spirit of Lewis Carroll*. Harmondsworth: Penguin.

Horne, D.
    1984   *The Great Museum: The Representation of History*. London: Pluto.

Howe, L.
    1990   *Being Unemployed in Northern Ireland: An Ethnographic Study*. Cambridge: Cambridge University Press.

Irwin, C.
    1991   *Education and the Development of Social Integration in Divided Societies*. Belfast: Department of Social Anthropology, Queen's University.

Jacobs, S.
    1987   Scientific Revolutions, Political Archetypes and Evolutionary Critique. *Midwest Quarterly* 28:190–204.

Kane, E.
    1968   Man and Kin in Donegal. *Ethnology* 7:245–57.
    1979   The Changing Role of the Family in a Rural Irish Community. *Journal of Comparative Family Studies* 10:141–62.

Karp, I., and S. D. Lavine
    1991   Introduction: Museums and Multiculturalism. In *The Poetics and Politics of Museum Display*, edited by I. Karp and S. D. Lavine. Washington, D.C.: Smithsonian Institution Press.

Kennedy, P.
    1891   *Legendary Fictions of the Irish Celts*. London and New York: Macmillan.

Kenney, M. C.
    1991   Neighborhoods and Parades: The Social and Symbolic Organization of Conflict in Northern Ireland. Ph.D. dissertation, Department of Anthropology, University of Michigan.

Kinsella, T.
    1969   *The Tain*. Oxford and Dublin: Oxford University Press with Dolmen Press.

Kratz, C. A.
    1989   Genres of Power: A Comparative Analysis of Okiek Blessings, Curses, and Oaths. *Man* (n.s.) 24:636–56.

Kuhn, T. S.
    1962   *The Structure of Scientific Revolutions*. Chicago: University of Chicago Press.
    1979   Metaphors in Science. In *Metaphor and Thought*, edited by A. Ortony. Cambridge: Cambridge University Press.

Lacy, B.
    n.d.   *The Siege of Derry*. Dublin: Eason.

Lakoff, G., and M. Johnson
    1980   *Metaphors We Live By.* Chicago: University of Chicago Press.

Leach, E. R.
    1958   Magical Hair. Reprinted in *Myth and Cosmos: Readings in Mythology and Symbolism,* edited by J. F. Middleton. New York: Natural History Press, for the American Museum of Natural History, 1967.

Lee, R. M.
    1981   Interreligious Courtship and Marriage in Northern Ireland. Ph.D. thesis, University of Edinburgh.

Lenin, V. I.
    1916   Imperialism, the Highest State of Capitalism: A Popular Outline. Translated by Y. Sbodnikov. In V. I. Lenin, *Collected Works,* vol. 22. London: Lawrence and Wishart.

Leslie, G. R.
    1979   *The Family in Social Context.* Oxford: Oxford University Press.

Lévi-Strauss, C.
    1964   *Totemism.* Translated by R. Needham. London: Merlin.
    1961   La geste d'Asdiwal. *Les temps modernes,* 16, 2, 179:1080–1123.

Leyton, E.
    1975   *The One Blood.* Institute of Social and Economic Research, Memorial University of Newfoundland.
    1976   Opposition and Integration in Ulster. *Man* (n.s.) 9:185–98.

Ligoniel
    1981   *The Last of the Mill Villages: Ligoniel.* Written by the people of Ligoniel. Belfast: Workers Educational Association.

Livingstone, J., and J. Beardsley
    1991   The Poetics and Politics of Hispanic Art. In *The Poetics and Politics of Museum Display,* edited by I. Karp and S. D. Lavine. Washington, D.C.: Smithsonian Institution Press.

Loftus, B.
    1990   *Mirrors: William III and Mother Ireland.* Dundrum: Picture Press.

Longley, E.
    1990   *From Cathleen to Anorexia: The Breakdown of Ireland.* Dublin: Attic.

Lundy, J., and A. MacPoilin, eds.
    1992   *Styles of Belonging: The Cultural Identities of Ireland.* Belfast: Lagan.

Lyons, F. S. L.
    1979   *Culture and Anarchy in Ireland, 1890–1939.* Oxford: Clarendon Press.

Macaulay, Lord T. B.
    1855   *The History of England from the Accession of James the Second.* Reprint. Edited by C. H. Firth. London: Macmillan, 1914.

Major, J., and A. Reynolds
    1993   *Joint Declaration, Downing Street.* Belfast: Her Majesty's Stationery
          Office.

Malinowski, B.
    1963   The Foundations of Faith and Morals. In *Sex, Culture, and Myth.* Lon-
          don: Rupert Hart Davis.

Manning, F. E.
    1976   The Rediscovery of Religious Play: A Pentecostal Case. In *The Anthro-*
          pological Study of Play: Problems and Prospects, edited by D. Lancy and
          B. A. Tindall. Cornwall, N.Y.: Leisure Press.
    1977   The Salvation of a Drunk. *American Ethnologist* 4:397–412.

Marsh, P.
    1978   *Aggro: The Illusion of Violence.* London: Dent.

Marsh, P., E. Rosser, and R. Havre
    1978   *The Rules of Disorder.* London: Routledge.

Marx, K.
    1844   Towards a Critique of Hegel's *Philosophy of Right:* Introduction. In *Karl*
          Marx: Early Texts, edited and translated by D. McLellan. Oxford:
          Blackwell.

McCartney, P.
    1988   *The Siege of Derry, 1689.* Derry: Guildhall.

McCormick, W. J. McK.
    1984   *Christ, the Christian, and Freemasonry.* Belfast: n.p.

McFarlane, W. G.
    1978   Gossip and Social Relationships in a Northern Ireland Village. Doc-
          toral thesis, Department of Social Anthropology, Queen's University,
          Belfast.
    1986   "It's Not as Simple as That": The Expression of the Catholic and Protes-
          tant Boundary in Northern Irish Rural Communities. In *Symbolizing*
          Boundaries: Identity and Diversity in British Cultures, edited by A. P.
          Cohen. Manchester: Manchester University Press.

McNeill, R.
    1922   *Ulster's Stand for Union.* London: Murray.

McWhirter, E.
    1983   Contact and Conflict: The Question of Integrated Education. *Irish Jour-*
          nal of Psychology 6:13–27.

Mead, G. H.
    1934   *Mind, Self, and Society.* Chicago: University of Chicago Press.

Menola-Kallio, A.
    1984   Feminine Identity and Collective Representation. In *Plenary Papers of*
          the Eighth Congress for the International Society for Folk Narrative Re-
          search. Bergen.

Messenger, J. C.

    1969   *Inis Beag: Isle of Ireland.* New York: Holt, Rinehart and Winston.

    1989   *Inis Beag Revisited: The Anthropologist as Observant Participator.* Salem: Sheffield.

Michelburn, J.

    1705   *Ireland Preserved; or the Siege of Londonderry.* London.

Midgley, M.

    1979   *Beast and Man: The Roots of Human Nature.* Hassocks: Harvester.

Milroy, L.

    1980   *Language and Social Networks.* London: Blackwell.

Mitchell, B.

    1990   *Derry: A City Invincible.* Eglinton: Grocers' Hall.

Moody, T. W.

    1968   *The Fenian Movement.* Dublin: Mercier.

Morgan, H. J.

    1990   Deceptions of Demons. *Fortnight* 320.

Moxon-Browne, E.

    1983   *Nation, Class, and Creed in Northern Ireland.* Aldershot: Gower.

Murray, D.

    1985   *Worlds Apart: Segregated Schools in Northern Ireland.* Belfast: Appletree.

NICC (Northern Ireland Curriculum Council)

    1990   *Cross-curricular Themes.* Belfast: NICC.

Nill, M.

    1985   *Morality and Self-interest in Protagoras, Antiphon, and Democrites.* Leiden: Brill.

O'Brian, G.

    1918   *Economic History of Ireland in the 18th Century.* Reprint. Philadelphia: Porcupine, 1977.

Ó Danachair, C.

    1957   Some Distribution Patterns in Irish Folk Life. *Béaloideas* 25:108–23.

    1965   Distribution Patterns in Irish Folk Tradition. *Béaloideas* 33:97–113.

    1977   Some Marriage Customs and Their Regional Distribution. *Béaloideas* 42–44:136–75.

    1979   Irish Tower Houses and their Distribution. *Béaloideas* 45–47:158–63.

O'Donnell, E. E.

    1977   *Northern Irish Stereotypes.* Dublin: College of Industrial Relations.

O'Hearn, D.

    1983   Catholic Grievances, Catholic Nationalism: A Comment. *British Journal of Sociology* 34:438–45.

    1985   Again on Discrimination in the North of Ireland: A Reply to the Rejoinder. *British Journal of Sociology* 36:94–101.

O'Rahilly, T. F.

1957   *Early Irish History and Mythology.* Dublin: Dublin Institute for Advanced Studies.

Orr, J. E.

1949   *The Second Evangelical Awakening in Britain.* Edinburgh: Marshall, Morgan and Scott.

Ortony, A., ed.

1979   *Metaphor and Thought.* Cambridge: Cambridge University Press.

O'Sullivan, S.

1966   *Folktales of Ireland.* Chicago: University of Chicago Press.

Paisley, I. R. K.

1959   *The "Fifty-nine" Revival: An Authentic History of the Great Ulster Awakening.* First published 1981. Belfast: Martyrs Memorial Free Presbyterian Church.

Patrick, J.

1973   *A Glasgow Gang Observed.* London: Eyre, Methuen.

Piellon, M.

1984   The Structure of Irish Ideology Revisited. In *Culture and Ideology in Ireland,* edited by C. Curtin, M. Kelly, and L. O'Dowd. Galway: Galway University Press.

Poole, M. A.

1983   The Demography of Violence. In *Northern Ireland: The Background to the Conflict,* edited by J. Darby. Belfast: Appletree.

Popper, K.

1959   *The Logic of Scientific Discovery.* London: Hutchinson.

Preston, D. L.

1981   Becoming a Zen Practitioner. *Sociological Analysis* 42:47–55.

Reddy, M. J.

1979   The Conduit Metaphor: A Case of Frame Conflict in Our Language About Language. In *Metaphor and Thought,* edited by A. Ortony. Cambridge: Cambridge University Press.

Redfield, R.

1947   The Folk Society. *American Journal of Sociology* 41:293–308.

Robinson, G.

1992   *Cross-community Marriage in Northern Ireland.* Belfast: Centre for Social Research, Queen's University.

Robinson, P.

1988   *Their Cry Was "No Surrender."* Belfast: Crown.

Robinson, P. S.

1986   Hanging Ropes and Buried Secrets. *Ulster Folklife* 32:3–15.

1984   *The Plantation of Ulster: British Settlement in an Irish Landscape, 1600–1670.* Dublin: Gill and Macmillan.

Rosch, E.

1977a   Linguistic Relativity. In *Thinking: Readings in Cognitive Science*, edited by P. N. Johnson-Laird and P. C. Wason. Cambridge: Cambridge University Press.

1977b   Classification of Real-World Objects: Origins and Representations in Cognition. In *Thinking: Readings in Cognitive Science*, edited by P. N. Johnson-Laird and P. C. Wason. Cambridge: Cambridge University Press.

1972   Universals in Color Naming and Memory. *Journal of Experimental Psychology* 93:10–20.

1978   Principles of Categorisation. In *Cognition and Classification*, edited by B. B. Lloyd and E. Rosch. Hillsdale, N.J.: Lawrence Erlbaum.

Rosch, E., C. B. Marvis, W. Gray, D. Johnson, and P. Boyes-Braem

1976   Basic Objects in Natural Categories. *Cognitive Psychology* 8:382–439.

Rose, R.

1971   *Governing without Consensus: An Irish Perspective*. London: Faber.

Ryan, D.

1948   *Socialism and Nationalism: A Selection from the Writings of James Connolly*. Dublin: Three Candles.

Sahlins, P.

1989   *Boundaries: The Making of France and Spain in the Pyrenees*. Berkeley: University of California Press.

Samarin, W. J.

1972   *Tongues of Men and of Angels: The Religious Language of Pentecostalism*. New York: Macmillan.

Santino, J.

1983   Miles of Smiles, Years of Struggle: The Negotiation of Black Occupational Identity through Personal Experience Narrative. *Journal of American Folklore* 96:393–412.

1989   *Miles of Smiles, Years of Struggle: Stories of Black Pullman Porters*. Chicago: University of Illinois Press.

Scarman, Hon. Mr. Justice L., G. K. Lavery, and W. Marshall

1972   *Violence and Civil Disturbance in Northern Ireland in 1969: Report of the Tribunal of Inquiry*. Belfast: Her Majesty's Stationery Office.

Scheper Hughes, N.

1979a   Breeding Breaks Out in the Eye of the Cat: Sex Roles, Birth Order, and the Irish Double Bind. *Journal of Comparative Family Studies* 10:207–26.

1979b   *Saints, Scholars, and Schizophrenics: Mental Illness in Rural Ireland*. Berkeley and Los Angeles: University of California Press.

Schon, D. A.

1979   Generative Metaphor: A Perspective on Problem Setting in Social Policy. In *Metaphor and Thought*, edited by A. Ortony. Cambridge: Cambridge University Press.

Schopenhauer, A.

1970   *Essays and Aphorisms*. Translated by R. J. Hollingdale. Harmondsworth: Penguin.

Scullion, F.

1981   History and Origin of the Lambeg Drum. *Ulster Folklife* 27:19–38.

Shanks, A.

1988   *Rural Aristocracy in Northern Ireland*. Aldershot.

Shearman, H.

1942   *"Not an Inch": A Study of Northern Ireland and Lord Craigavon*. London: Faber.

1948   *Anglo-Irish Relations*. London: Faber.

Sluka, J. A.

1989   *Hearts and Minds, Water and Fish: Support for the IRA and INLA in a Northern Irish Ghetto*. Greenwich: JAI.

Smith, A. D.

1984   National Identity and Myths of Ethnic Descent. *Research in Social Movements, Conflict and Change* 7:95–130.

Stein, H. F.

1986   Cultural Relativism as the Central Organising Resistance in Cultural Anthropology. *Journal of Psychoanalytic Anthropology* 9:157–75.

Stewart, A. T. Q.

1977   *The Narrow Ground*. London: Faber.

Suttles, G.

1968   *Social Order of the Slum: Ethnicity and Territory in the Inner City*. Chicago: University of Chicago Press.

Tara

n.d.   *Ireland Forever*. Belfast: Century Services.

Taylor, D.

1984   Ian Paisley and the Ideology of Ulster Protestantism. In *Culture and Ideology in Ireland*, edited by C. Curtin, M. Kelly, and L. O'Dowd. Galway: Galway University Press.

Taylor, L. J.

1985   The Priest and the Agent: Social Drama and Class Consciousness in the West of Ireland. *Comparative Studies in Society and History*, 271 (October 1985), 696–712.

Tonkin, E.

1992   *Narrating Our Pasts: The Social Construction of Oral History*. Cambridge: Cambridge University Press.

Toulouse, T.

1985   Veblen and His Reader: Rhetoric and Intention in *The Theory of the Leisure Class*. *Centennial Review* 29:248–67.

Turner, V. W.

    1962   Three Symbols of Passage in Ndembu Circumcision Ritual: An Interpretation. In *Essays in the Ritual of Social Relations*, edited by M. Gluckman. Manchester: Manchester University Press.

    1965   Ritual Symbolism, Morality, and Social Structure among the Ndembu. In *African Systems of Thought*, edited by G. Dieterlen and M. Fortes. Oxford: Oxford University Press.

    1982   *From Ritual to Theatre: The Human Seriousness of Play.* New York: Performing Arts Journal Publications.

UYUC (Ulster Young Unionist Council)

    1986   *CuChulain, the Lost Legend: Ulster, the Lost Culture.* Belfast. Ulster: UYUC.

Walker, G.

    1689   *A True Account of the Siege of London-Derry by the Reverend Mr. George Walker, Rector of Donoghmore in the County of Tirone, and Late Governour of Derry in Ireland.* Second edition. Reprint. Londonderry: Douglas, 1786.

Waller, W.

    1937   The Rating and Dating Complex. *American Sociological Review* 2:727–34.

Wallis, R., S. Bruce, and D. Taylor

    1986   *No Surrender: Paisleyism and the Politics of Ethnic Identity in Northern Ireland.* Belfast: Department of Social Studies, Queen's University.

Weiner, R.

    1980   *The Rape and Plunder of the Shankill: Community Action, the Belfast Experience.* Belfast: Farset Co-operative Press.

Whelan, K.

    1992   The Power of Place. *The Irish Review* 12:13–20.

White, T.

    1971   Brum's Mobs. *New Society* 181:760–63.

Whyte, J. H.

    1986   How Is the Boundary Maintained between the Two Communities in Northern Ireland? *Ethnic and Racial Studies* 9:219–34.

Whyte, John

    1991   *Intepreting Northern Ireland.* Oxford: Clarendon.

Williams, D., ed.

    1973   *Secret Societies in Ireland.* Dublin: Gill and Macmillan.

Willis, R. G.

    1967   The Head and the Loins: Lévi-Strauss and Beyond. *Man* (n.s.) 2:519–34.

    1972   Pollutions and Paradigms. *Man* (n.s.) 7:369–86.

    1978   Magic and "Medicine" in Ufipa. In *Culture and Curing: Anthropological Perspectives on Traditional Medical Beliefs and Practices*, edited by P. Moreley and R. Wallis. London Peter Owen.

Willmott, P., and M. Young

    1957   *Family and Kinship in East London.* Harmondsworth: Penguin.

Wirth, L.

    1938   Urbanism as a Way of Life. *American Journal of Sociology* 44:1–24.

    1956   *The Ghetto.* Chicago: University of Chicago Press.

Woolgar, S.

    1983   Irony in the Social Study of Science. In *Science Observed: Perceptions on the Social Study of Science,* edited by K. D. Knorr-Cetina and M. Mulkay. London: Sage.

Woolgar, S., and D. Pawluch

    1985a   Ontological Gerrymandering: The Anatomy of Social Problems Explanations. *Social Problems* 32:214–27.

    1985b   How Shall We Move beyond Constructivism? *Social Problems* 33:159–62.

Wright, F.

    1973   Protestant Ideology and Politics in Ulster. *European Journal of Sociology* 14:2, 213–80.

    n.d.   *Integrated Education and New Beginnings in Northern Ireland.* Belfast: Corrymeela.

Index

Page numbers in italics indicate illustrations